T0339107

A Decade of Ethiopia

A Decade of Ethiopia

Politics, Economy and Society
2004–2016

By

Jon Abbink

BRILL

LEIDEN | BOSTON

The chapters on Ethiopia 2004–2015 were previously published in Brill's *Africa Yearbook. Politics, Economy and Society South of the Sahara 2004–2015*. The chapter on Ethiopia 2016 will be published in the forthcoming *Africa Yearbook. Politics, Economy and Society South of the Sahara 2016*.

Library of Congress Cataloging-in-Publication Data

Names: Abbink, J., author. | Bach, Jean-Nicolas, author.
Title: A decade of Ethiopia : politics, economy and society, 2004–2016 / by
    Jon Abbink ; with the cooperation of Jean-Nicolas Bach.
Description: Leiden ; Boston : Brill, 2017. | "The chapters in this book on
    Ethiopia 2004–2015 were previously published in Brill's Africa Yearbook :
    Politics, Economy and Society South of the Sahara 2004–2015. The other
    chapters are published here for the first time"—Title page verso. |
    Includes bibliographical references and index.
Identifiers: LCCN 2017016927 (print) | LCCN 2017018280 (ebook) | ISBN
    9789004346826 (Paperback) | ISBN 9789004345881 (pbk. : alk. paper) | ISBN
    9789004346826 (e-book)
Subjects: LCSH: Ethiopia—Politics and government—21st century. |
    Ethiopia—Social conditions—21st century. | Ethiopia—Economic
    conditions—21st century.
Classification: LCC DT388 (ebook) | LCC DT388 .A23 2017 (print) | DDC
    963.07/2—dc23
LC record available at https://lccn.loc.gov/2017016927

Typeface for the Latin, Greek, and Cyrillic scripts: "Brill". See and download: brill.com/brill-typeface.

ISBN 978-90-04-34588-1 (paperback)
ISBN 978-90-04-34682-6 (e-book)

Contents

Acknowledgements

This is the fifth volume in the series "*A Decade of ...*", based on the country chapters in the *Africa Yearbook. Politics, Economy and Society South of the Sahara* of the past 13 years, including the new 2016 chapter. Previous monographs were on Mozambique, Ghana, Namibia and Nigeria.

While no contents editing was done on these individual chapters on Ethiopia, a brief introduction was added on some key political and socio-economic background factors that will remain influential in shaping the country's future societal development, and that would need further research and also policy attention. Additional features in this volume are a list of general readings on the country, as well as an index.

I join my predecessors in this series in thanking Joed Elich, Franca de Kort, Ellen Girmscheid and Debbie de Wit of Brill Publishers for their continued support and efficient logistic and administrative assistance for the *African Yearbook* project during the past years, and Peter Colenbrander and Carol Rowe for their very professional language editing of the chapters.

I also thank my colleague Jean-Nicolas Bach for having authored one of the chapters (on 2014) in the year that I was unable to do so.

Ethiopia 2004–2016: Vagaries of the 'Developmental State' and Societal Challenges

This Introduction contains a brief recapitulation of the 'state of play' in contemporary Ethiopia, with a view towards the future of this important African country. Four domains are briefly highlighted: political system, economic record, international role, and societal developments.

The decade or so described in this collection saw the emergence of Ethiopia as a (self-designated) 'developmental state', for a large part defined and shaped by the ideas and policies of the late Prime Minister and ruling EPRDF party leader Meles Zenawi, who died in August 2012. The process has known remarkable features, like significant economic growth, as indexed by GDP and foreign direct investment, and infrastructural overhaul of the country (large dams for hydro-electricity, roads, railway lines, emerging industrial parks, and large-scale agrarian plantations). Significant social and political changes and enduring controversies also occurred, as documented widely in a flood of press articles and scientific literature. Indeed, Ethiopia is perhaps one of the more dynamic countries in Africa: its regional clout, its great diversity, its growing economy and potential (with a population of c. 100 mln, 2nd in Africa), its being the center of the AU headquarters, and its importance in continental politics, e.g., with military actions across the border (Somalia), and participation in 'peace-keeping' or stabilization forces.

In view of its new economic dynamics and regional pivot position, Ethiopia seems also to be regarded by many donor counties as more or less 'too big to fail', explaining the comparatively high amounts of development assistance and humanitarian aid that it receives annually, despite its highly contested authoritarian trajectory and negative human rights profile. It has indeed its political problems

© KONINKLIJKE BRILL NV, LEIDEN, 2017 | DOI 10.1163/9789004346826_002

and dilemmas.[1] Domestically, there are several problematic constants that illustrate continuity in political culture and governance practices and are perhaps holding back further political and social progress.

The Ethiopian *political system* has a number of original traits, based on the recognition of ethnic identities as politically constitutive and as a basis for administrative units and budget allocations. There is a formal multi-party system, but nowhere – at the time of writing – has an opposition party or any party outside the ruling Ethiopian Peoples' Revolutionary Democratic Front (EPRDF) ever been a member of the government or of any regional or local administration (Only the Afar Region may have been an exception for a couple of years).

Despite the opening up of politics for a couple of years since May 1991, after the TLPF-EPRDF, winning the civil war, took over power from the *Derg* regime of Mengistu Haile-Mariam, the authorities have not been successful in establishing a free, democratic system. Politics has remained a high-risk business in the country. The 2005 elections at the beginning of the decade under discussion were both a highlight and low point of the Ethiopian 'democratization process', announced in 1991 with the new EPRDF-led regime. In 2005 there was, for the first time, significant electoral campaigning between various parties, and 174 opposition party members were elected in the 547-seat parliament, the 'House of People's Representatives'. This came as a kind of shock to the ruling party. However, the experiment, while promising, was not repeated in 2010, when only one opposition member returned. After the 2015 elections, opposition presence in parliament dropped to zero, giving the ruling party EPRDF and its various constituencies based on ethno-regional

---

1   Cp. E. Fantini & L. Puddu, "Ethiopia and international aid: development between high modernism and exceptional measures", in: T. Hagmann & F. Reyntjens, eds, *Aid and Authoritarianism in Africa: Development without Democracy*. London: Zed Press 2016, pp. 91–118.

provenance, a free hand as single party. It proceeded to expand its rule by extending hegemonic discourse (e.g., on the developmental state and ideology) within the state bureaucracy and the educational institutions, and of course guarded and implemented by the armed forces, special units and police. In recent years, there is the deep-rooted perception in Ethiopia of politics (and business) as strongly dominated by the Tigrayan population group, holding all key positions and having privileged access in the business world. Whether true or not, this is a constant refrain one hears in the country.

The 'democratic deficit' perpetuated by the political impasse – not seen as such by the ruling party, of course – was one of the enduring controversial and tension-generating elements in the country. The Executive became all-dominant, and apart from authoritarian and monolithic politics in the parliament and in government planning and the bureaucracy, there emerged an oppressive atmosphere in the mass media, in civil society and in public life in general. Many people physically fell victim to it due to imprisonment, disappearance, or death (documented in human rights reports).[2] Regrettably, in the past decade, the country saw harsh and exaggerated laws being promulgated in many domains, especially after the 2005 elections: the 'Freedom of the Mass Media and Access to Information Proclamation' (no. 590, 2008), the 'Charities and Societies Proclamation' (no. 621, 2009), and the 'Proclamation on Anti-Terrorism' (no. 652, 2009), and recently the 'Computer Crime

---

2 Some of the latest: HRW, "Ethiopia; year of brutality, restrictions", 12 January 2017 (at: https://www.hrw.org/news/2017/01/12/ethiopia-year-brutality-restrictions); Freedom House, "Ethiopia: attack on civil society escalates as dissent spreads", 23 July 2016 (at: https://freedomhouse.org/blog/ethiopia-attack-civil-society-escalates-dissent-spreads), and also the US State Department's *Ethiopia 2015 Human Rights Report*, 2016 (at: https://www.state.gov/documents/organization/252893.pdf). And cp. John Aglionby, "Ethiopia's economic gains tainted by violent repression", *Financial Times*, 6 February 2017.

Proclamation'(2016),[3] all with hard and unrelenting clauses that were quite unprecedented and perhaps going beyond what was judicially acceptable. Opposition voices, views and politics were made suspicious and frequently labelled as subversive. Often excessive and intimidating force was used against supposed opponents or suspects.

For many observers, even to those sympathetic to its ambitions, it was never clear why the EPRDF regime's obsession with maintaining such a repressive, undivided monopoly on the exercise of power and such heavy-handed control on everything was needed, or would in any way further national economic development or socio-cultural progress. The negative effects that this authoritarianism had on public debate, on (ethnic) group relations, human rights, and indeed on interpersonal relations in the country in fact did much to hold back wider social, cultural and economic development opportunities, equity, public trust, and ethnic cooperation.

Politically speaking, *hegemonic* rule in the classical Gramscian sense was aimed at,[4] with the ruling EPRDF's ideological outlook and mode of doing politics inculcated in the system[5] and spread via regular training and evaluation sessions in state and parastatal

---

3   See: ARTICLE 19 – Free Word Centre, Ethiopia; Computer Crime Law. Legal Analysis, London: Article 19-FWC. At: https://www.article19.org/data/ files/medialibrary/38450/Ethiopia-Computer-Crime-Proclamation-Legal-Analysis-July-(1).pdf.

4   Already outlined clearly in the 1993 party document *Our Revolutionary Democratic Goals and the Next Steps* (in *Ethiopian Register* magazine, June 1996) and in the 1997 *Guideline for EPRDF's Organizational Structure and Operation,* in: *Ethiopian Register*, September 1997. Both were prepared by the party's *Dirigitawi Ma'ekel* (Organisational Centre). See also the 124-page study *The Development Lines of Revolutionary Democracy.* Addis Ababa: EPRDF office, unpublished, 2001.

5   Cf. also R. Lefort, "Free market economy, 'developmental state' and party-state hegemony in Ethiopia: the case of the 'model farmers", *Journal of Modern African Studies*, vol. 50, no. 4, 2012, p. 681.

organizations. Many have 'internalized' this ideology or accept it because of intimidation or seeing no alternative.[6] Political life remains marked by suspicion and conflict, as evident by the always tense and highly contested elections, which were usually labelled as inherently biased by the opposition parties. It is further evidenced in recurring 'ethnic' clashes, especially in the countryside, and continuing public protests and demonstrations against top-down state-supported land appropriation. The protests, notably in 2016, featured attacks on property, especially ruling party-owned establishments and several foreign-owned large commercial farms. Many hundreds of people were killed in harsh repression. This unrest culminated in the declaration of a nation-wide 'state of emergency' in October 2016,[7] a radical measure installing a 'Command Post' with authority over everything and free from the usual judicial restraints. Political and social tensions became as serious as they had ever been under the EPRDF regime, and provoked a major crisis, revealing to many observers the cracks in the political system. Unhelpful was that the protesters and opposition activists were often quickly but incorrectly labelled as 'terrorists', probably to delegitimize the popular struggle for rights and economic equality. Within the ruling party EPRDF, the four constituent units and the Central Committee have also been arguing and reshuffling their positions in the past

---

6 Cp. Mattes, Robert & Mulu Teka, "Ethiopians' Views of Democratic Government: Fear, Ignorance, or Unique Understanding of Democracy?", Afrobarometer Working Paper no. 164, 2016. At: http://afrobarometer.org/sites/default/files/publications/Working%20papers/afropaperno164_ethiopia_democracy.pdf.

7 Although *not* the entire country was hit by protests. See also J.N. Bach, "État d'urgence en Éthiopie: nouveau *far East*, vieux *far West*", *L'Afrique en Question*, no. 28, October 2016. And: "Ethiopia: The slow death of a civilian government and the rise of a military might", in *Addis Standard*, 24 January 2017 (http://addisstandard.com/analysis-ethiopia-the-slow-death-of-a-civilian-government-and-the-rise-of-a-military-might/).

years, precipitated first by the death of PM and EPRDF leader Meles Zenawi in 2012, and of late (2016) by the violent dissent and upheaval in the country. But the unity front was maintained so far.

In terms of *economic development* the EPRDF regime largely followed an authoritarian command economy, with shades of a post-Communist plan economy, driven not primarily by developing or following domestic/international demand, but by 'supply side' economics: blue-print planning of economic activities and export business sectors for the future (especially for export of hydro-electricity from the big dams), of infrastructure, top-down industry park development, and massive plantations (e.g., for sugarcane). Secondary export sectors under development were gold production, potash, leather, sesame, a.o. Other foreign currency earners, e.g., *qat*, were more left to the private market. No doubt, a long-term vision was there, including one of poverty reduction, but the ambitions were sky-high and not 'inclusive' enough for the population as a whole. Remarkably, in the drive to commercialize agrarian production via large-scale land ventures given out mostly to foreigners, the focus on *coffee* production and supply chain development was somewhat diminished, although here, with its quality coffee, Ethiopia had a great comparative advantage, and could strive to become world producer no. 1. Coffee is still a major export revenue earner and is for 95% produced by small-scale farmers, showing that not all is dismal in the smallholder sector. New mineral resources were also sought, but with mixed success. For instance, oil exploration so far yielded few if any exploitable quantities, and the large natural gas reserves still await exploitation.[8] In the last couple of years, more emphasis was put on industrialization, via industrial park outlays, with the facilities (to be) leased out to international and domestic entrepreneurs and companies. Despite slow start-up processes, bureaucratic delays, and lack of reliable energy supply, the Ethiopian economy

---

8 A new agreement on exploitation and export was signed in July 2016 between Ethiopia, Djibouti and China.

has performed remarkably in the past decade or so, if measured on GDP figures. It grew in all spheres – agriculture, services, the production sector, infrastructure, etc. – and the state bureaucracy, while time-consuming and cumbersome for investors and perhaps over-regulated, was one of the more competent in Africa. The strong presence of China played a major role in the economy: as financier, source of expertise, investment, and as political-economical 'role model'. Despite practical problems and security issues, many foreign investors retain an interest in Ethiopia,[9] attracted in part by 'abundant labour supply' (or rather, low wage rates) and tax breaks in the start-up phase.

A disadvantage becoming more apparent in the past few years is the rapidly growing national debt burden, accumulating, especially, to China. The massive credits have kept the Ethiopian state busy investing – in railways, light-rail, roads, dams, state plantations, etc.), but in 2016–17 figures came out showing the increased vulnerability of the national economy to this debt burden.[10] The figure of the debt to China as of December 2016 stood at c. *$ 17 bn*.[11]

There is also concern about the absorptive capacity of the Ethiopian economy in view of the rapid population growth and the entry of close to 2 mln youthful job seekers on the job market annually. While youth employment programs are being developed and implemented, some with EU and World Bank funding, it is hard to discern the required productive expansion of the economy that would allow them all to find a job. This already is causing the

---

9   See e.g. the bi-weekly *Precise Consult International Investor Newsletters.* At: www.preciseethiopia.com.

10   One recent example is the Ethiopian Railways Corporation, see *The Reporter* vol. 21, no. 1064, 28 January 2017, pp. 1–2.

11   See: "Ethiopian scholar warns country's overstretched economy risks collapse". Online at: http://www.africareview.com/Business---Finance/ Scholar-warns-Ethiopia-overstretched-economy-risks-collapse/-/ 979184/3134930/-/p2iwwy/-/index.html.

exodus of tens of thousands of people every year to the Middle East, Europe, and elsewhere. Ultimately, however, the entrepreneurial skills and ambitions of a young generation will be the boon of the Ethiopian economy, provided they get the freedoms to develop, get access to credit and facilities, and are protected in their property rights.[12] The young generation is also less interested in politics as such, and tries to make its mark not only in economic ventures but also in social activities and cultural performance, showing remarkable dynamism (e.g., in graphic arts, youth movements, the fashion world, performative arts, or music).[13]

Long-term vulnerability of another kind also looms in the background: the vagaries of drought and food insecurity in the country – with every year an appeal to international donors for humanitarian and food aid for 5 to 9 mln people -, as well as growing ecological fragility and decline. These are permanent long-term threats, coupled with the exponential population growth and unknown risks[14] in the future that obviously affect a wider region than Ethiopia alone. However, despite this significant, in fact dramatic, population increase and the death of thousands due to malnutrition, there were no real mass famines in the past two decades. This shows that overall agrarian production improved and that mitigating emergency mechanisms to get food aid moving were instituted. But unfortunately, national food security was not achieved. While Ethiopia has

---

12   One example: Ms. Bethlehem Alemu and her *SoleRebels* shoe company, see: "Ethiopian shoe designer hopes for repeat success with coffee", at: http://money.cnn.com/2017/01/31/smallbusiness/ethiopia-shoes-solerebels-coffee-bethlehem-alemu/

13   Especially of course in Addis Ababa.

14   See for instance: J. Ferrie, "Indian Ocean Dipole? The obscure climate phenomenon driving drought in East Africa", IRIN, 22 February 2017, on: https://www.irinnews.org/news/2017/02/22/indian-ocean-dipole-obscure-climate-phenomenon-driving-drought-east-africa.

committed itself to the development of a 'green economy',[15] with plans outlined on paper, especially the issue of environmental pollution is quite serious, proceeding virtually unchecked. It is a quite under-studied issue and not yet the subject of serious public awareness or policy measures.[16]

The growth figures, the promise of state capacity, and the commitment shown by the Ethiopian government towards 'development' – often in over-ambitious or somewhat unrealistic fashion – led the international donor countries and organizations (World Bank, IMF, UNDP, a.o.) to largely continue political support for the regime. That the donors, including the Western countries, hereby always act responsibly and good faith must be seriously doubted.[17]

The *position and role of Ethiopia in African and international affairs* has seen continuity and change over the past decades. Emperor Haile Selassie (d. 1974) was a pioneer in the AU (then OAU) and for several decades a figurehead of African identity and interests on the world scene, and the current EPRDF regime has sought to revive, or increase, Ethiopia's international role again, after the stagnation under the *Derg* government of Mengistu Haile-Mariam (1974–1991). In its 'international obligations' and role in the wider African region, Ethiopia's post-1991 regime, building on the initial credit of 'having defeated the military dictatorship' of the *Derg*, was seen as 'functional' and 'helpful'. This applied even more so regarding post 9/11 terrorism threats and insecurity emanating from Somalia and the adjacent Middle East, and as compared to Eritrea's or South Sudan's problems of instability, intractability, and high migrant flows. But there were continuing problems, such as the unresolved

---

15   See: W. Davison, "Ethiopia powers up ambitions for green, climate-resilient industry", *The Guardian*, 23 July 2015.

16   Just one recent example: W.A. Zeleke, "Concerns about lead exposure toxicity in Ethiopia", on: http://www.zehabesha.com/concerns-about-lead-exposure-toxicity-in-ethiopia/, 3 January 2017.

17   Cp. Fantini & Puddu, *ibid.*, 2016, p. 114.

Ethio-Eritrean 'border issue' – where Ethiopia still refuses to comply with a post-war 2003 ICJ judgement – and the interference of Ethiopia in Somalia partly in response to Islamist threats. There is also the difficult question of the Nile waters, where Ethiopia's basically unilateral decision to build the huge 'Renaissance' dam on the Blue Nile (providing ca. 59% of the Nile downstream flow) whatever the consequences, put the relationship with Egypt on a new level of tension. The March 2015 'Declaration of Principles' (signed between Sudan, Ethiopia and Egypt), aimed to share the Nile waters and amicably discuss any disagreements, has not resolved the issue. The Blue Nile issue with Egypt was wholly predictable: Egypt simply cannot afford major changes in the Nile River levels, as this would threaten its existence.

Ethiopia is well-connected globally. A series of major foreign dignitaries visited the country recently, including US President B. Obama (2015), German chancellor A. Merkel (2016), and French President F. Hollande (2013), and Ethiopia's PM travelled to, among others, China, Japan, the US, India and Germany. It receives substantial sums of development aid and has concluded many cooperation agreements with these and other countries. Apart from permanently hosting the AU and being prominent in the IGAD, Ethiopia is internationally active in the framework of the UN, having recently provided peacekeeping troops for the UN missions in Darfur, South Sudan, Liberia and Ivory Coast. Its troops, which had unilaterally intervened in Somalia since 2006, were brought under the AMISOM umbrella in 2014. Ethiopia also played a role in the mediation efforts in the 2014–16 South Sudan bloody civil strife, and the country in 2016 successfully campaigned to be elected as a non-permanent member of the UN Security Council in 2017.

Ethiopian society in the past decade went through major changes, as yet not fully explored and studied. But new social groups, new identity issues, and elements of a new social structure emerged. More people were educated and connected to global media and markets, developing new aspirations and expectations, especially among a young and savvy urban generation. While Ethiopia had set as its developmental aim to be a 'middle income' country by 2020, it did not talk of creating 'middle classes' – a social category the EPRDF ideology does not like, or at least, does not want to see emerging as an independent social force.[18]

The hesitant emergence of new regional elites, often coupled to new 'ethnic' administrations on the district or 'Zone' level claiming autonomy or 'recognition, could also be discerned. The ethnic-based politics of the country engendered new reflections and debates on ethnic traditions, 'heritage', and difference among groups, developing new conceptions of collective identity and staking claims in the political and social domain. Ethno-regional identities, whether based on real or imagined differences, were being forged in ongoing competitive local politics on land, borders and (federal) budgets. Ethno-nationalist rivalries are under the surface and could become more of a danger to Ethiopian unity.

In addition, competitive relations between religious constituencies – Muslims, Evangelicals-Pentecostals, and Orthodox – continued to be felt, but were less apparent in the public sphere due to more government control. In view of the many violent incidents in the recent past, it would be an illusion to think that Ethiopia, despite its heritage of religious accommodation and pragmatic toleration, would be immune to religious radicalization, as evident in the Muslim and sometimes in the Evangelical-Pentecostal or Orthodox communities. A perusal of the Internet products of religious polemical debates – if not mutual insults – suffices to demonstrate this. The government, in line with is mandate to protect the secular

18   The EPRDF rather speaks of a 'middle income people', or 'middle income group'; see C. Nallet, *Classes Moyennes Éthiopiennes. Étude Empirique d'une Assignation Catégorielle Incertaine*, Bordeaux: Université de Bordeaux (PhD thesis), 2015, pp. 129–130.

constitution of the country,[19] has so far successfully contained and repressed religion-based violence, although sometimes it has also let local conflicts between Muslims and Christians run out of control.[20] Reflecting global trends, religious radicalization is nonetheless a persistent underlying threat, due to the influence of foreign and also domestically based radical ideologues who subvert the societal script of co-existence and toleration and are not always free from supremacist discourse. In the ongoing rivalry between religious constituencies there also seems to be emerging a notable trend towards social and religious conservatism and group conformism, especially towards women. As regards social structure, the point is, however, that new 'middle-class' and religious identity groups of a younger generation have emerged, which are an important factor in reshaping Ethiopian urban society.[21]

The problems of identity politics are well-known, and are 'inherited' from the past but for a large part the result of the ethno-political model followed by EPRDF. In the light of a quite problematic historical legacy, such Ethiopian identity issues are not easily 'solved'. But they are now becoming more of a liability, not only because

---

19   Cf. J. Abbink, "Religious freedom and the political order: the Ethiopian 'secular state' and the containment of Muslim identity politics", *Journal of Eastern African Studies*, vol. 8, no. 3, 2014, pp. 346–365; T. Østebø, "Islam and state relations in Ethiopia: from containment to the production of a 'governmental Islam'", *Journal of the American Academy of Religion* vol. 81, no. 3, 2013, pp. 1029–1060; and M.T. Corazza, "State and religion in the constitution and politics of Ethiopia," *European Journal for Church and State Research*, vol. 9, 2002, pp. 351–395.

20   See for example an incident on 29 November 2011, reported (somewhat polemically) on the website www.solidaritymovement.org/111215-our-muslim-and-christian-leaders-must-stand-up.php. However, such clashes have diminished over the past years.

21   Cf. M. di Nunzio, "What is the alternative? Youth, entrepreneurship and the developmental state in urban Ethiopia", *Development and Change*, vol. 46, no. 5, 2015, pp. 1179–1200.

of 'essentialized' group differences injected by would-be elites into the political process, but also due to their getting in the way of *national,* trans-regional economic development. This appears to be increasingly evident as national plans and policies often clash with ethno-regional interests and override the authority or scope of local and regional administrations. It is in fact dubious if the country can develop a new unifying narrative from the ensemble of fragmented identities, now invested with historical resentment and cultural pride. 'Development' cannot provide that narrative, at least not for long, because it is a discourse of *material* change, not of cultural content and social or historical identity. The Ethiopian developmental state model of today will deliver quite a number of goods, but has no good formula to respect and defend the constitutional and cultural rights of ethnic groups, minorities and ethno-regions within the national venture of economic progress – seen by many as being pushed through with overly coercive measures. Some administrative levels also occasionally register their opposition to certain schemes (e.g., of land appropriation in Oromiya or Amhara Regions), but are rarely in a position to prevent them or modify them.

In short, Ethiopia's potential and clout are important and growing, but major challenges on the domestic and international scene continue, especially regarding its wider regional role, its growing environmental problems, political and economic (in)stability, socio-economic inclusiveness, and justice and governance issues.

Ethiopia in 2004

With a population of about 72 million people and a relatively strong state, Ethiopia remains one of Africa's most important countries. Its position, however, continued to be weak due to chronic food insecurity, massive poverty, lack of productive capacity beyond agriculture, an ambiguous democratisation process and unresolved issues as to national identity and policy. There was also continued internal dissent, partly emerging from politicised ethnic differences, with opposition parties and civil society organisations struggling to gain a voice in national politics dominated by a ruling party that came to power through force of arms in 1991. Scattered rebel groups and occasional revolts necessitated a close watch on the security situation. There was also a growing challenge from religious revivalism and several instances of radicalisation among some Muslim youth groups.

Ethiopia's relations with neighbouring countries (Djibouti, Sudan, Kenya and Somaliland) were fairly good, but not with Eritrea and southern Somalia. The unresolved border problem with Eritrea remained in the headlines in 2004, and the insistence by the UN and Western donor countries that the conflict be brought to an end and on the recognition of the border determined in 2002 by the Ethiopia-Eritrea Boundary Commission (EEBC) of the Permanent Court of Arbitration was not productive. GDP growth in 2004 was significant, but the 2.8% annual population increase slowed down overall development. Ethiopia remained a relatively large recipient of donor aid, and continued to be, with Djibouti, a strategic partner of the US and other countries in the 'global war on terror'.

Domestic Politics

Ethiopia's *domestic politics* in 2004 remained firmly under the control of the Ethiopian People's Revolutionary Democratic Front

(EPRDF), especially of its core group, the Tigray People's Liberation Front (TPLF) of Prime Minister Meles Zenawi. The state apparatus, the army, the security service and the growing civil service, whose personnel were trained in the government-founded civil service college, were the bulwarks of support. EPRDF control did not preclude frequent elite rivalry and internal political tensions during the year, but this was less prevalent than in previous years. In view of these tensions – partly a result of lingering disagreements over policy towards Eritrea, which in 2001 had led to a major split in the TPLF and declining support for Meles in his own TPLF because of an Eritrea policy seen as too lenient – the prime minister sought to reform the EPRDF and seek more support among the other three 'ethnic' constituents of the coalition, the Amhara National Democratic Movement (ANDM), the Oromo Peoples Democratic Organisation (OPDO) and the Southern Ethiopian Peoples Democratic Front (SEPDF). The current leadership also opened up a little to opposition parties by holding several meetings on procedures for the 2005 elections and on campaigning.

Local conflicts in some regions were frequent, e.g., in Somali, Afar and Gambela (see below), three of the nine 'regional national states' (in Amharic 'killiloch', singular, 'killil') roughly based on ethno-linguistic criteria. Numerous unresolved disputes persisted regarding border demarcation, and, by implication, 'ethnic belonging' which has become the idiom through which 'resources', e.g., rights to land and budget, are secured. In 2004, there were dozens of boundary disagreements between communities (zones and peasant associations or 'qebeles') in Oromiya and Somali over 'who is an Oromo' and 'who is a Somali', a choice often difficult for people to make. The Somali region (the Ogaden) was unstable because of numerous changes in the regional government and a shaky security situation, with deadly ambushes by bandits and insurgent units on Ethiopian troops and garrison outposts. Ethiopian military action in the Ogaden was directed at eliminating armed activities, but human rights violations against non-combatants were a frequent result.

During the year, campaigning started for the May 2005 general elections for the House of People's Representatives (the national parliament, with 548 seats), with public debates in the state media (mass newspapers, television and radio controlled by the government) and the private, free press, and negotiations with opposition groups about 'levelling the playing field' for campaigning, especially in the countryside. But the government controls the National Electoral Board of Ethiopia (NEBE) that will supervise the electoral process and the registration of candidates and parties and handle complaints. A demand formulated by the main opposition party coalition (UEDF) in October 2004 to reform NEBE was not taken up by government.

In 2004, some 55 *political parties* were registered, among them the four parties in the EPRDF coalition. The EPRDF maintained its satellite ethnic parties in rural minority areas all across Ethiopia. The political opposition remained enormously fragmented, but gained public voice. The major opposition coalition, the United Ethiopian Democratic Front (UEDF), formed by 15 parties, the most important of which being the Coalition of Alternative Forces for Peace and Democracy in Ethiopia (CAFPDE) and the Oromo National Congress (ONC). CAFPDE, led by Dr. Beyene Petros, an MP and university lecturer in biology, reflected the southerners, and the Oromo National Congress, led by political scientist Dr. Merera Gudina, had its main support in western Oromiya. Many smaller parties, as well as the new four-party Coalition for Unity and Democracy (CUD), remained outside the broad opposition coalition.

CUD was formed in February 2004 from three existing parties: the All-Ethiopian Unity Party (AEUP), the United Ethiopian Democratic Party (UEDP) and the Ethiopian Democratic League (EDL), and a new one, The Rainbow Ethiopia Movement. This was founded by a number of influential intellectuals and opinion makers in Addis Ababa, e.g., former Ethiopian human rights council head Prof. Mesfin Wolde-Mariam and Dr. Berhanu Nega, the director of an important economic think-tank, the Ethiopian Economists'

Association. In September 2004, a new Oromo party was founded: the Oromo Federalist Democratic Movement (OFDM) led by Bulcha Demeqsa, a former World Bank official and banker. Apart from the need to forge a united challenge to the ruling party, the opposition faced the problem of building a support base in the countryside. In 2004, this process was actively 'discouraged' by the ruling party and its supporters in the rural areas. Opposition parties were the regular targets of attacks by government-related forces. For example, an AEUP member (Dessalegn Simegn) was killed in Ibnet district (Gondar area); on 29 April an AEUP member (Hailu Zelleke) was shot dead in Gishe Rabel; and on 15 May government militia killed the AEUP Youth League leader Getiye Alagaw.

Other opposition groups remained illegal and unregistered because they opted for armed struggle: for instance, the Oromo Liberation Front (OLF), a group aiming for the secession of an Oromo state; the Ogaden National Liberation Front (ONLF), a movement claiming autonomy for Somali-inhabited eastern Ethiopia; and various smaller groups. The OLF, a previous partner in government (1991–92), had made itself unpopular by siding with the Eritreans in the 1998–2002 war and accepting arms and training from them. In 2004, it kept its office in Asmara and had significant nuisance value for the Ethiopian army, with several raids and small-scale attacks, but was not a military threat.

Governance in Ethiopia remained marred by a lack of trained and qualified personnel, especially in the regions, by a lack of transparency, by personalism, and by tendencies to abuse public funds for personal gain, i.e., corruption. Democratisation was occurring and was rhetorically promoted, but an authoritarian style of politics often prevailed in practice, with parliament showing little independence from the executive led by the prime minister, a strong federal government hand in local and regional politics and in security matters and ongoing harassment and intimidation of opposition party members. The judicial system remained weak and overburdened, especially at the lower levels, but the slow development towards more autonomy by the judiciary could be discerned. In 2004, the issue of corruption of public officials and EPRDF-associated business people was a continuing point of debate and accusation. A government-installed federal ethics and anti-corruption commission dating from 2001 waged public campaigns against graft. Its activities were initially directed against political opponents and former TPLF central committee members like Siye Abraha, Bitew Belay and others who had opposed the Eritrea and economic policy of the Meles group in 2000–01. Its activities, like monitoring complaints by the public, providing information and education and suing people, had some effect in making people conscious of the problem and of the need to tread with caution, but corruption did not notably diminish.

Muslim and Pentecostal-Evangelical religious adherence continued to grow, and both groups showed revivalist, and, in the case of some Muslim groups, militant tendencies, with a potential to disturb the relatively amicable relations between believers. Muslim leaders like the chairman of the Ethiopian Islamic Affairs Supreme Council, perceived their religion to be the majority religion in Ethiopia, and Muslims started to demand a greater public role for it in the law and politics. In many towns, disputes occurred about the choice of locations for new mosques. In 2004, Wahhabist Islam remained prominent in the form of NGOs and of huge private, often foreign and informal, investments in mosque-building, Islamic schools, social programmes, and the training of religious teachers and leaders in Muslim countries (Saudi Arabia, Pakistan and the Gulf States). This brand of Islam continued to build support at the grassroots against the Muslim establishment (Islamic Affairs Supreme Council and its local branches). In the Alaba region in southern Ethiopia, where Wahhabist Islam is strong, a violent incident occurred on 1 February between Orthodox people and Muslims. A Christian student was killed and a convert to Christianity seriously beaten and his house ransacked. In nearby Besheno village, Muslims chased out 32 Christians. There was also a report about an Ethiopian Orthodox teacher who forbade Muslim pupils to use his (public)

school as a place for prayer being beaten and his family being harassed. Elsewhere in Ethiopia, some similar incidents occurred. The
presence of 'Takfir-wal-Hijjra' – like groups was reported in some
Ethiopian towns.

Pentecostalism continued to grow across the country, especially
in the south, with about 6 to 8 million adherents. They had some
trans-national material support and were disliked by both Muslims
and the Orthodox. Disputes about burial places, mosque or church
building sites, the loud playing of religious music and conversion
efforts were frequent. The Ethiopian Orthodox church was publicly
less prominent and remained internally divided because of the controversial patriarch 'Abune' Paulos (Gebre-Yohannis). Youth movements, however, were active in the church, pleading for revival and
renewal and a response to the Islamic and Pentecostal expansion.

The *domestic political debate* in Ethiopia in 2004 was dominated
by the perennial development issues (agriculture, health, infrastructure, capacity building) and by the stalemate over the 2002 border
decision by the EEBC of the Permanent Court of Arbitration (PCA)
in The Hague, handed down at the request of both countries after
the conclusion of the 1998–2000 war. Domestic legitimacy of the
government depended in large part on the perception among the
wider public of how this disadvantageous decision for Ethiopia
would be handled and diplomatically dealt with in the face of international pressure from donor countries, which insisted on unconditional acceptance of the PCA decision and even threatened the
country with sanctions. A core issue remained the status of Badme
town, where the war had started in 1998. In view of the national
consensus in Ethiopia, it appeared even more unthinkable in 2004
that Ethiopia would yield this Ethiopian-founded town to Eritrea.
Domestic public opinion in Ethiopia moved towards a more un-
compromising stand on the border issue, following the perceived
intransigence of Eritrea's government. The issue of Ethiopian access
to the sea (Assab port) was also rekindled and was set to gain prominence as the dispute lingered on. Prime Minister Meles Zenawi also

appeared to seek more support for his position outside his home base of Tigray, where more people showed dissatisfaction with his Eritrea policy, with the aftermath of the split in the dominant TPLF coalition party, and with the lack of improvement in living conditions. For instance, notable protest actions by citizens occurred in the Tigrayan town of Abi Addiy in March.

Ethiopia's 'experiment' in *ethnic democratisation* proceeded in 2004, but the federal authorities dominated by EPRDF kept all significant control of political power. Local-level conflicts were left to be tackled by the regional governments. There were credible reports of abuse of human rights, disappearances, torture and executions (planned or 'by mistake') by police and army, and usually carried out in an unpredictable manner and with impunity. Dozens of people in Oromiya, Somali and Amhara regions, many of them members of opposition parties were the victims. Thousands of people were also forced out of a job for non-economic reasons, evicted from homes or land without compensation and illegally detained without charge. Prison conditions remained very poor, without proper sanitation, food or medical facilities. On 21 January, an Oromo students' demonstration at Addis Ababa University, held after a riot during a contested Oromo cultural event on campus, was beaten up by campus police and 330 students were arrested and later expelled for the rest of the year. Students in several high schools and colleges in Oromiya region subsequently protested this incident, eliciting repression from government forces. On 18 May, another 18 Oromo students were arrested following an investigation into a grenade attack on 29 April in one of the university's dormitories, during which one student had died. Other incidents reported by human rights organisations were arbitrary arrests, beatings and humiliating treatment in southern Ethiopia (in Konso, Sidama, Wolayta). The 2004 US state department report on human rights was quite critical of Ethiopia, and in turn provoked a quite irritated denial from the Ethiopian authorities.

While Ethiopia saw significant improvement in *press freedom* after the fall of the Mengistu regime, many private, independent news magazines were subjected to harassment, pressure and arrest because of articles critical of government and the dominant party. Dozens of journalists were legally persecuted. A tendency to self-censor developed. However, this year, while several journalists were arrested, awaiting formal charges, in prison or were on trial, killings were, in contrast to some previous years, not reported. At least one journalist, from the 'Tobbiya' weekly, was beaten by police. As a result of harassment, beatings or threats, ten journalists fled the country or went missing in 2004. During the entire year, the Ethiopian Free Journalists' Association (EFJA) remained banned by the government, following an accusation in November 2003 that it had "failed to meet its legal obligations regarding registration" with the ministry of justice. This ban, likely proclaimed in view of the EFJA's criticism of the new draft press law, met with widespread protests, also internationally. The International Federation of Journalists (IFJ) urged government to reassess the move. The new draft press law brought forward by government to parliament in 2004 was seen as draconian and drew a wave of (inter)national criticism because of its proposed restriction of press freedoms. There were still no private television or radio stations, except Radio Fana, which is EPRDF-affiliated, but in June the licensing of private radio stations was announced.

Apart from the tension on the Eritrea border, the *security situation* in Ethiopia was marred by frequent local violent clashes, mainly between 'ethnic groups' and the state military, or among various ethno-regional groups, with hundreds of people killed. The worst example was in January and February in the western region of Gambela, where Anyuwa, Nuer, Majangir and highlanders were at odds. The tension escalated after killings in December 2003 and the renewed fighting in January-February resulted in the massacre of at least 200 to 300 people and widespread destruction of property. These 'ethnic clashes' emerged out of the deeply politicised antagonism – according to many, government-fuelled – of two dominant ethnic groups in the region, the Nuer and the Anyuwa, who already historically had a tense competitive relationship. The Anyuwa were the main victims of these killings, and thousands of them fled to Sudan. Elsewhere in the country, small-scale but repeated violent clashes occurred between pastoralists and cultivators, such as Mursi and Aari, Suri and Nyangatom, Oromo and Somali, Hamar and Boran.

No religiously inspired violence was reported, but there were a number of unresolved killings that might be related to religious beliefs. There were some apparently politically motivated incidents of grenade throwing at Addis Ababa University (29 April, during which one Tigrayan student died), in a business location in the town of Debre Zeit (on 3 May, one person killed), in the town of Ambo (15 April, 30 students injured), and violence in some other places (army beatings of students and protesters in Nekemte and Dembi Dolo towns in March). Violence by police or militia units was usually not prosecuted. Often, cases were delayed and then dismissed. This impunity impacted negatively on the domestic security situation.

The country has remained relatively free from international *terrorism* perpetrated by groups associated with al-Qaida. The government routinely accused OLF and ONLF of terrorism, as in several of the incidents mentioned above, but a relationship to Islamist terror groups was not clear. The radical Somali Islamist group 'Al Ittihad al Islami', previously operating in the Somali-Ethiopian border area ('Luuq'), was defeated in an Ethiopian military action some years ago and did not resurface, at least not in Ethiopia.

Foreign Affairs

There were hardly any interest groups or parties that could influence EPRDF policy. The party's position was strong due to a combination of entrenched political and economic power and a lack of alternative political forces. Only the internal dissent rumbling in the dominant party could lead to power shifts and foreign policy changes in the long run. The position of Meles Zenawi was, however, more closely tied to the proper handling of the *border conflict with Eritrea*. Ethiopia remained adamant in its insistence on a review of the 'illegal and unjust' basis of the EEBC's boundary decision of April 2002, but on 25 November Meles Zenawi presented a new peace initiative, the '5 Point Peace Plan' (5PPP), which proposed to address the underlying issues in the conflict and aimed at long-term normalisation between the two countries. Reversing Ethiopia's formal rejection in 2003, he declared Ethiopia's acceptance 'in principle' of the 2002 decision, despite its still being considered 'illegal and unjust'. The payment of dues to the commission was resumed, and a plea was made for starting the demarcation process. The general thrust was to break the stalemate that had emerged after the Eritrean government refused any dialogue or negotiations whatsoever on the modalities of border demarcation and subsequent peace, insisting the decision be implemented to the letter. Ethiopia saw in this an underlying attitude refusing any normalisation of relations between the two states. While the 5PPP relieved some of the international pressure on Ethiopia (including threats of divestment and sanctions), few people in the country itself, or Ethiopians in the diaspora, supported Meles's about-face: the caving in to pressure by an international community ignorant of the facts on the ground was widely rejected.

Relations with Kenya were generally good but showed signs of strain after several Ethiopian troop incursions on Kenyan territory in March and April in pursuit of OLF rebels, which resulted in a number of Kenyan deaths. Kenya in the same month also deported four Ethiopians accused of harassing or torturing Ethiopian political exiles in Nairobi.

Ethiopia, Sudan and Yemen strengthened their cooperation under the Sana'a Forum for Cooperation, aimed at creating a free trade zone and a common front towards Eritrea. In Somalia, Ethiopia supported the formation of a new Somali unity government within the IGAD context, but in March was also accused of providing arms to allied factions.

During 2004, the *Nile River* issue came under public discussion again because of Ethiopia's plans to harness more water from the tributary Blue Nile, which originates in Ethiopia's Lake Tana. In the context of the Nile Basin Initiative, a meeting was held in March of the ten riparian countries in Entebbe, Uganda, and a week later in Nairobi. Ethiopia announced it would plead for a more equitable sharing of the Nile waters, of which 86 % flows from Ethiopian sources (Lake Tana and the Blue Nile). A reconsideration, supported by Kenya and Uganda, of the 1929 and 1959 Nile Treaties thus looked increasingly likely.

On the northern border with Eritrea, the *United Nations Mission in Ethiopia and Eritrea* (UNMEE) kept a peacekeeping force in place near the Temporary Security Zone, a strip of demilitarised territory on Eritrean soil promulgated after the December 2000 'peace accord' (cessation of hostilities agreement). Despite the mounting tension in 2004, no serious incidents were reported. Minefields created during the war posed a great security threat and claimed the lives of dozens of people. In December 2004, the UNMEE force was reduced from 4,200 to 3,889 men. Direct traffic between the two countries across the zone was still not possible.

During the year, Ethiopia had *peacekeeping troops* under the UN flag in Burundi and Liberia. In November, Ethiopia offered troops for the UN-sponsored stabilisation force to support the newly elected government in Somalia, whose new president, Abdullahi Yusuf, an old friend of Ethiopia, had asked for 25,000 UN peacekeepers.

Many aid and development cooperation agreements were signed in 2004 between Ethiopia and donor countries, especially EU countries, Japan, the US and China (the latter in construction and infrastructure). In January an $ 11 m development aid agreement was signed with the UNDP. In April, a contract was signed with the Jordanian company SI Tech International to exploit the huge natural gasfields in the Ogaden region, with proven reserves of 12.5 bn cubic metres.

Ethiopian *diplomacy* centred on the Eritrean-Ethiopian border issue and regional Horn of Africa politics. In January, the UN appointed a special mediator, former Canadian Minister of Foreign

Affairs Lloyd Axworthy, to push for progress on the border issue. He had consultations with the Ethiopian leadership but Eritrea refused to meet with him. British Prime Minister Tony Blair visited Ethiopia in October for talks on the same issue and for furthering his initiative for the 'Commission for Africa', a major plan for a partnership between Western donor and African countries to speed-up Africa's development. In January, German Chancellor Schröder also paid a visit to Ethiopia. UN Secretary-General Kofi Annan was in Addis Ababa from 3–6 July to address the African Union summit on the UN's Millennium Development Goals and also to have bilateral meetings with the Ethiopian leadership on the border conflict with Eritrea.

Cross-border migrations in Ethiopia were limited to refugee movements in western Ethiopia (related to the Sudan conflict) and in the Somali region, where instability increased. In Dima town, southwest Ethiopia, about 19,000 Sudanese refugees were located. Following the Gambela 'ethnic clashes' in early 2004, a reported 4–5,000 (some sources said 10,000) Ethiopian Anyuwa fled to the Pochalla area in Sudan. The numbers of cross-border migrants in 2004 declined compared to previous years, and tensions between local people and incoming refugees were largely absent. More trouble was generated in resettlement areas within Ethiopia between locals and re-settlers. In Tigray region a small but regular influx of Eritrean refugees or deserters was registered, on top of those already displaced by war. In some inaccessible border areas, there were cross-border raids by local people, mainly pastoralists, e.g., Sudanese Toposa attacked villages and cattle herds of the Suri people in southwest Ethiopia at least three times in 2004, and the Ethiopian Dassanetch attacked Turkana people in northern Kenya on 16 and 20 October, with several people killed and cattle stolen. Such incidents caused no diplomatic ripples.

Socioeconomic Developments

Due to the good rains and the resulting higher *agricultural output* in 2004, a GDP growth rate of some 7% (according to IMF;

government claim 10%) was reported, up from −4% in 2003. Industrial production and services were slightly up as well. However, the long-run GDP growth trend tends to equal national population increase. Furthermore, the GDP growth figure only applies to the registered economy and excludes the large informal sector.

There was continued massive poverty in Ethiopia, with an estimated 48% living below the poverty line of $ 1 per day. Annual income per capita remained around $ 110. The number of street children increased, as did that of prostitutes. Poverty reduction plans and debt relief schemes were signed with several countries, e.g., Germany in December and with Sweden in May, with the ostensible aim of enhancing Ethiopia's effort to reach the UN Millennium Development Goals in 2015.

EPRDF-affiliated business conglomerates such as Mega-Net, Africa Insurance, Ambassel, Guna, Biftu PLC, Sur Construction, etc. increased their hold on the national economy, drawing frequent complaints from private business people. The other major economic player growing in importance was Saudi-Ethiopian billionaire-tycoon Mohammed al-Amoudi, chairman of the MIDROC Corporation and owner of dozens of enterprises, including the Addis Ababa Sheraton Hotel. The country's largest salt factory in the Afar region was opened in October, built by an EPRDF-affiliated share company.

The overall *economic and food security situation* of Ethiopia remained very precarious: the country could not feed itself. While the harvest of 2004 was good, significantly reducing the number of food-needy people, in December the government again announced a donor appeal for 387,482 metric tons of food aid for about 2.2 m people, valued at some $ 159 m. This was down from the 2004 aid appeal for 14 m people, but again shows the chronic food deficit of the country even in the best of times. Ethiopia also asked for $ 112 m of non-food assistance for urgent humanitarian needs.

The *public health* situation in Ethiopia remained highly problematic. Malaria epidemics were recorded in several areas, as the spread of the parasite-carrying mosquitoes widened. Incidence of

TB and other infectious diseases did not diminish. Economy and society were also seriously burdened by the HIV/AIDS pandemic, which in 2004 affected about 3 to 5% of the total population, some 1.5 to 2 m people, one of the highest absolute figures in Africa. There were about 750,000 AIDS orphans who had lost one parent or both. In 2004, AIDS-related deaths reached about 100,000 to 120,000. The reach of treatment was very low: as of June only about 4,500 people received anti-retroviral drugs. HIV-AIDS patients occupy some 40% of hospital beds. The health infrastructure, with 119 hospitals and 412 health centres, is stable but under-funded and understaffed, with a high turnover.

Costs for *education* took about 6% of the national budget ($509 m) and the sector's coverage and enrolment expanded significantly. Quality improvement, however, was a point of concern. In 2004, about 60% of eligible children went to primary school. High school attendance was 13%, university attendance 5–6%. The new regional universities (Jimma, Bahir Dar, Meqelle, Awasa) were consolidated, and new ones were built in Soddo-Wolayta, Dilla and some other towns in the south. The teaching load of university staff was doubled because of the requirement by the government that universities, especially Addis Ababa University which produces most of the MA graduates, treble the output of students, in line with the government's 'capacity building' programme. The research time of scientists was thus severely reduced, and salaries remained stagnant. State universities also had to continue the widely unpopular and de-motivating evaluation system ('gimgema') that gives students a very big say in the performance assessments of individual staff. Private university colleges served about 15–20,000 students, but had no all-round academic profile.

The World Bank and IMF maintained a close working relationship with Ethiopia, e.g., in the framework of nicely worded plans like the Poverty Reduction and Growth Facility (PRGF), the Sustainable Development and Poverty Reduction Programme (SDPRP) and the Poverty Reduction Support Credit (PRSC). Despite the failure of several phases of these plans, worth hundreds of millions of US dollars, all were extended according to schedule. The government also drew up a PRSP that found acceptance among the donor community, due to the country's meeting the benchmarks, and this allowed Ethiopia to receive additional funds from IMF. Disagreement arose, however, on the 'slow pace' of privatisation, on financial system reform and on government reluctance to open up the financial sector (banks, insurance) to foreign capital, where the government fears dominance and exploitation by foreigners. This, and the many bureaucratic hurdles in the legal and administrative system, probably accounted for Ethiopia's ranking in 2004, despite improvements, as a 'mostly unfree' economy on the US Heritage Foundation index. Notable in 2004 was the continued expansion of Chinese businesses in Ethiopia, e.g., the telecommunications companies Huawei (to set up a switch telephone network) and ZTE (to develop the cell phone system earlier awarded to the Swedish company Ericsson), as well as road construction contracts (April). EU firms repeatedly complained to the Ethiopian government about being excluded and about the aggressive business policies of Chinese firms on the Ethiopian market.

The approved *national budget* in 2003/2004 (the budget year runs from 1 July to 1 July) was estimated at $ 2.24 bn, with capital expenditures of $ 628 m (1 $ was ca. 8.60 Ethiopian birr in December 2004) and $ 919 m of recurrent expenditures. The budget deficit was some 7% and inflation was about 5.5%. The national debt in 2004 was an estimated $ 6.8 bn (not taking into account the proposed debt cancellations). Military spending was about 5–7% of the budget, education and health 7.5%.

Due to its prudent macroeconomic and monetary policies, its regular debt-service payments, the – relative to other African countries – low rate of corruption and the positive developments in selected sectors of the economy, Ethiopia received a comparatively large share of international and donor country aid, amounting to about 6% of GDP in 2004 (down from 8% in 2003). Still, the absorptive capacity of the country for aid was limited, and many programmes did not have the full desired effect because of a lack of facilities, employment, institutional support or skilled manpower.

Ethiopia was also eligible for the HIPC initiative, and in 2004 had benefited, via the IMF and the World Bank's IDA, from cumulative *debt relief* to the tune of $ 1.3 bn, as well as a larger number of grants-in-aid instead of loans. Another privileged area of donor support was capacity building in higher education, communication technology, the rural economy and administrative reform (decentralisation, local capacity building).

Ethiopia's economy continued to be marked by reliance on *agricultural production*, most of it in the smallholder sector, and showed little growth. While the weather in 2004 was favourable and more fertiliser was used, contributing to a 24% higher agricultural output, there was no marked structural improvement in the sector. Despite renewed extension services and peasant training programmes, investment remained low and poverty rampant. About 80% of the population worked in agriculture. Agriculture generated some 46% of GDP, and constituted 60% of export earnings through coffee, hides and skins, leather products, oilseeds, livestock and the stimulant ch'at (catha edulis). The service sector share in GDP was about 49%, that of industry 12%.

The government still followed the 1993 'Agricultural Development-Led Industrialisation' policy (ADLI), which places agricultural producers at the centre of the economy and sees them as the engine of growth. In view of the unpredictable, weather-dependent and smallholder-based nature of Ethiopian agriculture, this model has not worked well. There were signs in 2004 that the government started thinking about independent urban industrialisation to generate growth and serve the domestic market. In this respect, the example of China's economic development made a great impression on the Ethiopian leadership. The land tenure system of Ethiopia was again hotly debated among experts. The government, however, did not budge from its ideological principle of all land as state property: in its view, liberalising the land market would generate great inequality, drive many people off the land to the cities and create land-based power groups. At the same time, the government in 2004 moved to make the 'registration' of land rights possible, in terms of which parents can transfer their use of land to their children. Customary land rights and practices were not legally respected, although in certain areas they made a comeback in practice. There was investment in the rural sector by private agrarian entrepreneurs and also by party-linked business people, who started commercial farms (flowers, vegetables for export, dairy production, etc.), but in 2004 these comprised only 5% of agricultural production.

Compared to other African countries, Ethiopia has long been marked by a low rate of *migration* of rural people to the cities. The urban population in Ethiopia in 2004 stood at 16%. The new ethno-federal political order in Ethiopia, urging people to remain in 'their own' region, has tended to discourage internal migration. While this was still the case, more people were moving to the towns and cities. There was also a constant outflow of more educated but un- or under-employed or dismissed people to foreign countries (US, Canada, Gulf States, Saudi Arabia). Remittances from overseas were estimated to have reached about $ 220 m in 2004 and represented a vital part of the Ethiopian economy.

In the rural sector, Ethiopia embarked on the implementation of a large-scale, $ 220 m *resettlement programme* to meet problems of overpopulation, soil erosion, drought and recurring famine in the northern and central parts of the country. This programme, designed in 2003, envisaged the move to lower density areas by 440,000 households (or some 2.2 m people) 'on a voluntary basis'. The effort resembled the schemes instigated by the previous Marxist government, but the measure of coercion was less and site preparation seemed better. Still, success was limited: participation was less than expected, facilities were lacking, disease was rampant and some re-settled people had already returned to their places of origin (where they kept their rights to land for three years). In some locations,

tensions emerged between newcomers and indigenous populations, who used the land for extensive purposes like livestock herding, hunting, beekeeping, etc. and also as ritual or burial sites. The
other solution to relieve pressure on the land and on resources –
birth control policies – made only slow progress. The fertility rate
was an estimated 5.44 children born per woman, which was down
from seven 15 years ago. The government prepared a population
policy document in 1996, but continued opposition against family
planning and population reduction expressed by the Muslim community, the Ethiopian Orthodox church and other religious groups
made implementation difficult. Popular opinion was also reluctant.
In the countryside, however, many clinics now offered contracep-
tives and these were in high demand, especially among married
women, who carry the largest burden of daily work and childcare.

In 2004, Ethiopia also had a population of *internally displaced
persons (IDPs) and refugees* of some 275,000 people, down 29% from
2003. They were located chiefly in the Tigray and Somali regions.

Ecological problems persisted in Ethiopia, such as deforestation,
massive topsoil erosion and overuse of resources in many places. A
contributory background factor was the pattern of steadily declining rainfall connected to global warming and microclimate change.
Related factors are continued high population growth and policy
failures in agriculture. There was no significant growth in the agricultural sector, and most peasants perform additional non-agrarian
activities to survive. Land remained state property but could be
leased and given in use to peasants and urban dwellers. However,
it was often unpredictably redistributed at will by state agents on
criteria other than economic. An average holding was less than one
hectare, too small for proper sustenance and growth. The lack of a
land market and legislation to provide security of tenure for rural
producers contributed to the lack of investment in agriculture and
upkeep of the commons.

The pastoral sector in the lowland areas covers a large land surface and is the domain of several ethnic groups, such as the Afar,

Somali, Boran, Guji and smaller groups in the southwest, like the Mursi, Nyangatom, Hamar and Suri. In 2004, they continued to be marginalised, and earlier government plans to assist the sector with education, securing their grazing lands, credit schemes and improving security had not materialised. A World Bank- and government-supported 'Pastoral Community Initiative' was launched in 2004 to address the issue. The government agenda, however, was to move towards settling the pastoralists, regardless of the ecological consequences for fragile ecosystems.

Ethiopia in 2005

During the year, Ethiopia experienced a serious political crisis. National politics and public debates were not dominated by the enduring stand-off with Eritrea about the demarcation of the common border, but by highly controversial parliamentary elections in May and their dramatically violent aftermath. The democratisation process saw a decisive setback. While economic growth was realised in the formal sector and educational, infrastructural and export gains were made, not much progress was achieved in respect of food security, reducing mass poverty, achieving industrial take-off, easing ethnic/regional tensions or enhancing social stability. At the end of the year, Ethiopia faced a new challenge of responding to a critical international community with regard to its domestic post-election crisis and its perceived refusal to 'implement' the 2002 decision by the Permanent Court of Arbitration on the Ethio-Eritrean border. No progress was made on this issue, and moves by both parties heightened tensions. This prompted the UN and donor countries to repeatedly express their fears about a possible resumption of armed conflict. Good relations continued to be maintained with other neighbouring states.

Domestic Politics

The domestic political scene was completely dominated by the *parliamentary elections* on 15 May and their violent aftermath. This was one of the most contested and dynamic rounds of voting ever held in the country. All subsequent developments during the year were marked by the outcome: public attitudes, governance, the economy and relations with international donors were all negatively influenced by the awkward handling of post-election events.

These elections for 547 seats in the House of People's Representatives (HPR) and for the House of the Federation (the second chamber) were preceded by a *campaign* in which, for the first time, opposition parties gained access to the state media and could travel throughout the country and inform voters about the alternatives. The government had opened up the political process, although it remained in firm control. There were also televised debates between the main competing parties. Voter registration and turnout were very high (approx. 90%). Despite this, even before election day there were many incidents of targeted intimidation, negative press campaigns, arrests and occasional killings of opposition activists. Several government ministers also tried to 'ethnicise' the campaign, e.g., by intimating that the opposition campaign reflected a course similar to that of the Rwandan Interahamwe, a comparison widely rejected. In August, a local singer countered this with a song saying, "the Rwandan genocide will never happen here", and it was an instant hit.

From a technical point of view, the elections, organised and overseen by the National Electoral Board of Ethiopia (NEBE), went relatively smoothly and without violent incident, as far as could be ascertained from observers' reports. The *ruling Ethiopian People's Revolutionary Democratic Front (EPRDF)* and its affiliates, who were in solid control of all political institutions and centres of power, ran against a large number of *opposition parties*. The most important of these were the Coalition for Unity and Democracy (CUD) and the United Ethiopian Democratic Front (UEDF), two parties that had quickly grown in popularity in the six months before the elections. CUD was a party with a more national than ethno-regional programme and represented urban populations, middle classes and a substantial portion of the central and northern peasantry (many of Amhara, Gurage and mixed background, although not with a clearly defined 'ethnic' profile). The UEDF was a new coalition of mainly southern Ethiopians, Oromo and diaspora-linked parties attracted to federalism and ethnic rights issues. They pleaded for 'real federalism' and not EPRDF's centralist kind. A number of smaller ethno-regional parties closely linked to the ruling EPRDF, e.g., in the Somali, Gambela, Afar and Beni-Shangul regions, also gained seats. Smaller ethnic opposition parties were not successful, except the Sheko and Mezenger People's Democratic Unity Organisation (SMPDUO) from the southwest, which won a single seat. Despite intimidation and threats, especially in the rural areas of Amhara and Oromiya, the two main opposition parties, CUD and UEDF, won a substantial number of seats, 161, almost a third. CUD alone won 109 seats, UEDF 52. A new Oromo party, the Oromo Federal Democratic Movement, founded in September 2004, made a good showing with 11 seats. The remaining seats were for SMPDUO and an independent, making for a total of 174 opposition seats. In the final count, the EPRDF and its affiliates won 371 seats, thus retaining a clear majority. The outcome indicated that for the first time many rural people had dared to vote for the opposition. In locations where international observers were present at vote-casting and counting, the opposition usually won. The opposition also took virtually all urban areas. Addis Ababa region was a clean sweep for them, and the CUD leader Berhanu Nega, an economist of repute, was chosen by his party as future mayor.

The vote-counting process was non-transparent and highly contested and dragged on for three months. The CUD opposition cried foul, alleging that it was during this crucial phase that the ruling party – in control of the government, the state and NEBE – secured its victory. Accusations of *vote-rigging* followed and for 299, mainly rural, constituencies complaints were lodged. The grounds for the opposition's accusations were not always clear, and their often stubborn rhetoric did not help to ease tensions. Only in 31 cases did a repeat vote take place, and all these seats went to the EPRDF. In this new round even some high-profile EPRDF leaders who had lost their seats in the first round now regained their mandates. It was obvious that the EPRDF, which had as usual been confident of victory, had had a great scare at the good showing of the opposition and had underestimated the groundswell of opposition to their achievements as a government. In subsequent meetings between EPRDF leaders and their political cadres, the reproach was heard that they had not properly monitored the views of the people nor 'prepared' adequately to secure a victory.

Despite their good showing, it appeared unlikely that the opposition would gain an outright victory. CUD in particular refused to accept the final results, calling for a repeat of the elections and staging peaceful protests to express its dissatisfaction. Despite a ban on all *demonstrations* and gatherings declared by Prime Minister Meles Zenawi on election day, in early June students began to challenge the vote-counting process. The troubles started on the night of 5 June, when armed soldiers entered a student dormitory at Addis Ababa University at midnight to arrest CUD supporters, for unknown reasons. Other students then protested against this action and resisted, chanting, "The votes of our peasant fathers shall not be stolen, and election problems should be solved by legal means". On 6 June, government forces arrested dozens of peacefully demonstrating students. They also shot a young woman and a student at Kotebe college. After their deaths, a cycle of protests and violent suppression began. Most Addis Ababa residents were struck by the humiliating and brutal behaviour of police and special forces, who showed little regard for human life or property.

The post-election period was thus marked by *repressive state violence*, persistent threats against the opposition and lack of successful dialogue, in which neither government nor opposition were skilled. In June, police and special forces killed at least 42 people, and many thousands – mostly youngsters, some only 14 years old – were arrested with-out charge in night raids and transferred to improvised, ill-equipped detention camps. On 12 June, government militia shot and killed the newly elected MP Tesfaye Adane Jara (CUD) in Arsi Negele town, and other deaths of opposition members were also reported.

The *elections* were witnessed by more than *300 foreign observers*, from the US (non-governmental), the AU and the EU. The EU group was the largest and best prepared. The AU report was uncritical. The US and especially the EU reports complimented Ethiopia on the progress made, but stated that on the whole the elections could not be called free and fair and fell short of international standards. The EU observers and their mission head, European parliamentarian Ana Gomes, then drew heavy criticism and insults from the Ethiopian authorities, which stated that their report was "garbage" and that the observers had contributed to the election violence. Remarkable was the silence and inaction of the US, which continued to view all domestic developments in Ethiopia through the prism of the international 'war on terror' (with US troops stationed in eastern Ethiopia and Djibouti), seeing Meles Zenawi's regime, for some undisclosed reason, as a necessary partner. The US voiced only superficial concerns about the violence and the arrests of opposition figures. The only tangible act was to forbid the sale of Humvee vehicles to the Ethiopian police and military. However, there were reports that the government used newly acquired technology and skills for its security forces in its efforts to suppress domestic post-election dissent. The government had few if any answers to the frequent reports and questions by national and international organisations about human rights abuses, including killings, disappearances, summary executions, torture, abduction, destruction of property, humiliation and unjustified imprisonment of citizens during the course of the year.

The *independent press* also suffered in the clamp-down, and a general curtailing of news reports followed. Rumours and unverifiable stories began to circulate and created unrest and insecurity. About 13 journalists were in jail or accused of crimes, some for 'treason'. Virtually all non-government newspapers closed down. No independent radio and TV stations existed anyway. During the course of the year the government also targeted foreign journalists: well-known British correspondents from AP and 'The Guardian' were forced to leave the country, and correspondents from VOA and 'Deutsche Welle' had already been barred earlier in the year. Censorship and self-censorship increased notably, leading to a scarcity of information in the country.

After the final election result was made public by NEBE on 5 September, most *opposition* parliamentarians from CUD and some from UEDF *refused to take their seats in the HPR*, rejecting its legitimacy. While CUD called for peaceful protests and civil disobedience, a mass demonstration in early October in the central square of Addis Ababa was called off by them for fear of government violence.

In October, a *new government*, with the same party, prime minister and inner circle of trusted confidantes, was confirmed in power. Some remarkable ministerial appointments were made, e.g., that of former Oromiya region leader Kuma Demeqsa, who had a record of being dismissed from most previously held positions, as minister of defence, and of controversial figures such as Addisu Leggese as vice-premier and minister of agriculture and Tefera Walwa as minister of capacity building. The former information minister and EPRDF election campaign leader Bereket Sim'on, seen as quite a divisive person, was appointed special advisor to the prime minister. Some parliamentary procedures had already been changed in the intervening period, notably the rule that new parliamentary agenda topics could be proposed by 20% of parliamentarians: this was now raised to 51%, to minimise the impact of the opposition. Key Addis Ababa region services, such as the road transport authority, public rally permit office, NGO licensing bureau, authentication-registration bureau and quarantine service department, were also brought under the federal government, apparently to undermine the incoming CUD administration of the city. For the same reason, the government moved the seat of the Oromiya regional capital back from Nazreth to Addis Ababa.

A *second round of demonstrations* started in *November* and the government again responded with violent suppression. Another 40 to 50 people were killed, including several policemen (as in the June killings, exact numbers were unknown, because some people were not traced), and many thousands of opposition sympathisers from all over the country were detained and put in camps. On 15 November, the government admitted that it held over 5,400 people but had freed nearly 8,000 arrested earlier. However, during

December more people were arrested, and estimates were that a total of 18,000 people were being held. By this time, a large group of opposition leaders (including the entire CUD leadership, among them Berhanu Nega, Mesfin Wolde-Mariam, Yaqob Haile-Mariam, Hailu Shawel and Ms. Birtukan Mideqsa), civil society activists and journalists had been put in jail, accused of having incited the violence. They were later charged with 'treason' and 'genocide' – charges for which no credible evidence was available – and were repeatedly denied bail. A list of 131 accused was then prepared, which included Ethiopian intellectuals and critical opinion leaders in the diaspora. The government also started to undermine the two main opposition parties, CUD and UEDF, by fomenting internal dissent via 'moles' and by refusing to recognise the legal status of the CUD, which tried in vain to register with NEBE as CUDF after one of the four constituent parties had left the coalition.

Following the November troubles, opposition activists and supporters throughout the country were persecuted and harassed. Protests and clashes between citizens and security forces continued, notably in the Oromiya, Gambella and Amhara regions, as well as in various towns such as Awasa, Dessie, Ambo, Jimma, Neqemte, Bahir Dar, Gondar and obviously Addis Ababa, where high-school pupils were in the forefront.

Despite the relatively promising election campaign, the televised debates, the improved press reporting, and the opposition parties' substantial gains, *no decisive democratic breakthrough* on the national level was achieved in 2005. On the contrary, an authoritarian government incapable of dealing with dissent reasserted itself. The response of NEBE, the police, army and judiciary to the election-related unrest and disputes was not professional and led to an undue escalation of violence. Despite the show of force, the regime was weakened and lost much of its legitimacy. The political atmosphere turned from elation and optimism in the early part of the year to gloom and violence in December, and despite numerous efforts by Western donor countries, no negotiated end to the crisis was in sight. Many Ethiopians saw the crisis as a turning point, and stated that the regime had now shown its true colours and that to expect the establishment of real democracy and the rule of law was an illusion, only believed by gullible Western foreigners who did not wish to admit the mistake of having put their bets on the EPRDF.

Throughout the last months of 2005, several small-scale *bomb and hand grenade attacks* were reported, especially in Addis Ababa. They caused little damage and no injuries or deaths and no culprits were arrested. But city residents and observers suspected that the devices were planted by (pro-) government individuals to create unrest and justify even further clamp-downs. The election crisis, resulting in growing distrust of the central government, thus aggravated the overall security situation.

On the domestic front, the year also saw a continuation of *ethnic and regional tensions*, with local-level conflict flaring up, especially in the Gambela region and along the boundaries between the Oromiya and Somali regions. Hundreds of people probably died during the year in repeated clashes. Mediation efforts and judicial action were rarely tried or had no success. A solution to the long-standing Gambela crisis, which had led to repeated armed clashes between the army, the indigenous Anywaa people and the Nuer people (with their numbers constantly augmented by Nuer newcomers from Sudan) was not achieved. Nothing was heard of a government commission of inquiry to investigate the clashes of 2003–04 in which hundreds of people were killed. Ethnic tensions were also reported in the Afar area (e.g., with Issa) and in the southwest. In the Southern region disputes were frequent, especially on local borders. Small-scale rebel activities were noted in the Ogaden region, where the Ogaden National Liberation Front (ONLF) maintained a presence, in parts of Oromiya (east and west) where the insurgent Oromo Liberation Front (OLF) operated, and to a lesser extent in some parts of the northern Amhara region, where unrest intensified after the election crisis in the second half of the year. More bandit activities were reported in the remoter parts of the country and occasionally on some highways. The formula of 'ethnic politics', which gives political expression to ethnic identity on all administrative levels, did not ease ethnic tensions but sharpened them, making ethnic identity a contested resource and political instrument. Despite the positive recognition of ethnic heritage and culture by minority groups, local-level conflicts and confrontations, notably over borders and access to regional or zonal budgets, were frequent.

Ethiopians remained committed to *religion*, and with various shades of affiliation: about 40% adhered to Orthodox Christianity, 38–40% to Islam, 10–12% to Protestant-Evangelical Christianity and the remainder to traditional religions. Religious leaders of the Ethiopian Orthodox Church (EOC), the Muslim community and the Pentecostal-Evangelical movements were not prominent in the public or political sphere. For instance, hardly any statements or appeals about the election crisis, the insecurity, the ethnic tensions or the deadly violence were heard during the year. Fearing political repression, religious leaders rarely exerted themselves by calling for mediation or restraint. The position of the incumbent pro-government EOC patriarch continued to be contested within and outside the church. An indication of this was the frequent reports of worshippers leaving a church when he entered to lead the service. *Communal relations* between the three major religious blocs in general continued to be outwardly peaceful, but tensions under the surface remained. There were growing rivalries and in some areas violent clashes between Muslims, Orthodox and Pentecostals. In some places, disputes over new mosque and church buildings as well as over burial grounds were frequent. Precise information about religious conflicts was difficult to obtain, but in several places religious differences became enmeshed with the political strife of the post-election period. Christians and Christian evangelists were repeatedly harassed by Muslims. In one incident in September in the southeast, a bus was stopped by Muslim militants and passengers forced to cite the Muslim creed: one man was reportedly killed when he refused. In November, ten Christians were killed in Kore village in central Ethiopia by Muslim inhabitants allegedly incited by government cadres, and some 100 houses were burnt down. There were also skirmishes, but not killings, between Orthodox believers and Evangelicals. In the Ethiopian Christian community, Evangelist-Pentecostal affiliation continued to grow. In the Muslim community, the grassroots influence of stricter 'foreign-style' Islam (i.e., Saudi 'Wahhabi') increased, but radical or political Islam was not prominent in the public sphere. Involvement by Ethiopian Muslims in Islamist terrorist activity was quite rare.

Reforms to the *judicial system* were slow to materialise. The lack of funding and manpower continued undiminished, the case load of the courts was huge and the training and experience of most judges inadequate. Getting justice within a reasonable period was therefore impossible. Law enforcement was not strong, and an oft-heard opinion was that "there is no law in this country". Citizens' perceptions of the independence of the courts and judges were unfavourable and bribery was a problem. According to the US state department human rights report for 2005, police and security forces, as a direct extension of the political power-holders, also showed contempt for court orders, e.g., those relating to the release of prisoners held without charge or found to be wrongly accused. Abuses by the police and in prisons, including frequent cases of beatings and torture, mostly occurred with impunity. In March, a 530-page report entitled "Comprehensive Justice System Reform Program" was offered to the government by a Dutch consultancy office, but the chances that the long list of recommendations will be implemented are likely to be slim. Prison conditions were marked by overcrowding, lack of food and poor hygiene. The trials of former 'Derg' (Mengistu regime) officials dragged on into their 15th year, thereby protracting the denial of justice to the accused.

Foreign Affairs

In what seemed to become an unsolvable stalemate, the *conflict with Eritrea* was marked by an almost total lack of progress and creeping deterioration, mainly as a result of additional restrictive measures imposed by the Eritreans on the United Nations Mission for Ethiopia and Eritrea (UNMEE) forces. Eritrea insisted on unconditional, non-negotiable demarcation of the border as determined in the April 2002 Permanent Court of Arbitration (PCA) decision, despite the fact that in the decision no details for a realistic demarcation on the ground were given. Predictions by international observers and experts that "war might well break out soon" were heard throughout the year, usually following Eritrea's threats and predictable rhetoric about Ethiopia's refusal to implement the PCA border decision. This was Eritrea's excuse to keep hundreds of thousands of soldiers in the army, keep Eritrean society militarised and delay domestic democratisation indefinitely. Ethiopia did not budge either, sticking to its November 2004 'Five Point Peace Plan' calling for a wider discussion of normalisation and border demarcation issues. Some 300–400,000 landmines remained in the border area, and dozens of local people were killed by mines. Tens of thousands of displaced people on both sides of the border continued to live in under-equipped camps. There were no economic or air links between the two countries. International mediation efforts by Canadian UN special envoy L. Axworthy and later by retired US General C.W. Fulford were not successful. The conflict remains unlikely to be resolved while the two current regimes remain in power. The UNMEE maintained a presence of about 3,200 personnel in the 25 kilometre-wide security zone along the 950 kilometre border. Observers noted that Eritreans crossed into the zone and reinforced their positions. Ethiopia was also reported to have occupied an area inside the zone. Due to the restrictions imposed by Eritrea, UNMEE effectively controlled only about 40% of the zone in December. There were discussions about further reducing the UNMEE force.

With its other neighbours – Sudan, Djibouti, Somalia, Somaliland and Kenya – Ethiopia maintained relatively good and uneventful relations. Djibouti remains the main seaport for Ethiopia, a status it has had since Ethiopia trapped itself into becoming landlocked in

1993 by recognising Eritrea, without border adjustments. Controlling contraband trade in goods was an enduring problem, with several government officials also involved. Relations with Somalia improved, as the government intensified contacts with the new Somali president Abdullahi Yusuf, a long-term ally. Ethiopia continued to keep a close watch on Somali Islamist insurgent groups in the border area, such as 'al-Itihaad al-Islami'.

Ethiopia pursued a course of good relations with self-declared independent Somaliland, in view of its growing use of the port of Berbera. It also expanded contacts with Sudan and undertook negotiations over future oil supplies from Sudan to Ethiopia. On the Kenyan border, there were trans-border clashes between Ethiopian and Kenyan agro-pastoral groups (e.g., Somali, Boran, Degodia, Gabbra), resulting in dozens of deaths. Drought in the last few months of 2005 aggravated the problem.

Ethiopia remained active in IGAD, the sub-regional organisation of northeastern African countries, although its contribution was insignificant in 2005. One prominent issue was the Nile question, where no breakthrough was achieved as to the future use of its waters by the member states cooperating in the Nile Basin Initiative (NBI). Prime Minister Meles confirmed in February that the current situation, based on old colonial treaties favouring Egypt, was untenable as Ethiopia, the source of 85% of the Nile's waters, was denied rights to use water from the Blue Nile for agriculture. Planning started for the building of a large dam at Kara Dombe on the Blue Nile.

Relations with the *Western donor community* deteriorated sharply because of the government's harsh suppression of post-election demonstrations, its treatment of the opposition and the worsening human rights situation. Donor country policy circles had no clear idea of what long-term conclusions to draw from the political crisis. Several EU countries announced a freeze or cutbacks in development aid and the re-channelling of funding, but no radical measures were taken. The crisis had negative effects on the economy, the investment climate and on Ethiopia's international standing, with even the World Bank making critical notes on the government's over-reaction and the damage to governance and operational reliability. The EPRDF and Prime Minister Meles thought that the country just had to revert to 'business as usual', but this was unlikely to happen.

The trend among the Ethiopian leadership to re-orient itself towards Asian countries, notably China, was strengthened. China, asking no questions about human rights and searching for oil and resources for its own economic expansion, was seen as *the* model of development for more than one reason: developing fast economically while retaining authoritarian one-party rule. China's business interests in Ethiopia notably increased, and Ethiopia also announced closer military cooperation with that country.

Socioeconomic Developments

Macroeconomic figures were contradictory, but Ethiopia probably achieved a GDP growth of 6–7%, down from earlier projections of 8.7%. GDP per capita remained basically stagnant, mainly due to high population growth. In the second part of the year, agriculture, the mainstay of the economy, suffered from drought conditions, resulting in less production and thus in a downward trend in growth. Due to the weather conditions, there was an average reduction of 1.2% in agricultural output per capita, mainly in staple crops. However, export crops like coffee and flowers recorded a significant increase compared to 2004. The emergence of the flower export businesses, set up both by Ethiopians and foreigners, was a new and promising phenomenon, which in 2005 accounted for revenues of about $ 20 m, compared to zero five years ago. Encouraging was the overall growth in the *value of exports* by 7.6%. But imports – mainly oil – increased by 32.6%. The value of coffee exports was $ 340 m, a growth of 35.8% growth due to higher world market prices and increased production. Non-coffee exports such as sugar, oil seeds, the stimulant 'ch'at', hides and skins, livestock, gold and flowers, grew by 21.8% to some $ 390 m. Industry, distributive services and other services also recorded growth rates of 6.9%, 7.6% and 6.3% respectively. Tourism took a dip because of the political disturbances.

The growth figures and *prudent financial management* kept hopes high among certain donors, such as the US, World Bank and IMF, for take-off growth and governance improvements. However, the stumbling blocks were government's continued refusal to open up capital and financial service markets to foreign capital – motivated by a probably justified fear of domination by outsiders – and the political crisis, which negatively affected governance, accountability and the investment climate and raised security costs. Economic growth was inhibited by the increasing cost of oil imports, which reached about 7.5% of GDP and were expected to rise by some $ 280 m (or 11% of GDP, 20% of total imports).

Demographic issues remained the subtext of much of Ethiopia's economic woes: with a persistent 3% annual growth rate, the *population* reached 75 m in 2005, putting undiminished stress on natural resources and on already overburdened infrastructural and government service facilities. Of the population, 43.9% was under the age of 15, and the median age was 17.7 years. Population pressure also contributed to environmental problems, conflicts over land and water and to food insecurity: in most rural areas, especially the pastoralist sector, parents had great trouble in feeding their many children adequately, even though the year started out with good harvest prospects. In the last three months of the year, however, drought conditions exacerbated the food situation. (Even in normal harvest years, at least 2.5 m Ethiopians need food aid).

The *national budget for* the Ethiopian financial year (1 July 2004–30 June 2005) was about $ 3.5 bn, 22% of which was destined for the regional states. The current account deficit was reported to be 11.6% of GDP, or about $ 420 m. The country's overall trade balance deficit increased by 4% of GDP and reached about a quarter of total annual GDP. The country imported almost three times the sum earned from exports, $ 3.4 bn versus $ 850 m, the deficit being compensated for by donor grants and a variety of borrowing schemes. Foreign reserves fell from five months worth of imports to 3.7 months. Inflation on an annual basis reached 10.5%, more than double that of last year and caused by higher prices for fuel, building materials, food staples, services and imported goods.

The *foreign debt* remained more or less stable at approximately $ 6 bn, with external debt service payments taking 6.5% of export earnings. Ethiopia again made calls for debt cancellation (from which it had already benefited to the tune of $ 9.2 bn over the past 15 years), and in July the G8 summit discussed Ethiopia as one of the countries eligible for a 100% multilateral debt write-off, which would mean the cancellation of Ethiopia's $ 161 m debt with the IMF, ADB and World Bank. But the decision was not executed, partly due to the political crisis. In December, several key donors (EU, UK and World Bank) threatened to withhold direct budget support of $ 375 m, one-quarter of projected total donor funding. The government counted on higher levels of donor funding for the coming years, but this was unlikely to materialise in view of the political crisis and the limited absorptive capacity of the administration. Foreign direct investments showed a notable increase of 40–50%, creating tens of thousands of jobs in sectors such as horticulture, aluminium, plastics production, mining, transportation and services.

About half the population remained below the *poverty line*. The effects of the Sustainable Development and Poverty Reduction Programme, the earlier PRGF of the IMF and related plans developed in the framework of the UN MDGs, were not very visible and indeed were seen by many to be illusory.

Although the 2005 grain harvest was relatively good, 2.6 m people were again dependent on emergency *food aid*, while there were 5.1 m beneficiaries under a new government scheme, the Productive Safety Net Programme, although this has yet to guarantee adequate assistance. The food shortage could be largely remedied – with foreign funding – from domestic sources. Food insecurity thus remained a persistent problem, despite government efforts to increase production, agricultural extension, irrigation, dyking, etc. The 2005 UN-donor appeal for humanitarian assistance was for almost $ 272 m, of which $ 159 m was for food aid. Emergency food aid requirements in December were estimated at approx. 340,000 tonnes. UNICEF made appeals for a total of $ 91 m to combat malnutrition and the spread of disease among children in the wake of famine conditions. Donor food aid support again illustrated Ethiopia's continued food aid addiction.

Chinese and *Malaysian* companies were given concessions to explore oil deposits in the Gambella area and the Ogaden. The ambitious Kalub gas project, a joint venture with the Jordanian company SI-Tech International to exploit the large natural gas reserves (118 bn cubic metres) in the Ogaden did not make progress and was on the verge of collapse in December.

The two *main players in the Ethiopian economy* remained the *EPRDF*, among whose members and cronies were owners of, or large stakeholders in, many core business conglomerates in construction, media, trading and infrastructural works, and the *Saudi-Ethiopian tycoon* Mohammed al-Amuddin, who expanded his mega-business empire with new acquisitions and activities in various fields such as construction, hotels, mineral exploration and food and drinks factories. He also had many overseas interests. Other business people continued to complain about the power, privileges and insider knowledge of these two business blocs. On the 2005 Corruption Perception Index of Transparency International, Ethiopia shared rank 137 with seven other countries (out of 159), a drop for the third consecutive year.

In some areas of national policy, such as *education*, progress was made. According to government figures, primary school coverage reached about 60–65%. However, concerns about declining quality were repeatedly voiced by parents and education experts, and the drop-out rate was some 18%. Secondary education coverage reportedly reached 30%. Violence in secondary schools was a growing problem. Universities saw a 14% higher enrolment, and 13 more regional universities were being built. Quality concerns were also heard about university education, with universities again required to take in greatly increased numbers of students, leading to similar problems as in 2004: a notable increase in the workload of teachers, alarming staff shortages, decline in student achievement and a severe reduction of the research capacity of staff. Many of the graduates could not find work. The opening of Addis Ababa University and a few others in the south where protests were organised was delayed by several months because of the post-election turmoil. In late 2005, the government announced that more than 600 Nigerian teachers were to be hired for higher education institutions.

The *public health situation* remained critical, the most serious diseases being malaria, TB, infections, diarrhoea and HIV/AIDS, which claimed an estimated 100,000 lives during the year. About one in every 35 Ethiopians was infected (approx. two million). The government started to provide antiretroviral drugs to a select number of people. This donor-funded programme was set to be expanded in coming years. Maternal mortality rates remained among the highest in Africa. The health sector received significant investments, e.g., with the building of more rural health stations and the training of more people, but equipment and staffing were still insufficient to deal with the grave challenges.

The ongoing social crisis was reflected in *urban unemployment*, which stood at about 40%, with youths between 16 and 24 comprising the majority of the unemployed. The government and its media outlets often called them 'adegena bozenewotch', an insulting Amharic term meaning 'dangerous vagrants'. Although new schemes to alleviate youth unemployment were tried, they have had little success yet. During the election demonstrations, the young urban unemployed supplied many of the street protesters, more to vent their anger and their hopelessness than in support of the opposition.

Internal *migration* to the cities or to other regions in Ethiopia remained limited. The population of the urban areas was about

20% of the total. The number of internally displaced persons (*IDPs*) was between 150–165,000 people, including 62,000 displaced in the Tigray region by the 1998–2000 border war with Eritrea, some 50,000 people uprooted by 'ethnic clashes' in Gambella, as well as tens of thousands of people displaced by inter-ethnic conflicts in the Somali region (e.g., Mieso area), along the border between Somali and Oromiya regions and by small-scale clashes elsewhere. The brain-drain to Western countries continued unabated, as did the outflow of low-skilled workers, domestic servants, etc., to the Middle East. The reasons for this were abject poverty, want of opportunities to improve one's life, ethnic discrimination in the regions and overall political insecurity.

Ethiopia in 2006

Ethiopia struggled with the aftermath of the controversial 2005 parliamentary elections and with enduring economic, environmental and food security problems. It was involved in a short but intense war with a new Somali Islamist movement active in southern Somalia. Economic growth and infrastructural investment was registered, but poverty and unemployment did not undergo notable reduction. The legitimacy and popularity of the incumbent political leadership appeared to decline, coupled with a tendency to political repression and intolerance of opposition. The political process showed no meaningful signs of opening up or conciliatory effort and took on a grim character. International human rights agencies heavily criticised the human rights record. Donor countries and the World Bank slowly resumed development support to the government, although they tried to avoid direct funding to the federal government. There was no solution to the border dispute with Eritrea. Ethiopia maintained stable relations with its other neighbours (Somaliland, Djibouti, Sudan and Kenya).

Domestic Politics

Ethiopia's domestic politics was marked by the continued *political crisis* that emerged after the 2005 elections. These elections had led to a dramatic stand-off and to massive repression of opposition groups, notably the Coalition for Unity and Democracy Party (CUDP, formerly CUD), and this continued in 2006. The government, dominated by the former insurgent movement, the Ethiopian Peoples Revolutionary Democratic Front (EPRDF), remained in power, had a large majority in the parliament and continued to implement its economic and political programmes uninfluenced by opposition ideas or calls for compromise. While the opposition had almost a third of the parliamentary seats, its influence was marginal, as EPRDF and its allies block-voted on all issues brought to the parliament, the House of Peoples' Representatives. In addition, some opposition leaders and activists, including MPs, claimed that they were the target of repression and sometimes persecution. In the countryside, dozens of people sympathising with, or members of the opposition disappeared or were on occasion killed under mysterious circumstances. Opponents often made the accusation of targeted killing. One case in point was the assassination in October by police or militia of a CUDP-affiliated youth activist, the 16-year old Wondwossen Gutu, in Addis Ababa. Another was the mysterious death of a top airforce instructor, Daniel Beyene. As with past killings, the culprits were not found and judicial proceedings were not initiated, feeding the idea of the impunity of the security forces. The EPRDF tried to tighten its grip on the rural population by continuing to organise people in administrative units with a duty to report to higher levels.

The *mass trial against opposition leaders* and civil society members that had started after their arrest in November 2005 continued. Convincing evidence against the accused (who included diaspora activists and academics critical of the government but not known for violent agendas) was not produced, and a series of inconclusive court meetings and appeals dragged on. All the prisoners were denied bail. The Ethiopian political leadership made frequent prejudiced remarks about this trial, confirming the impression that it was a political trial meant to silence key opponents. Few if any independent observers continued to speak of Ethiopia as a country 'on the road to democracy'. The leadership mostly ignored pleas for national dialogue and the release of the accused made by the EU, US and the visiting UN commissioner for human rights, Louise Arbour.

At the beginning of the year, in the aftermath of the violent repression in November and December 2005, *anti-government protests* were only carried on via demonstrations, strikes and symbolic actions by high school students in several towns, resulting in frequent

beatings, several deaths, arrests, intimidation of parents and teachers and the closure of schools. In January, a Christian religious
celebration ('Timqet') went awry when people began to chant anti-
government slogans. Police responded with force, killing three people, among them a 12-year old child, beating up dozens of others and
making 42 arrests.

During the course of the year, opposition parties further fragmented into factions due to disunity, the divisive activities of government supporters and harassment in the countryside. The CUDP,
in the absence of its major leaders, was taken over by new people
more favourably disposed towards the government. This was denounced by the diaspora branches of the party. Many observers
noted that the party had now been co-opted and was no longer 'opposition'. The second-largest opposition party, the United Ethiopian
Democratic Front (UEDF) more or less held its own, but the Oromo
National Congress, one of its constituents, was the target of consistent subversion. The opposition voice in parliament was therefore
much weakened.

Opposition demands that the National Electoral Board of
Ethiopia (NEBE), which had overseen the elections of 2005 but had
not satisfactorily resolved outstanding problems, be depoliticised
and its membership evenly balanced between government loyalists and independents or opposition members, were rejected by the
government.

Early in the year, the formation of a new and somewhat unexpected alliance of opposition parties was announced: the *Alliance
for Freedom and Democracy* (AFD), made up of the CUDP (its diaspora section), the Oromo Liberation Front (OLF), the Ogaden
National Liberation Front (ONLF), the southern Sidama Liberation
Front (SLF) and the Ethiopian Peoples Patriotic Front (EPPF). This
alliance, formed among the diaspora, was received with mixed feelings both in Ethiopia and among Ethiopian communities abroad.
It gathered groups that advocated peaceful democratic struggle
(CUDP) and those that did not exclude violence and had combat

groups in the country (OLF, ONLP, EPPF). Its position on the unity of Ethiopia was not clear. The OLF and the ONLF perspectives seemed to dominate this alliance. Its formation in Utrecht, the Netherlands, was reputedly 'witnessed' by a major political figure from Eritrea (a presidential advisor), which further prevented the AFD from gaining substantial support in Ethiopia. The second big Ethiopian opposition party, the UEDF – a mixed coalition of democratic ethno-regional parties – was also invited into the AFD but ultimately refrained from becoming a member. The AFD called on government to take up dialogue. Predictably, the government refused.

All this meant that the political scene in Ethiopia remained frozen. There was continuation of rhetoric on 'democracy' but in reality a hardening of positions. The attitude of the ordinary population moved towards a mixture of cynicism, despair and disdain for politics, augmented by growing anti-Americanism due to the US's perceived indifference towards domestic repression and injustice.

As with other African countries, *debates in cyberspace* on Ethiopian politics and society were increasingly prominent. Websites of opposition groups and Ethiopian diaspora communities continued to be vocal and influential, although apart from furnshing valuable first-hand information on developments in the country some of them also provided forums for exaggerated rhetoric and even insults across political, ethnic and community lines. The Ethiopian government blocked several of the critical websites and web-logs.

This was also the 'year of *defections*': dozens of diplomats, army personnel, civil servants, judges and journalists left or fled the country. This could further erode the standing and legitimacy of the government. The high number of defecting diplomatic personnel (more than 60) was remarkable. The defectors cited repression, bad governance, corruption or personal intimidation and dissatisfaction as their motive. Several defecting diplomats also revealed secrets of the regime in memos of internal meetings at embassies and ministries. Revealing also was a 52-page document (in Amharic, published on some diaspora websites) with instructions for Ethiopian embassies on how to pressurise or neutralise diaspora opposition voices abroad. According to some observers, these concrete plans of action could lead to interference in the internal affairs of the states where the embassies are located.

The *human rights and civil liberties* situation remained bad. Throughout the year a constant stream of reports and news items on the abuse of rights by police, militia and army was published. The annual US state department report on human rights in Ethiopia was very critical. Politics and the legal system continued to be marked by unpredictability, lack of transparency, difficult access to justice and lack of timely and fair judicial process. Constitutional rights were often ignored. According to documented local human rights reports, hundreds of people were arrested on vague charges (or none at all), shot, extra-judicially killed, abused, allegedly tortured or made to 'disappear'. Few of the cases of this and past years were brought to a court of law, meaning justice was often denied to the victims and the bereaved. Leaders of the Oromo Mecha-Tulama Association, arrested in 2004, remained in prison without being charged.

The planned reform of the *legal sector did not make much progress*. The justice system was not free from political (government) pressure or intimidation and also struggled with the case load. A verdict was passed in the 12-year 'Red Terror' trial against 57 (27 *in absentia*) former leading officials of the Mengistu regime: all were found guilty of 'genocide, treason and murder'. Final sentences would come in early 2007. In December, a first verdict *in absentia* was also passed on former dictator Mengistu Haile-Mariam – he was sentenced to life imprisonment. This was later appealed by the state prosecutor. Mengistu remained in Zimbabwe under the protection of President Mugabe.

Overall, the regime's rhetoric was still full of references to 'democratic values', 'rule-of-law', 'justice', 'progress', etc. and some work was done to realise these ideals. In the eyes of most Ethiopians, however, the record was very disappointing. A revealing example of undue government pressure was the case of the *inquiry commission* into the 2005 post-election violence. This commission was handpicked in January 2006 by government and headed by two reputable, independent judges with no political connections. They had to report on the question of whether government forces had used excessive force in the June and November 2005 disturbances. After extensive research based on documents and on interviews with all parties, including eye-witnesses and police and army people, they concluded that 193 people, many of them uninvolved bystanders, including women and children, had been killed, six policemen had died, 763 people had been injured (often seriously) and that about 30,000 mostly young people had been arrested and put into remote prison camps. In its 3 July judgment, the commission decided (by a vote of eight in favour and two against) that government had indeed used excessive force and abused its powers. The report was not accepted by government. Even before its final version was ready, the commission had experienced serious intimidation while it was reviewing the evidence and writing its report. This led the chairman and the vice-chairman (and later some other members) to flee the country. Then the remaining commission members revised their opinion under pressure and collaborated in 'rewriting' the report, this time with conclusions absolving the government of blame. Although the rewriting happened outside the legal mandate and time frame of the commission (until 7 July), this report was duly 'approved' by parliament in late October.

The CUDP leadership arrested in November 2005 remained behind bars the entire year. Their trial on 'treason' and 'genocide' charges made little progress, with constant delays in court sessions and hearings. The prisoners' health deteriorated owing to bad conditions and inadequate medical attention. There was no credible evidence against them. It was feared in Ethiopia that false witness statements and forged papers (a trusted practice in past trials in Ethiopia) were being prepared. Western donor countries continued their criticism of this political trial, which has done the government much damage.

The *mass media* suffered from continued pressure and unpredictable harassment. The independent press endured further intimidation and arrests of journalists and newspaper vendors. At least 14 journalists were on trial on various charges ranging from 'defamation' to 'attempted overthrow of the constitutional order'. In a preposterous move, the government in June dismissed the TV presenter of the nation's popular children's programme, the aged *Ababba* Tesfaye, who was held responsible for one derogatory 'ethnic' utterance by a young child in his programme. While the urban population had at least some, although declining, access to independent information, the majority of Ethiopians had little or none to news or opinions other than those of the government.

Local-level *group conflicts* were evident in some areas of the country, notably Gambela and the Somali and Oromiya regions. In Gambela, an unsolved conflict between Nuer and Anywaa people again led to looting, displacement and killings in January and March. On 11 June, some 25 people were killed in an ambush on a bus by armed rebels near Gambela. In the Oromo and Somali areas of southern Ethiopia, resource and border conflicts re-emerged in which several dozen people were killed. For instance, in Oromiya clashes in early June took place between the Guji and the Boran (approx. 150 people killed), and on 29–31 May, 39 people were killed in the Somali region (Daroor area) in a dispute between two Garhaji subclans. There were also smaller clashes in the southern region: violent riots in the southern towns of Dilla on 3–4 April (killing 11 people) and in Bule (3 April). Clashes between students and police occurred in Meqele (in early June), Nazreth (on 2 June, with one student killed) and Asella (on 7 June, again with one student killed). Government troops kept the lid on further communal clashes, but they often came too late and were sometimes also claimed to be taking sides. On 3 January, the government through the ministry of justice announced that it would seek to develop alternative dispute resolution mechanisms based on local community structures. In urban areas in the first few months of the year there were a dozen bomb attacks, which killed 12 people and injured 100 more. No one claimed responsibility for these attacks.

As in previous years, *regional or ethnic rebel movements* were active in the Oromo, Somali and Amhara regional states, reflecting continued discontent with policies, political interference and repression by the central government as well as socioeconomic problems. No significant attempts to negotiate or address the underlying grievances were made. Among the most important movements were the OLF, the ONLF and the EPPF, a small and shady nationalist group operating in northern Ethiopia. An assessment of their field strength is difficult to make, but as in previous years the nuisance value of these movements was significant. Their programmes did not always have a clear national vision, and appeal to certain sections of the Ethiopian public. Some of these movements have their own problematic political and human rights records.

The Somali Region 5, a large territory with 3.9 m inhabitants, remained unstable, with the central government frequently changing personnel and clan groups clashing with each other, e.g., in September, under the impact of resource competition, internal disunity and partly due to divisive state politics. The separatist ONLF has some support in rural areas but followed a risky strategy of armed confrontation and had no constructive, inclusive programme for either the Somali region or for Ethiopia in general.

A relatively recent type of conflict – at least for Ethiopia – was *religious clashes*, some between Ethiopian-Orthodox and Pentecostal-Evangelical believers, others between Christians and Muslims, with Muslims increasingly showing antipathy toward Christians living in their midst. On 15 April, a church in Jijiga town was bombed, injuring five people. In incidents similar to those reported in 2004 and 2005, some Christians were killed, among them several Muslims converted to Christianity, and their property destroyed. For example, in Dembi town in western Ethiopia on 1–2 October a violent clash caused the death of five people and the destruction of two churches. Another clash occurred in mid-October in Bora and

Beshesha in western Ethiopia, where 11 Christians were hacked or burnt to death allegedly by militant, Wahhabist-inspired Muslims. Security forces were not decisive in suppressing or preventing such violence, but reconciliation efforts started after the incidents.

For unclear reasons, more and more foreigners and tourists reported stone-throwing incidents and acts of harassment, notably by children and young male adults in villages and towns, suggesting that anti-foreigner feelings were on the rise in Ethiopia.

The three main religious denominations remained Orthodox Christianity (45%), Islam (38%–40%) and Protestant-Evangelical Christianity (about 10%). Adherence to Evangelist-Pentecostal Christianity and to Islam continued to grow. The number of people belonging to traditional religions declined, although as part of political, ethnic-nationalist movements in some places, indigenous religion seems to have made a modest comeback (e.g., the 'Waqefeta' belief among Oromo in central Ethiopia).

Foreign Affairs

The Ethio-Eritrean 'border conflict' was not solved: no movement of any kind was registered in the two positions. Eritrea, however, kept up rejectionist rhetoric, insisting on literal execution of the 2003 decision of the Ethiopia-Eritrea Boundary Commission (EEBC) at the Permanent Court of Arbitration (PCA) in The Hague without talks on implementation and adjustments on the ground. Ethiopia did not concede anything either. While Ethiopia is legally in a weak position since it had committed itself to the PCA decision beforehand, it insisted that the mandate was not properly carried out and mistakes in the decision should be rectified. The stalemate continued, despite another round of international efforts by the UN and the EU to mediate. No compromise could be reached on any talks, with Eritrea further isolating itself diplomatically and Ethiopia refusing to acknowledge a controversial border line and the impending loss of Badme town, where the fighting in 1998 had started. Ethiopia remained vigilant in the border zone, while Eritrea further restricted the activities and movements of the UN Mission for Ethiopia and Eritrea (UNMEE) teams and patrols. The Temporary Security Zone (TSZ) along the border was frequently penetrated by Eritrean soldiers. In October, some 1500 soldiers with 14 tanks moved into the demilitarised security zone, officially to 'harvest crops'. The mandate of UNMEE was renewed by the UN, but its forces were further reduced from 3,373 to 2,300 people. Meaningful patrolling of the zone became impossible, also because of Eritrea's prohibition since 2005 of UN helicopter flights.

In the *Somali conflict*, the Eritreans supported the rising Islamist movement, the Union of Islamic Courts (UIC), with training, advisors and weaponry. The rise of the UIC caused great concern in the region, notably in Ethiopia, because of repeated threats made by the UIC towards Ethiopia, Somaliland and Puntland: they openly clamoured for a forceful 'reunification' of all Somali-inhabited areas and for an 'Islamic state' as well as calling for Muslim revolt within Ethiopia. The Ethiopian government, pursuing its long-term policy, supported the Transitional Federal Government (TFG), the legal government of Somalia since November 2004 seated in Baidoa and threatened by military assault from the UIC. When the UIC forces – taken over by a radicalising 'jihadist' leadership originating in the former 'Al Ittihad al Islami' movement – attacked Baidoa in December, the Ethiopians and TFG forces retaliated and war ensued. In one week of fighting the UIC was defeated and melted away but it later regrouped elsewhere, developing a radical/terrorist agenda under Islamist leadership. The military defeat of the UIC was a setback for the Eritreans but did not change their rhetoric or practice and their continuing support for UIC and other Ethiopian opposition movements elsewhere. A few days after the start of its military operations in 21 December, Ethiopia announced it would leave Somalia on condition that an AU peacekeeping force was installed.

Ethiopia had the *support of the US government* despite its worrying political and human rights record, obviously because of its pro-US international stance notably in the anti-terror campaign. Military and intelligence cooperation continued, for example with the US combined joint task force stationed in Djibouti. In the US congress, scepticism about Ethiopia's domestic policies gained momentum and a number of congressmen tried to get a critical bill on Ethiopia drawn up in late 2005, the Ethiopia Freedom, Democracy and Human Rights Advancement Act (H.R. 5680), on the agenda. This bill suffered delay, being put on hold in July, and it had not been adopted by the house of representatives by year's end.

The EU and the Ambassadors' Donors Group continued to express its misgivings on Ethiopia's political record, especially on the so-called 'treason/genocide' trial against the democratic opposition, but did not interrupt attempts at crisis diplomacy or halt economic support. In January, however, the UK said it would suspend $ 88 m in direct budgetary aid. In the course of the year, EU countries as well as the World Bank (in July) resumed aid programmes in an adapted format, e.g., trying to divert the flow to other, lower-level targets, such as the protection of basic services programme via local governments and NGOs, instead of to the federal government. During a visit to Ethiopia on 15–17 February, EU Commissioner Louis Michel called for renewed political dialogue and democratisation. Two EU diplomats were expelled after being arrested on 19 October near the Kenyan border with an Ethiopian human rights lawyer working with the EU Commission who was fleeing to Kenya to avoid persecution. This lawyer, Ms. Yalemzewd Beqele, was still in prison at the end of the year.

Relations with China intensified, especially in the economic sphere (information technology, trade, investment) and in military cooperation. In May, a Chinese company started drilling for oil in the Gambela area. Politically, China did not engage the Ethiopian government in any sense.

The Nile question continued to be controversial, with Ethiopia (the source of the Blue Nile, the main tributary) pushing for a greater

role and share in its use of the waters for irrigation and power generation. The Nile Basin Commission (NBC), founded in 1999 by the
relevant countries, did not make significant progress. Two points
of controversy were not resolved: the status of the old Nile treaties concluded before 1999 and the giving of prior notification by a
member country of any national development project to the other
member states.

Socioeconomic Developments

Food security in Ethiopia was not achieved and, as in any good year
(with sufficient rainfall), 2–3 m people required food aid. Structural
problems in Ethiopia's agricultural economy relating to land tenure,
insecurity of title to land, low productivity, taxation, population
pressure and lack of arable land persisted. Some experiments were
made – on the basis of studies by various ministries – in adapting
the policy of state ownership of all land. But as controlling the rural
population remains vital to the current government, fundamental
changes were not in the making, despite a move towards defining
more possession and use rights (e.g., via registration and transfer
to children). In order to combat recurrent food insecurity, the government went on with a 'safety nets programme', supported by the
World Bank, in which people do food-for-work projects such as
building wells, small irrigation systems or soil erosion prevention
schemes. In February, the FAO called for $ 18.5 m of food aid for
some 1 m people affected by severe drought in the Somali region
and in parts of Oromiya.

Urban unemployment was around 30–40% and rural unemployment went unregistered. Job creation in a few economic sectors
such as the flower business, construction and small enterprises continued, but could not address the magnitude of the problem. In the
farming areas, for instance, unemployment aggravated generational
tensions, with young men demanding money and the premature
partition of the land by their parents.

The *public health situation* remained critical, despite an extension of health facilities across the country. Continued population growth (2.5%–2.7% per annum with a fertility rate of 5.5 children per woman) offset investment gains. Major diseases were HIV/AIDS, malaria, diarrhoea and TB. Several outbreaks of meningitis (in January in Wolaitta region) and cholera (in April, leading to 52,000 cases) were registered. Due to low salaries and sub-standard working conditions in many hospitals and clinics, Ethiopia suffered from a lack of doctors and other qualified medical personnel, many of whom emigrated.

The HIV/AIDS crisis continued, with 4% (almost 3 m) people infected and probably another 100,000 estimated deaths (ill-recorded, owing to incomplete statistics and public shame about the disease). New treatment and prevention initiatives were tried, one of them under the the 2005 US-funded emergency plan for AIDS relief ($ 20 m annual budget) under which several hundred thousand people were tested and counselled, and a slight decline in the infection rate was noted. Other NGOs and some civil society groups were also engaged in anti-AIDS programmes. For rural women, a major health risk remained birth complications, which often went untreated. Local food scarcity and famine caused additional deaths from malnourishment or infectious diseases. In early August, in parts of the Amhara, Southern, and Somali regional states, the worst flooding in decades caused the death of at least 600 people and made more than 10,000 destitute, notably in and around Dire Dawa.

The *education sector* continued to grow in terms of facilities, number of schools and number of pupils enrolled. Whether overall progress in the qualitative sense was made remained unclear. As with other Millennium Development Goals, the measurement is difficult if not inadequate. The building of many regional universities went on, but funding to make them into mature centres of learning was strained. In February-March, teachers across the nation were obliged to follow a series of cadre lectures on EPRDF policies in education and afterwards had to sign that they would implement them.

This was not popular and was seen as a party control measure. In view of the still widespread abuse of children and the custom of 'forced marriage' (by abduction), notably in the rural south of the country, the government in October released a 'national action plan on sexual abuse and exploitation of children'.

Economic growth in Ethiopia, as in previous years, was significant. Estimates of GDP growth ranged from 5%–9%. This is difficult to determine in view of different figures given by government spokespersons, shaky statistics and lack of a visible rise in overall wealth levels. The World Bank in March 2007 mentioned a figure of 5.5% growth for 2006. The grain harvest was comparatively good because of sufficient rains. Foreign direct investments also increased. Exports rose, infrastructural works were carried out, entrepreneurial activities were on the rise and new housing projects were completed in urban areas (slum clearance in Addis Ababa was halted for the time being after the 2005 elections). Still, productive industrial investments lagged and did not absorb the swelling number of school leavers and unemployed in the towns and the rural sector. Neither did the urban formal sector have the capacity to provide jobs to the many higher education graduates. Most of the unemployed disappeared into the large informal economy or went into hawking or petty crime. Remittances by Ethiopians abroad represented largely invisible foreign investments, of which the annual amount was estimated to be some $ 400–$ 450 m in the past two to three years. This money went to relatives of the migrants, helping them survive, improve housing and make small business investments.

Tourism was a growth sector and was reported to have earned more money than in the previous year, but the figures were unknown. It is the third largest foreign exchange earner after coffee and oilseeds. In the new 2006 Plan for Accelerated and Sustainable Development to End Poverty (PASDEP), the government announced its goal to make the country one of the top-ten tourist locations in Africa by 2012.

Ethiopia continued negotiations on WTO admission, but opinions, including in high political circles, were divided on the balance of benefits and drawbacks of membership. Some felt it might open the door for global capitalism – especially via the financial sector (banks) and in tourism – to add another African country to its hunting ground. This would lead to the national economy being dominated by international capital, to profits being repatriated abroad, to socio-cultural problems and to the growth of a small trading and entrepreneurial elite linked to the political leadership to the detriment of ordinary Ethiopians and the middle class.

The growth figures and the government's cautious financial management are in fact what prevented donors from giving up on or backing out of Ethiopia. Despite its major political and economic problems, the country is still seen, notably by EU diplomats, as a test case in Africa that 'must succeed'. In addition, Ethiopia is protected against serious pressure or sanctions by its close association with the US campaign against global terrorism. The new US ambassador, D. Yamamoto, stated on 20 September that Ethiopia was seen as an "important strategic partner". This became evident during the Ethiopian military campaign in Somalia in December, condoned by the US.

The Ethiopian *state budget* in 2006 (the budget year is from 7 July to 6 July) was approximately ETB (Ethiopian birr) 35.4 bn ($ 4.1 bn). State revenues were $ 2.65 bn, 53% of which was to be domestically generated by taxation and 34% by foreign aid and loans. On 23 June, the auditor-general noted in his report that $ 83 m of the 2006 budget was unaccounted for. In November, the auditor-general was dismissed.

Ethiopia's GDP stood at $ 13.3 bn. Agriculture contributed some 48% to this, the service sector about 40% and industry only 13%. The agricultural sector employed, as in previous years, about 80% of all productive workers, while industry was slightly up at 8% due to an industrial growth of some 7%. Annual inflation was 12% and was reflected in the significant rise not only of prices for imported consumer items, but also in the prices of food staples, cooking oil, meat, cereals, butter, fruits and fuel (petrol and kerosene for cooking). Poverty in both the urban and rural sectors was widespread, with income inequalities rising, but some reduction in the percentage of the poor was registered, albeit with an estimated 40% still living below the 'poverty line' of $ 1 a day. It is still not clear what the exact impact and overall results of GDP growth are for the country. Ethiopia remained the seventh-poorest country in the world.

Ethiopia again had to pay more for its oil imports, an estimated $ 800 m. A growing volume of oil imports came from Sudan. The development of the huge natural gas fields in the Ogaden (Kalub and Hilala) did not see any progress. In August, after a new round of bidding by international companies to develop the reserves, Malaysia's Petronas won the contract.

Coffee exports earned some $ 350 m, but the world market price was faltering and many farmers switched to other products such the stimulant leaf *ch'at*, and to petty trade. Flower exports grew by 70%, generating earnings estimated at $ 35 m. Horticultural products earned about $ 32 m. Other foreign currency earners were the traditional export products such as hides and skins, *ch'at*, leather products, gold, livestock and oilseeds.

Overall annual exports brought in $ 1.085 bn, a milestone, because for the first time the $ 1 bn mark was passed. But imports were again much higher at $ 4,105 bn. The national debt rose to $ 6,038 bn, despite another round of debt cancellation with, notably, the World Bank, Russia and the IMF (which wrote off $ 161 m in January). The national debt was about 80% of annual GDP. Debt service payments amounted to almost 7% of GDP. Military expenditure – at least the figure publicly known – was about $ 296 m, or almost 4% of GDP. In reality, considering the substantial and growing security apparatus and the cost of the war in Somalia in December, it was probably much higher. There was a balance of payments deficit of – $ 3,384 bn. This was closed with foreign aid to the tune of $ 1.6 bn and with various domestic and international borrowing schemes.

In *infrastructure*, progress was made in road building, electrification of towns and villages and in the installation of telephone lines as well as cellphone network coverage. Internet connections grew slightly, but access to the Web was seriously restricted. In September, the monopolistic Ethiopian Telecommunications Corporation (ETC) signed a contract of $ 1.5 bn with three Chinese companies for all telecom investments in the country for the period 2007–11. The relevant 'suppliers credit memorandum of understanding' envisaged a loan by China repayable in ten years. The deal, implying exclusive reliance on Chinese telecom technology, drew criticism especially among workers and expert technicians with the ETC. This company also came in for much criticism from customers due to its grave mistakes in billing, bad management, waste of equipment, poor services and corruption. Disgruntled employees created a website to air their grievances. In a rare move, the new general manager appointed in October admitted mistakes and promised improvements.

Throughout the year, problems of *corruption* and other abuses of public office at all levels of state institution were regularly reported. Most common was embezzlement of state funds, preferential treatment in business deals and bribes under contracts with foreign companies and development aid. The situation has not reached the unmanageable proportions known elsewhere in Africa, but corruption did not diminish either. Ethiopia was ranked in the 130–138 bracket (on a scale of 158) on TI's Corruption Perceptions Index, roughly the same position as in 2005.

The economy continued to be dominated by a few big businessmen and by companies led by government party members. Dozens of big private enterprises remained in the hands of shareholders and managers closely affiliated with the EPRDF. Several banks, such as the Wegagen, Nib and Dashen banks, were also party-affiliated.

Migration was substantial, both internal in response to to local ethnic conflicts, lack of opportunity, poverty and instability, as well as trans-border to the Middle East or further abroad. The port of

Bossaso in Puntland, Somalia was a magnet for many Ethiopians trying to get to the richer shores across the Red Sea. The risks of the sea voyage in ill-equipped fishing boats, managed by human traffickers, were great and often led to human casualties: dozens of people drowned during the crossing and an uncertain future awaited them once they arrived. As in previous years, there were also refugees from neighbouring countries in Ethiopia: some 75,000 Sudanese, 15,000–20,000 people from southern Somalia and a growing number of Eritreans. Towards the end of the year, it was reported that dozens of young Eritreans were crossing the border into Ethiopia (as well as into Sudan) every month. By late 2006, their number was upwards of 10,000. The internally displaced (from previous wars, 'ethnic' clashes and the Somalia campaign) were estimated to be between 150,000 and 200,000 (mostly in Somali, Tigray and Gambela, and to a lesser extent in Oromiya and the southern region). This reflected the overall instability in the country and in the wider region.

Continued population pressure contributed to *environmental problems*, conflicts over land and water and food insecurity. While in the cities there were slight indications that birth rates were stabilising and in some cases slightly declining, in the countryside the average number of children born to a woman was still close to six. Land scarcity was getting worse and was aggravating food insecurity as well as communal conflicts.

Due to population growth, conversion to farmland and the drying out of rural areas, forest cover in Ethiopia this year further diminished by some 140,000 ha, falling below 13 m ha (including coffee and other plantations) of the total land area of 109 m ha. Since 1990, an estimated 14% of forest cover has been lost. Ongoing deterioration of the environment was a dangerous process undermining the basis of Ethiopia's livelihood and was not adequately tackled.

Ethiopia in 2007

This year saw the Ethiopian millennium. Ethiopia's domestic and international situation remained highly unstable and was marked by violent tension. The political space was monopolised further by the ruling party, the Ethiopian Peoples Revolutionary Democratic Front (EPRDF), while the fragmented opposition was further undermined. The government released major opposition figures from prison after a questionable trial but made no further meaningful 'reconciliation' moves. Domestic ethnic and social dissent persisted, sometimes in violent form. The EPRDF continued to organise among the rural population, co-opting them into party structures. In the wake of Ethiopia's 2006 invasion of Somalia, a protracted terrorist campaign was mounted by remnants of the defeated Islamic Courts Union, targeting Ethiopian troops, Somali civilians and government officials. The redistribution effects of economic growth were limited and poverty remained widespread. Spiralling inflation severely affected the poor and middle class. There was drought, especially in the south. There were no solutions to the structural problems of the rural economy, climate change and the ecological crisis. The US and China provided international support for Ethiopia, while the EU continued to provide development funds. Relations with Eritrea were poor, with no headway being made in the border conflict, while the proxy war in southern Somalia and elsewhere intensified. Ethiopia's relations with its other neighbours were mainly stable.

Domestic Politics

The ruling EPRDF continued to dominate *Ethiopian politics*, with no rapprochement with the internally fragmented opposition parties, which were further undermined. The EPRDF used its majority in parliament to push through its political programmes. The parliamentary opposition had no impact on policy, its spokesmen even admitting they had only a symbolic presence.

General *political life* in Ethiopia remained volatile and hazardous. Close associates of opposition leaders were frequently harassed, killed or made to disappear. Opposition parties could not function properly, with offices being closed and members persecuted, while membership in them was often seen as a 'crime', notably in the countryside. The Oromo opposition party, Oromo Federalist Democratic Movement (OFDM), was also frequently harassed.

The CUD's (*Coalition for Unity and Democracy*) former *party name* was assigned by the government-dominated national electoral board to a splinter 'CUD' group close to the government. The original core membership (people like Birtukan Mideqsa, Berhanu Nega, Mesfin Wolde-Mariam, Muluneh Eyoel, Yaqob Hailemariam, Hailu Araya and Hailu Shawel) was left to try to found a new movement.

One positive event was the release in July of 35 major opposition (CUD party) leaders and supporters, jailed since late 2005. They were acquitted of charges of genocide and incitement to violence, but convicted of the attempted overthrow of the constitutional order. They were sentenced to life imprisonment. However, after mediation by a group of 'elders' (including Ethiopian-American Professor Efraim Isaac) and donor country diplomats, they were pardoned on 20 July, but only after signing an admission of 'partial responsibility' for the post-election violence in 2005. This conditional release was curious, seemingly intended to humiliate the opposition. The case had always been political and none of the charges was convincing. The government appeared to respond to pressure from donor countries and the diaspora to release the prisoners but used the occasion to reassert control. On 11 July, an ex-TPLF (Tigray People's Liberation Front) senior leader, Siye Abraha, was also released, for lack of evidence, after six years in jail.

The government continued to take risks by neglecting the domestic constituency, showing no interest in building political consensus and inclusiveness beyond the ruling party cadres, and enforcing its policies on the basis of its 'party vanguard ideology' and the attempted cooption of the masses.

While *dissatisfaction with government policies* remained high, as confirmed in a July 2007 Gallup poll, anti-government protests were sparse and declined during the year due to repression and preventive action by the well-developed security services. The general population, meanwhile, realised that the window of opportunity provided by the 2005 elections – relatively free and promising but closed down and 'won' by the government – had been shut. The regime had chosen, instead, to consolidate its power, privilege and exclusive rule. There were no indications that this would soon change. Local elections were postponed to 2008.

The *independent mass media* shrivelled further. The private press did not recover from the government assault during the post-2005 election crisis, when most independent media had been forced to close and only a few papers continued under precarious conditions. The only other survivors were state or party papers. Self-censorship continued, and several editors were again arrested, with others still languishing in jail. People in rural areas did not gain access to independent information, a deficiency the government had no interest in remedying. Uniquely in Africa, the state has complete control over internet provision and telephone services (with some 900,000 cell phones in use). Academic freedom was also subject to government interference and control.

Criticism by the diaspora of the Ethiopian government continued. The government took diaspora community debates and websites very seriously, especially where they were likely to impact host country politics, as in the case of US Congress resolution HR 2003 (Ethiopian Democracy and Accountability Act). No independent Ethiopian websites were favourably disposed to the government and many of the most critical sites remained blocked by the state-controlled Ethiopian Telecommunications Corporation, the sole internet provider in the country. Ethiopia lagged further in the ICT revolution in Africa: the network expanded, but the internet was not an open or reliable source of information.

Not surprisingly, the *human rights record* of Ethiopia remained very poor. Violent and unpredictable actions by the police, army and secret services led to insecurity, fear and self-censorship. Human rights organisations, domestic observers as well as the human rights bureau of the US State Department reported dozens of extra-judicial deaths as well as beatings disappearances, and many cases of intimidation and threat. For example, security forces killed Gemechu Bencha (16) in Gue (Wollega) on 3 January for alleged Oromo Liberation Front (OLF) sympathies. Degaga Gebissa, a United Ethiopian Democratic Front (UEDF) party sympathiser, was killed by police in Meta-Robi. On 5 March, Tseggaye Ayyele, an opposition Ethiopian Democratic Party (EDP) member, died in Debre Marqos prison after being tortured.

This type of incident deterred people from becoming politically active or standing up for their constitutional rights. All independent observers expressed serious concern about the political process. Government paid only lip service to the rule of law and respect for citizens' rights. The government and/or dominant party (they overlap in all significant respects) proceeded with the *large-scale cooption of the rural population* into the ruling party, evidently to increase control and ultimately forestall a repeat of the free choice in the 2005 election, which had taken the regime by surprise. The structure used was, from the top down: the regional state; the zone; the 'woreda' (district); and the 'qebele' (local community), which was further divided into the 'nu'us-qebele', the 'gott'' and finally the 'mengistawi mewwaqir' (comprised of 4 or 5 families, of which one reported to a higher-level party representative). In schools, the civil service and other institutions, regular briefing sessions, supposedly administrative but really largely party-political, were held to 'instruct' employees on correct policy, with no opportunity for debate or opposition activity. Consequently, Ethiopian political culture did not change much, except for the reinforcement of autocratic rule. It seemed unlikely that democracy would soon be achieved.

The *Ethiopian millennium* (2000 EC, Ethiopian calendar) was celebrated on 12 September in Ethiopia and among Ethiopian diasporas around the world. Despite this major symbolic national occasion, there was a feeling of malaise and gloom among the general population and the fragmented and weakened opposition parties. Pessimistic jokes and anecdotes circulated about the missed chances of this millennium as well as the high cost of living associated with it: it was often nicknamed the 'minim-yellem' ('there is nothing') millennium. Official pronouncements about the number of foreign guests expected – up to 400,000 – were widely off the mark. At most, some 40,000 people, mainly diaspora Ethiopians, arrived. The celebrations were low-key, and there was no public debate about the history of Ethiopia and the challenges facing it in the new millennium. Indeed, the programme along these lines envisaged by scholars at Addis Ababa university was cancelled. The main 'attraction' was the appearance on 12 September of international pop star Beyoncé Knowles and other foreign singers for a crowd of young people. Her audience with the patriarch of the Ethiopian Orthodox Church was highly contentious among many believers. Many Ethiopians noted the irony of foreign stars being invited to take centre stage by the government-appointed Ethiopian millennium committee for the unique Ethiopian millennium, instead of Ethiopian artists. Ethiopia's most popular singer, Teddy Afro, chose to give his millennium concert in Jimma (Oromiya region). In the context of the millennium, the release of opposition figures was one good sign, but was not aimed at promoting national reconciliation or reinstating the prisoners to their elected positions. For instance, economist Berhanu Nega, voted in as mayor of Addis Ababa in 2005, was denied his position, as regime cronies had filled the vacancies.

On 9 December in the southern town of Awasa, the millennium celebrations took the form of a 'Nations, Nationalities and Peoples' Day'. This well-organised national event was meant to showcase the country's ethnic diversity and official state versions of ethnic harmony and identity. Dozens of ethno-cultural groups performed, and high-level politicians spoke of the benefits of the federal constitution and the ideals of a multi-ethnic Ethiopia.

There were still too few judges, and too few experienced ones in the *legal sector*. An unsuccessful attempt was made to reform the parallel structure of federal courts and regional state courts. Commercial law was still underdeveloped or poorly applied, for example, in the very weak protection of property rights. Court orders to release suspects were frequently ignored by the federal police. Some progress was made in the legal sector but the pace was very slow and important judicial decisions on political issues, land and other national policy matters were still influenced by government. Indeed, after the 2005 elections, the street violence and the mass arrests of opposition politicians and other civic activists, the tendency by government was to tighten its grip on the major federal courts and their judges. Many senior judges followed informal party directives in their verdicts. A general popular complaint was that "there is no law". On 11 January, after a 12-year trial, former President Mengistu was sentenced to life imprisonment for 'genocide' and other crimes. The state prosecutor lodged an appeal. There were few developments in cases involving past government human rights abuses, imprisonment without charge and political killings.

While the ethno-federal political system recognised local ethnic identities as politically relevant, it also encouraged lower-level *'ethnic' or communal conflict*. As in previous years, there were under-reported but violent clashes that left scores of people dead, often in the same areas: for example, the conflicts between the Guji and the Koré and Buiji continued, as did those involving the Suri-Dizi in the southwest and those between Oromo and Somali. In early February, clashes, apparently arising from cattle raiding between Gabra and Borena pastoralists in Oromiya region, resulted in at least 16 deaths. Tensions in Gambela (Anyuwa/Nuer) remained strong. Some clashes had roots in the past or were related to natural resource competition. The government was unable to contain the violence or offer solutions, except to repress the worst outbursts militarily.

In general, communal relations were marked by a further drawing of lines. For instance, the Silt'i people (a Gurage-speaking group) were no longer part of the 'Gurage' cluster, but separate. This process of independent-identity construction in this case went hand in hand with Islamisation aided by foreign funding.

From May to November, Ethiopia's central statistical authority undertook a national population census (the first since 1994), the results being expected in 2008. While primarily meant to yield data for policy purposes, it was expected to have clear political implications in respect of the relative 'strength' of ethno-linguistic groups.

Regional and ethnic *insurgent movements* were active, including the Oromo Liberation Front (OLF) (in west and east Oromiya region), with its leadership in exile: the low-key Ethiopian People's Patriotic Front in the north; and the militant Ogaden National Liberation Front (ONLF), which adopted all-out terrorism. It made its presence felt in March with two bombings in Jijiga and Dhagabur, with 17 civilians killed, including children, and on 24 April with an ill-advised attack on an oil exploration site in the east: nine Chinese and 65 Ethiopians (labourers, cooks, guards, villagers) were killed in a calculated massacre. Whatever the 'political' motivation for this action, the result was that ONLF lost any goodwill it might have had. The incident also effectively broke up the so-called Alliance for Democracy (AFD), formed in 2006 between the OLF, the ONLF, part of the diaspora-CUD and two other minor fronts. After the attack, the AFD was no longer heard of and will have little further impact on Ethiopian politics. The Ethiopian government response to the April attack was predictably harsh: a massive search-and-destroy clamp-down on the Ogaden and the rooting out of ONLF units and their presumed supporters. As the sparse reporting from the area made clear, this resulted in human rights violations against the civilian population, including destruction of villages; arbitrary arrests and abuse; road blocks; and restricted access to pastures and wells, which led to a humanitarian crisis. At year's end, this campaign was still in full swing, with the ONLF suffering major blows. Some commentators reproached the ONLF for taking such a 'criminal risk': they knew that retaliation against the Ogadenis would follow and would expose the civilian population (including many non-Ogaden clan Somalis) to a military campaign.

Religious relations were stable, but dangerous tensions continued under the surface. The three main denominations remained Orthodox Christianity (45%), Islam (38–40%) and Protestant-Evangelical Christianity (about 10%). Evangelist-Pentecostal Christianity and Islam continued to grow. The number of people subscribing to traditional religions declined, although these did revive modestly as part of political, ethnic-nationalist movements in some places, for instance the 'Waqefeta' belief among certain Oromo groups in central Ethiopia. Tensions between the religious communities increased where largely foreign-sponsored Islamist ('Wahhabi' and other) networks and groups that deliberately advanced a confrontational Islam were active. Evangelical-Pentecostal Christians also spread their message but in less overtly political and aggressive ways. They were notably active among Ethiopian Orthodox believers. The new Islamists and new Christians continued to agitate against time-honoured local cultural traditions – part of a long-term process of confrontation – and this might lead to major clashes in the future, endangering the Ethiopian model of religious coexistence. On 26 March, a Christian evangelist was beaten to death by militant Muslims in Jimma, an area of major clashes in 2006.

An audible sign of the growing religious competition and intolerance was the 'urban sound wars' as mosques, prayer houses and churches of various denominations tried to create the loudest soundscape in town and thus disturb the public peace. As in other spheres, the government was reluctant or uncertain about how to tackle the threat of religious radicalisation. It was aware of the sensitive issue of growing religious clashes, due in part to its invasion of Somalia (Somali radicals may have built connections with Ogaden-Somali rebels), although allegations by radical pro-Islamists and Somali nationalists, and some Western journalists, that 'Christian Ethiopia' was fighting 'Muslim Somalia' were wide of the mark.

A policy of public debate, education and targeted measures against intolerance and militants to counter this 'radicalisation' was not pursued.

Foreign Affairs

The main issue was *Ethiopia's involvement in southern* Somalia to buttress the internationally recognised Transitional Federal Government (TFG) against a coalition of Islamist militant forces. This situation went from bad to worse. Prime Minister Meles Zenawi admitted in press interviews that the intervention was perhaps mistaken, because the weakness of the TFG had been underestimated, as had the extent of 'guerrilla' activity by the Islamist movement. Remnants of the Islamic Courts Union regrouped under the Alliance for the Re-liberation of Somalia, based in Asmara, Eritrea, and also comprising assorted hard-core Islamists, moderate groups and diaspora elements opposed to the TFG and the Ethiopian presence. However, in a media interview on 6 September, Zanawi called the invasion "a tremendous success". He would not say when the Ethiopian forces (15,000–18,000 in number) would leave. Apparently, as long as the Islamists – with their close ties to Eritrea and other international connections – are perceived as a national security risk for Ethiopia, the Ethiopians will not leave Somalia alone. The conflict was asymmetrical, with Islamists avoiding frontal attacks but engaging in hit-and-run attacks on police stations and army check points and bomb attacks on markets, cinemas, and government offices and personnel. Possibly hundreds of Ethiopian soldiers were killed during the year. Islamist groups also carried out targeted killings of community leaders, elders, employees of foreign NGOs, TFG administrators and Somali women activists, with many bystanders as victims. After terror attacks, Ethiopian forces indiscriminately returned fire on a massive scale, in the process often killing yet more non-combatants. As in other cases of asymmetrical warfare, the distinction between innocent civilians and combatants became more blurred. The AU, in one of its greatest ever failures, could not muster the agreed-upon modest stabilisation force of 8,000 people (itself 20–30,000 troops too few) to help TFG extend its authority. Only 1,400 Ugandan troops and a Burundian force of 800 were in place. Most Ethiopian troops, while battle-hardened, hated being in Somalia, and often took out their anger over Islamist violence and instability on the population and its property. Many gross abuses were reported, although independent verification was difficult. Amnesty International's reports on human rights abuses in Somalia had a basis in fact, but were often too hasty and backed by insufficient information. The Ethiopians did their best to support the TFG to extend its powers and bring stability, but could not prevent the slow slide into what the population perceived as 'nationalist resistance'.

There was no improvement in *Ethiopian-Eritrean* relations. Mutual vilification, with the Eritrean president playing a major role, continued, and no normalisation was attempted. The Ethiopia-Eritrea boundary commission completed its work on 30 November, and, exasperated at both parties, declared that, in the absence of demarcation on the ground the border described on paper in its hotly contested 2002 arbitration decision would be the actual border, This was an unprecedented and questionable move. The Eritreans, meanwhile, continued to undermine and push out the UN Mission in Ethiopian and Eritrea (UNMEE) mission. While the border situation remained tense, no hostilities erupted. With the ending of the boundary commission, however, the threat of conflict has grown. The Eritrean leadership demanded that the world community put pressure on Ethiopia to recognise the border. This did not happen, as the Eritrean leadership remained highly unpopular because of its untactical, autocratic and dogmatic approach.

Relations with other neighbours (Sudan, Kenya, Djibouti and Somaliland) were stable. On 12 September, Ethiopia announced it was willing to deploy 5,000 soldiers as part of a joint UN-AU peace-keeping force in Darfur.

Most *Western donor countries* displayed their usual indifference to the actions of the Ethiopian political elite and events in Ethiopia, and did not push forward the democratisation agenda, apart from their usual weak pronouncements. On 6 July, a committee of EU parliamentarians criticised the "massive human rights violations" in the country. In August, Ethiopia suddenly ordered Norway to recall six of its eight diplomats, because Norway allegedly had leaned too much towards Eritrea in mediating the border dispute. In response, Norway said it would cut its aid to Ethiopian by a third.

However, *international development aid* continued to flow (some $ 1.2 bn in 2007), and the trappings of development – more schools built; economic growth in the form of more roads, offices, commissions, agencies, development projects and buildings (including condominiums in Addis Ababa's poorer neighbourhoods, which are not much liked by the urban dwellers because of their poor quality and uncertain services) – lulled donors' doubts about the reality of the growth.

Consistent with the decision by the *World Bank* and donor countries in 2005–06, aid flows were directed to local authorities instead of the federal government. This intensified the government's efforts to recapture and control local authorities and make them more dependent on federal structures, thereby countering the intent of the World Bank and donor countries.

Further support for Ethiopia came from *the US*, which provided political cover for Ethiopia's actions against the Islamist threat in Somalia and the threat of terrorism in the Horn in general. The ONLF attack in April on the oil exploration site in eastern Ethiopia reinforced the US's determination to support the Ethiopian government as an important ally in the global fight against terrorism. In the US Congress, however, there was criticism of US government support for a regime that was provoking more and more enmity among its own population and was so heavily reliant on force to contain challenges to its rule. Debate on the critical house resolution (HR 2003, Ethiopian Democracy and Accountability Act) took place, but the resolution was not brought to a vote in the senate. Though the resolution was fairly modest, calling on Ethiopia to respect its constitution, be transparent and accountable in governance and respect the human rights of citizens, it was forcefully opposed by some prominent Republicans, particularly Senator James Inhofe.

China was also a major source of support, by extending economic aid and project support at discounted prices. A Chinese industrial park of $ 500 m was planned near Dukem.

Socioeconomic Developments

GDP was about $ 17 bn, substantially up on 2006. According to IMF figures, Ethiopia registered 5.5% growth, but the ministry of finance and economic development talked of 10.9%. As population growth was 2.5%, real growth was about 3%. This was evident in the construction boom; the expansion of roads, telecom, educational facilities; and agricultural investment. Much of the growth came from donor funds and from foreign investment in the booming flower industry and in mining. Export of flowers netted $ 168 m. However, not enough derived from increased agricultural productivity or industrial investment. The prime minister claimed in December that the 16.7% increase in the defence budget would not harm growth.

The chief factor in growth was, as always, the natural conditions affecting the performance of the *agrarian sector*. The main harvest was above average, although rainfall sharply declined towards the end of the year. Coffee production was down, but revenue from coffee exports was some $ 410 m). Negotiations with the US Starbucks chain resulted in the certification of certain Ethiopian coffee brands, allowing for higher prices. However, neither stability in the agricultural sector, the stated aim of the government since 1991, nor food security was attained. Ethiopia's agricultural economy (60% of export revenues, 49% of GDP, 80% of employment) remained vulnerable to drought and was beset by issues of state ownership of land and land scarcity.

The growth in *the construction sector* was fed by overseas remittances (amounting to $ 591 m in 2007, or 4.4% of GDP) and the smart use of local banks, which deployed domestic savings on which interest below the inflation rate was paid to account holders as loans to investors enjoying state support (and often political allies of the government). Virtually all growth in the sector was thus based on credit and not on productive long-term investment. The building boom led to a shortage of building materials and cement. A large new cement factory was opened in Dire Dawa. In August, Malaysia's Petronas finally signed a deal with the government to develop the *natural gas reserves* of eastern Ethiopia.

The World Bank, through the IDA, maintained one of its largest programmes in Africa in Ethiopia, with 24 active projects worth more than $ 2.3 bn (including $ 800 m in grants). Based on evidence provided by the Ethiopian government, the World Bank claimed that efforts to improve basic services were showing results, with primary school enrolments and the percentage of people with access to clean water increasing and child mortality going down. Also, the percentage of Ethiopians living in *poverty* was said to have decreased to 39% of the total population (78 million). This is at variance with the perceptions of ordinary people, who often said they had never seen such poverty. This reflects the huge and growing gap between rich and poor.

The state budget in 2007 (the budget year is from 7 July to 7 July) was ETB (Ethiopian birr) 45 bn, approximately $ 4.4 bn. State revenues were $ 2.9 bn and expenditures $ 3.7 bn. The current account deficit was $ 1.85 bn. Public debt was somewhat up, reaching 55% of GDP. Of this, external debt was almost $ 3.8 bn.

The rate of tax revenue to GDP was about 15–17%, a low ratio below the African average, but up from previous years. The efficiency of the tax regime left much to be desired and can only be improved if the big party-affiliated companies are more efficiently taxed and as more informal sectors of the economy are brought into the formal sphere.

The *trade deficit* increased 15% to $ 1.3 bn. Imports rose to $ 4.5 bn (mainly because of higher oil prices). Exports rose 0.7% to $ 1.2 bn. Declining coffee exports were offset by higher sales of flowers, pulses, oilseeds and khat. In February, Russia announced the cancellation of Ethiopia's remaining debt of $ 161 m.

Corruption, lower than in other African countries, was growing and was evident up to the highest levels in business, the civil service and the administration. According to the Corruption Perceptions Index, Ethiopia took 138th place (out of 179), one place lower than last year. A national ethics commission tried to keep track of the worst offenders, but the problem was endemic.

The positive words by the international financial institutions came at a time when *food security* was as remote an ideal as ever. The situation was not substantially different from that under the previous two regimes and indicates that only some sectors benefited from the economic growth. Again, millions of people were in danger of famine, a danger government policy could not substantially alleviate. The successes claimed by donors probably arise from their focus on what was happening in the cities (road construction, several new enterprises), not on the average people and economic conditions in the countryside, where progress is slow and misery unabated.

Ethiopia was still negotiating with the WTO for membership, a difficult process, because government was reluctant to allow the penetration of foreign capitalism and competition into the banking and other key sectors. For this, they probably had good cause – the competition would seriously dent domestic banks and other interests.

Ethiopian *social and educational conditions* remained critical. On the UN's Human Development Index Ethiopia took 169th place (out of 177). According to official figures, mass poverty declined somewhat due to economic growth, but was still rampant, and social inequality increased significantly. The number of beggars did not decrease. The hugely wealthy elite of political and economic entrepreneurs ('developmental capitalists', or in Amharic 'limatawi balehabtoch') became more pronounced. The local view was that in principle such a class could and should not emerge, because development with largely foreign funds should not lead to private wealth. While the new elite were building huge villas and ordering Hummer vehicles for private use, much of the rural and urban population continued in grinding poverty, with unemployment and social welfare issues inadequately addressed.

Slow progress was registered in the education sector, where expansion in the number of primary schools could be claimed as a success. Here, the Ethiopian government was on course to meet the Millennium Development Goals. As in previous years, the quality of education faltered, and was seen as secondary to numerical expansion. The expansion of 'universities' in many small provincial towns continued, but they had sub-standard facilities, student dormitories and services, no proper libraries or laboratories, and insufficient qualified staff. The government's focus on numbers, which looked good to donor institutions and representatives, damaged the quality of education and will have little long-term effect.

The *health sector* also *saw* some investment, with more rural clinics built and new plans launched, and many more people gaining access to clean water. However, this could hardly keep up with rapid population growth or make major inroads into existing public health problems such as HIV/AIDS (a stable 4.5–5% infection rate, or approx. 1.6 million people), TB, malaria, typhoid and other infectious and diarrhoeal diseases. Urban healthcare was further bifurcated, with private hospitals for the rich and understaffed and badly paid state hospitals for the rest of the population. Doctors complained of low salaries and long working hours but got short shrift from the prime minister, who, in a statement viewed with disbelief by many, claimed that doctors could go anywhere they wanted and that healthcare workers were more important. Most Ethiopian doctors already work abroad and there is only one qualified doctor in the country per 36,000 people. Prostitution remained widespread, notably in Addis Ababa and provincial towns. Thousands of girls turned to it as a last resort. In addition to the domestic market, demand from Arab sex tourists was also large. Prostitution was a major public health issue due to the high HIV/AIDS infection rates.

Urban unemployment remained high, and was conservatively estimated at 40%, mainly youths. Workers' rights were poorly protected under the 2004 labour law, and sudden dismissal without compensation or right to other employment was frequent. The only labour union, Confederation of Ethiopian Trade Unions (CETU), remained under government control and was not heard from in 2007. Civil servants were still legally barred from membership in unions.

In several areas (Afar, Wolayta, Tigray, Amhara), *floods and landslides* occurred, displacing tens of thousands of people and killing dozens. Several of these disasters resulted from overexploitation and erosion in areas of overpopulation. Various UN agencies and NGOs provided emergency aid. Victims of the 2006 floods in southern Ethiopia complained they had received insufficient aid to rebuild their livelihoods.

Environmental deterioration, including loss of wildlife areas and biodiversity, continued virtually unabated and was the focus of no major policy initiatives. Bunding, reforestation and terracing occurred, but on a modest scale. More land was cultivated, more forest was cut down. Only 2.5% of the country is now covered by forest, compared to about 35% 50 years ago. Erosion increased, and was very visible to the casual traveller. As a result, the long-term livelihood of the rural masses was further jeopardised.

Internal and external *migration patterns* changed little. There were population movements into and out of the country. An estimated 6,000 Eritreans fled across the disputed border to Ethiopia to escape military service and repression. Camps in the north (e.g., Shimelba) contained 15,000 to 20,000 Eritrean refugees. There were still some 68,000 Sudanese refugees and displaced people in

Ethiopia, but thousands were repatriated. The fighting in southern Somalia led to an influx of 50,000–80,000 Somalis into Ethiopia. The government continued its population resettlement schemes from drought-prone to 'under-utilised' areas in the southwest (at the expense of local communities).

Ethiopia also remained a major source country for international migration. This included brain-drain migrants as well as the outflow through human trafficking and adoption (the distinction is sometimes blurred). Political refugees and labour migrants also left the country. Large numbers of Ethiopian women went to Middle Eastern countries, despite warnings, and ended up in Lebanon, Egypt, Saudi Arabia, Yemen, Sudan, Djibouti or South Africa as domestic servants. Abuse was frequent, and several girls ended up as prostitutes. Within Ethiopia, many rural children migrated to the cities, often to work as domestic servants for relatives (usually they also got primary education while in town). Internal displacement due to 'ethnic' conflicts occurred in various places in the south and east of the country.

Many Ethiopians tried to cross the Red Sea, for example, via the Puntland port of Bosasso. Here, human traffickers transported people for a high price in unseaworthy vessels, the frequent result being shipwreck or people jumping overboard when the coast guard approached. On 12 February, one such boat capsized as it approached the Yemen coast and at least 30 Ethiopian and Somali migrants were drowned. On 16 February, another vessel capsized, with 112 people drowned. More such incidents followed throughout the year, raising the death toll to 600–700.

Ethiopia in 2008

Political life continued its slide towards autocracy, with the leading Ethiopian People's Revolutionary Democratic Front (EPRDF) monopolising political space in parliament and in government organs across the country. Disregarding opinions of the opposition and critiques by experts, commentators, the remaining independent press and donor countries, the government displayed a curious mixture of insecurity, authoritarianism and arrogance in its behaviour, which did not augur well for national politics. The ruling party's intention to fight for survival and complete dominance at all costs was no longer hidden, while for the international community the overriding mantra was 'economic growth'. The EPRDF was centred on Prime Minister Meles Zenawi, the undisputed leader who took no risks and showed no interest in national compromise or inclusive politics. No observer could claim that Ethiopia was on the right political track, as respect for human rights, civil liberties and equity registered no significant progress. The popular opposition leader Birtukan Mideqsa, released in 2007, was again imprisoned on flimsy grounds, as part of further moves to undermine and fragment the legal opposition.

The crucial problems of domestic political reconciliation and democratisation, settling the border issue with Eritrea, the Ogaden insurgency, and the quagmire in Somalia, where Ethiopian troops were engaged for a second year running, were thus not solved. One exception was Ethiopia's announcement of the withdrawal of its troops from Somalia by the end of the year, with in fact only a few thousand remaining on 31 December.

While Ethiopia's economy grew substantially and showed dynamism despite the government's more restrictive policies, the food insecurity of millions of people, mass poverty, shaky health and education sectors, ecological decline and the fair distribution of the benefits of economic growth remained major challenges. Socioeconomic inequalities were still huge. Weather conditions varied, with relatively good harvests but with regional crises in food production again necessitating food aid. Donor countries again provided major financial support packages to Ethiopia, largely out of habit rather than based on a long-term programme and a critical appraisal of the facts or evaluation of the use and impact of the funds. Foreign relations with Sudan, where oil imports played an important role, grew closer (with Meles supporting the rejection of the ICC warrant against President Omar al-Bashir) and relations with Djibouti, Kenya and Somaliland remaining stable. The strained relations with Eritrea saw no improvement.

Domestic Politics

Ethiopia, the most complex and important country in the Horn of Africa, took further predictable steps towards *authoritarianism*, with the closing down of much of the political space for democratic politics and the forceful reassertion of one-party control by the *ruling EPRDF* (with the Tigrai People's Liberation Front/TPLF at its core). The government and the dominant EPRDF (the difference was often difficult to discern) were very good at the rhetoric of 'democracy' and 'good governance', but there was very little to show for it.

Human rights, opposition party activities, civil society space and associational life were constantly under threat, and although limited possibilities still existed, the overall political picture was bleak and worrying. A growing number of voices from within the country, diaspora groups, rights organisations and among international analysts spoke of an emerging dictatorship, and the government indeed did little to disprove this lament. Prime Minister (and TPLF/EPRDF chief) *Meles Zenawi* entered his 17th year in power. Domestic or international criticism and appeals to the government to show responsibility and inclusive statesmanship were ignored, as was evident in

highly symbolic acts such as the reincarceration of prominent opposition leader Ms. *Birtukan Mideqsa* on 29 December, based on an
intentional misunderstanding of one of her statements, and the dubious conviction of popular singer *Teddy Afro* (Tewodros Kassahun)
on 5 December on fallacious charges of 'manslaughter' (for allegedly
accidentally killing a street vagrant with his car in 2006). No credible
evidence had been produced in court in his case, and evidence dis-
proving his guilt, such as clear testimony that on the said day he was
nowhere near the scene, was ignored by the court. He was jailed for
six years, presumably because of the great and unwelcome appeal of
his songs to the Ethiopian public.

Opposition parties were also *harassed*, notably in the countryside, and civil society organisations obstructed. Opposition members or people critical of particular policies were often unjustly
dismissed or forced out of their jobs. Labour union freedom was
nonexistent, academic and university life was under worrying pressure and the independent media were pushed back further. Security
services earned overtime in developing informant networks, surveillance and in reporting on opposition figures and other critical
voices. There were also some suspected political disappearances
and reportedly more than a dozen extrajudicial killings. All this was
clearly contrary to the country's 1994 constitution. Several thousand political prisoners, most of them Oromo, were reportedly still
in prison. In March, the civil society activists Daniel Bekele and
Netsannet Demissie, part of the large group of opposition figures
arrested after the dramatic 2005 elections, were released, although
only after being condemned for 'incitement' and under certain
conditions.

On 8 October, a bill was pushed through parliament that significantly enlarged the *powers of the executive* (the Definition of Powers
and Duties of the Executive Organs, proclamation 471/2005). This
gave the government all power to dismiss, dissolve or reorganise
all federal organs and offices in the country, without scrutiny by
parliament.

The largest *opposition parties*, Coalition for Unity and Democracy (CUD) and United Ethiopian Democratic Front (UEDF), experienced *further fragmentation*, not least due to constant harassment by the government. Their irrelevance in parliament, where they were routinely ignored and bypassed by the ruling party and by government ministers, became glaring. They were also much under-reported in the state-controlled media. The opposition had no chance to introduce legislative proposals into parliament (which lacked the formal right to initiate legislation). Some former opposition leaders left the country (for instance, CUD leader and 2005 mayor-elect Berhanu Nega) while others attempted to create a new party from the remnants of CUD, the *Unity for Democracy and Justice Party* (UDJP). The UEDF, a coalition of ethno-regionally based parties, also descended further into crisis on account of its heterogeneity, leadership squabbles and lack of visibility in parliament. Oromo Federal Democratic Movement (OFDM) leader, veteran economist Bulcha Demeqsa, was the most rhetorically energetic member of the opposition. Building an opposition party base in the rural areas was next to impossible, due to constant harassment, threats and arrests, invisible to the foreign diplomatic community indifferent to or blissfully ignorant of what happened outside Addis Ababa.

In mid-September, the EPRDF held its 7th congress in Awassa and duly re-elected Meles Zenawi as chairman. Reports were made on the various party activities, including the massive membership drive that marked the transition of the EPRDF from a cadre party to a 'popular' party, although nothing changed in the leadership structure.

Confirmation of the reassertion of dominant (TPLF/EPRDF) party rule was provided by *local elections* on 13 and 20 April for the 'qebeles' and 'woredas' (districts), and for 20 vacant parliamentary seats. The EPRDF fielded 3.6 m of the 4.5 m candidates (1 out of 20 Ethiopians). As critics had predicted, it was a clean sweep for the EPRDF, which won a Soviet-style 99% of the vote and in the process forced all local officials and administration workers to become party members. In a majority of constituencies, opposition party candidates were not even able to run. This 'organisational operation', well-executed by thousands of party cadres, was partly triggered by earlier World Bank and donor country strategies developed after the 2005 election crisis to redirect donor development funds straight to local authorities instead of to the federal government. The government response was to 'recapture' the local authorities and coopt them fully into the national and ruling party structures. This wholesale politicisation of the countryside further diminished the trust between people and led to a silencing of critical voices. A climate of fear and avoidance in social and political life was noticeable in the country.

During the year, there were several more mysterious *bombings* of taxis, buses, petrol stations, bars and hotels, killing about 40–50 people. As in previous years, hardly any perpetrator was caught, except in two cases: after a bus bombing near Humera (eight killed, 27 injured) people "in the pay of Eritrea" were arrested, and after a bombing in Jijiga on 20 September (four killed, 20 injured), when people "working for the insurgent Ogaden National Liberation Front (ONLF)" were apprehended. Details of these cases remained unclear.

The government also introduced *a new draft* NGO law severely restricting the range of activities in which local NGOs could participate and limiting their access to foreign funding (no more than 10% of the budget). Clearly, contrary to government claims about legally "regulating and strengthening the NGO sector", the opposite was intended: amazingly NGOs were prohibited from taking part in domestic debates on or from contributing to advancing human and democratic rights; equality between peoples, sexes or religions; children's rights and the rights of the disabled; conflict resolution and reconciliation; or criminal justice issues. The law was an unprecedented effort to restrict citizens' rights to organise and to form grassroots organisations aimed at supporting people in the pursuit of their rights and a further step to consolidate the government's/

party's monopoly on social and cultural activities, even internationally. The argument that "only the government should provide services" in these fields seemed weak, since government had no record of doing so and was unable to fill-in the gaps. The effect was thus another step in undermining independent civil society. The law was considered by many a regrettable and costly mistake, as it would significantly increase the misery of the Ethiopian people and preclude the inflow of millions of dollars to the country. By thus politicising the NGO sector, the government further confined the sociopolitical space for groups not adhering to the party line. Debate on the NGO law in parliament was stifled and a predictable majority vote was expected in January 2009.

A major controversy, again showing that everything – including professional services and institutions – was politicised to a dangerous degree, arose over the *2007 census figures*, of which a preliminary report by the central statistical authority became available in November. The data showed a curious mix of facts and fiction, making everybody unsure about its exact value. The first point was the relatively low total population figure of 73.9 m in 2007. Most previous estimates (based on extrapolation) had expected 78–80 m at least. For instance, the UN Department of Economic and Social Affairs estimated Ethiopia's 2007 population at 80.8 m. The lower population figure made the GDP growth figures look more favourable. However, the main bone of contention was the reduction of the population of Amhara region, credited with the lowest population growth rate (1.7%) of all regions. Its population was nearly 2 m less than regular projections on the basis of growth rates suggested. This was a puzzling decline in view of the national annual growth rate of about 2.6%, unless there was mass starvation or out-migration from Amhara region, which was not the case. Addis Ababa's population was also estimated as being quite low, little different from the 1994 census figure, which was also puzzling in view of the substantial in-migration from rural areas.

The *legal system* showed continued dependence on the government, and judges were not immune from pressure from above, notably in cases involving alleged political opponents. Lower civilian courts were able to operate independently, but suffered from a lack of manpower and facilities and were faced by a large backlog of cases. Bribery occurred frequently. Prison conditions were substandard, often appalling, and prisoners' rights were not respected. Birtukan Mideqsa, the most prominent prisoner, was held in solitary confinement and was only allowed to see her four-year old daughter on a few occasions. Reform of the judicial system was nowhere visible and the enormous backlogs continued.

In the long-running *trial* (since 1991) *against 57 former 'Derg' top government members*, the federal high court pronounced sentences on 11 January, ranging from 23 years to life imprisonment. On 26 May, in the appeal case involving some of these people, including former dictator Mengistu Haile Mariam, the sentence was changed by the court from life imprisonment to *death* in 18 cases. In the case of Mengistu, there was no chance he would be extradited from his exile in Zimbabwe to face his sentence.

On 4 December, the *new media law* (adopted by parliament on 1 July) was gazetted, confirming severe restrictions on news gathering, publishing and broadcasting. In terms of the law, the government demanded certification, prohibited relevant government office information from being divulged to the independent press, determined what was considered transgression of the right to gather and publish critical news and on what subjects, and made it easier to apply the defamation clause. Journalists guilty of this and other infringements of national security and public order (to be determined by the government) could be criminally tried and imprisoned. The effect will probably be that journalists and editors will increase self-censorship. During the year, several of the few remaining independent journalists were harassed or arrested, including Alemayehu Mahtemework of the magazine 'Enqu' on 2 May, simply because he had a story on singer Teddy Afro. On 22 August, chief editor Amare Aregawi of the 'Reporter' was arrested, but was released after a week. But on 31 October he was violently attacked and beaten unconscious by unknown assailants while collecting his son from school.

Other newspaper editors were also arrested, held for some time, released on bail or fined, or had their licences revoked. Dozens of journalists remained in exile. Several papers continued to be banned or went out of business during the year, but about 20 new ones appeared, including party or government papers. Independent newspapers were not well-distributed outside the cities and hence the information deficit, notably among the rural population, remained substantial.

During the year, the Ethiopian Telecommunications Corporation (ETC) continued as the sole internet service provider. *Internet access* was the lowest in Africa. Many websites, notably of the unreservedly critical Ethiopian *diaspora*, were *blocked* and e-mail traffic routinely checked with the help of Chinese technology and advisors. Internet speed was also very slow and the connections unreliable, except at the ECA offices and for other international organisations and at certain government colleges, such as the civil service college. The extension of internet through projects such as Schoolnet and 'Woredanet' nevertheless continued. *Cellphone network coverage* in the countryside (controlled exclusively by ETC) expanded significantly. Cellphone use also greatly increased. Frequent power cuts affected not only these services but also the economy in general.

As part of the government's rhetorical enactment of 'national harmony', the third *Nations, Nationalities and Peoples' Day* was celebrated in Addis Ababa on 8 December, this time organised by the Oromiya region authorities, with cultural performances by the 76 official ethnic groups in Ethiopia. The speeches and performances were almost identical to those of the previous year. One of the speeches asserted that Ethiopia now was "a country in which justice and the rights and equality of its peoples are ensured and where development and progress hold out real hope", words that provoked ripples of suppressed laughter through the crowd.

Ethnic relations were not as harmonious as represented, as was evident in the frequent clashes between groups in rural areas throughout the year, reflecting persistent *ethnic and regional tensions*, for instance in southern and western Ethiopia. Clashes seemed endemic in the Ethiopian ethno-political system because it politicised the group identities of all ethnic/linguistic groups, pitting them against each other. A few examples: a clash between Guji and Sidama near Wondo-Guennet on 3 April left 18 people dead; another between Issa Somalis and Afars in the area of Mille and Adaytu village from 10–12 June saw 32 people killed and 26 wounded. The number of victims of subsequent Ethiopian army operations was not known. The background to the conflicts was persistent drought and the gradual encroachment of Issas on Afar land. Another conflict erupted between the agro-pastoralist Guji Oromos and the sedentary Burji people on 6 August and again on 17 September, killing at least five people, displacing many, with 17 homes razed and dozens of livestock taken. It also led to Burji vacating several villages or towns, including Soyoma and Hagere-Mariam, in the face of the onslaught by heavily armed and well-organised Guji, who had been fighting with other ethnic groups as well over the past years. Government security forces acted only belatedly, after repeated requests by the Burji. In Gambela region, police and militia fought local inhabitants resisting the relocation of their villages, resulting in 11 deaths and 29 injured. The Gauwwada ethno-linguistic group also engaged in a major fight with police and government forces in early February, after leaders had asked for a special district for the group: 33 people were killed, 49 injured. Somali and Oromo pastoralists also fought regularly, mostly competing for land and other resources around their 'borders'. In general, pastoralists faced difficulty in the face of the persistent bias of the government towards settled agricultural peoples over pastoral livestock herders.

Various ethno-regional insurgent movements continued their activities but did not threaten the national army, except perhaps the ONLF, which faced a major counter-offensive. The Oromo Liberation Front (OLF), active in parts of Oromiya region, and the small Ethiopian People's Patriotic Front (EPPF), in the Amhara region near the Sudan border, were a nuisance to the government but did not make a dent in the military situation.

The domestic situation was further marred by the harsh government campaign to suppress the *ONLF insurgency*, which had challenged the government in 2007 with a disastrous terror attack on an oil field, unleashing a full-blown and ongoing offensive by the Ethiopian army. According to several international human rights groups and backed up by refugee interviews and aerial photographic evidence of scorched villages and fields, in this massive campaign serious and often avoidable human rights abuses were perpetrated against civilians. The campaign curbed the role of the ONLF, but precipitated local food security problems, huge social and economic damage and deep resentment among Ethiopian Somalis. Foreign NGOs were hindered in their work and due to this pressure 'Médecins Sans Frontières' terminated its operations on 26 August. While the ONLF was not an Islamist movement, the government – with its secularist leanings – became more aware of the dangers of Islamist radicalism due to the Front's possible connections with Somali extremists, and it started reconsidering its previously fairly lenient policies towards the radical Muslims who were emerging in the country. Christian-Muslim tensions were a potentially dangerous issue, fuelled by foreign-educated radical Muslim leaders and activists. Especially worrying were the growing religious polemics, notably by Muslims against Christians and so-called 'unbelievers', and by some Christian groups responding in kind, in dozens of tracts, audio-CDs and DVDs. This trend further challenged the Ethiopian model of religious coexistence.

Religious tensions thus remained just below the surface, with Wahhabi-Salafist groups as well as other Islamist revivalists building their strength through conversion programmes ('da'wa'), religious education and training (much of it foreign-funded), and calls for dissociation from Christians and other non-Muslims. A violent incident occurred on 2 March when Muslim extremists in Nesebo (Arsi) attacked congregants at two Protestant churches with machetes,

killing one man and seriously injuring 15 others. Despite their growing impact, 'Salafist' extremists were by no means universally popular among the Ethiopian Muslim population (35–40% of the total).

The Evangelical-Pentecostal churches expanded further at the
expense of the Ethiopian Orthodox church. The latter, still the largest denomination, saw consolidation of religious renewal movements within it and both denominational streams also adopted a
more self-conscious and at times polemical presentation of their interests and views vis-à-vis other religious communities. According
to the 2007 census, Christian denominations formed about 62% of
the population.

Foreign Affairs

The three crucial foreign policy issues were: the war in Somalia,
the tension with Eritrea and obtaining the accustomed number of
donor loans and grants without provoking too much criticism of
the political and human rights record. On the first issue, important
changes did occur, none on the second, and on the third, business
continued as usual, with a weak and inconsequential donor community babbling on about the deteriorating condition of democracy and human rights in the country. For the rest, the relations with
neighbours Kenya, Sudan, Djibouti and Somaliland were stable and
on the whole free of conflict.

The *war in* Somalia between the Somali Transitional Federal
Government (TFG) and its Ethiopian supporters on the one hand
and the radical Islamist insurgents ('al-Shabaab', 'Hizb ul Islam')
backed by Eritrea and some Muslim countries on the other, remained
bloody and chaotic, with the two parties matching each other on
the battlefield. Many civilians died in the crossfire. The Ethiopian
military, however, gradually withdrew from the fighting in order
to force the TFG to take matters into its own hands. The financial
and human costs may also have weighed too heavily on Ethiopia.

After the accord reached between TFG and the Somali opposition (Alliance for the Re-Liberation of Somalia (ARS-Djibouti) in June, Ethiopia announced it would withdraw its forces by December, and in fact largely did so (with the rest leaving in January 2009). Its military regrouped just across the border and continued to train Somali TFG units.

On the Eritrea-Ethiopia border issue, the ideological and judicial stalemate continued: no talks were held. The EritreaEthiopia Border Commission (EEBC) closed its doors, but no delimitation of the border on the ground was made. The UN Mission in Ethiopia and Eritrea (UNMEE) also folded, withdrawing after Eritrea sabotaged all supplies to it, including fuel, and withdrew its cooperation. Eritrean troops also reoccupied the temporary security zone along the border, and the area remained very tense, with troops vigilant on both sides. A solution was not likely under the two current regimes.

Relations with the *donor community and the* EU proceeded predictably, with the usual sums of aid money forthcoming, disbursed with little critical evaluation. Britain especially was rather lenient, sending another $ 220 m on ODA to Ethiopia. In July, a report by a retired British colonel and consultant (M. Dewar) advised the government on modernising its internal security.

Meles Zenawi made several *foreign visits*, for instance to the India-Africa summit in New Delhi on 8–9 April, to South Africa on 18–19 June, to the 11th AU summit in Egypt on 29–30 June and to the G8 summit in Japan on 8–9 July. Among the *foreign dignitaries* visiting Ethiopia were the Finnish minister for foreign trade and development, the French secretary of state for foreign affairs and the Chinese assistant foreign minister.

Ethiopia also remained pivotal in IGAD, but this regional organisation did not accomplish much during the year, except in showing its exasperation at the Somali TFG for its lack of success in achieving unity of purpose or extending its authority.

Negotiations in November in Uganda on a new *Nile River* agreement to replace the 1929 and 1959 accords stalled following disagreement among member states of the Nile Basin Initiative.

China remained a very important partner of Ethiopia in political and economic affairs. Chinese investments this year were estimated to be at least $ 350 m, up from only $ 10 m in 2003.

Relations with the US in the last year of the Bush administration remained good, as the American perception of Ethiopia as a valuable regional ally in the global anti-terror campaign did not change, despite persistently critical voices in the US congress on Ethiopia's domestic policies. The extent of material support by the US to Ethiopian war efforts in Somalia was not known but was probably significant (unconfirmed reports even claimed that the US gave Ethiopia about $ 80 m per month for this).

Socioeconomic Developments

A *famine threat* continued to plague Ethiopia: 3.5–6.4 m people were variously estimated to be in need of emergency food aid, although 2008 was not a year of persistent nationwide drought. Failure of seasonal rains in several areas (Tigrai, Gedeo, Sidamo), but also recurring faulty government policies to foresee and plan for it were responsible. After a government call for $ 425 m, foreign donors, mostly the US, again supplied emergency food aid. This year's harvests were not bad, but domestic food production saw no noticeable increase, certainly not on a per capita basis. All land remained state property, with peasants having usufruct rights, transferable to children under certain conditions.

The *export* of coffee, oil seeds, hides and leather products and flowers brought in larger sums than in the previous year. For example, coffee sales rose 60–70%, although in some areas coffee production was affected by local droughts. Flower exports reportedly rose by about 130% and netted $ 185 m, lower than the projected $ 280 m, as sales dropped towards the end of the year due to the widening global economic crisis. The full extent of the global economic downturn had, however, not yet affected Ethiopia by December. Additional exports were horticultural products, gold and livestock.

Exports remained competitive due to the low wage costs: on average a labourer earned $ 60–80 a month. Total *export earnings* reached $ 1.3 bn, but offsetting the benefits of export growth was the strong increase in imports to about $ 6 bn.

The Ethiopian economy remained heavily *state- and party-dominated*: the IMF estimated in a 2007 report that about 55% of all enterprises were public ones, and this figure did not decline in 2008. One example was the big EPRDF-party business conglomerate Guna (export of sesame seeds, natural gum, coffee, pulses and spices; and production, import and distribution of construction materials, industrial and agricultural inputs): figures released on 27 July revealed that it had netted a gross profit of $ 4 m during the past year, an increase of more than 200% on previous years. A new tack in government policy was the promotion of micro- and small-scale enterprises, stimulated by donor agencies.

In mid-April the government launched a *commodities exchange*, with a centralised electronic price listing system for agricultural products. The intention was to improve domestic market efficiency and distribution. At the end of the year, the government also moved to take over coffee marketing, because it saw coffee traders hoarding to raise prices. Many trading licences were revoked.

As *macroeconomic figures* differed markedly across institutions (IMF, government, UNESCO, UNDP, World Bank, Economist Intelligence Unit), they were considered only tentative. Undeniably there was continued substantial growth in Ethiopia. According to US figures, the country's GDP reached $ 25 bn (with almost half generated by the agricultural sector and 13% by industry). The IMF (in April 2009) claimed a GDP growth rate of 11.6% for 2008, in continuance of the performance of the last five years. There remained, however, the paradox that despite this growth 3–4 m people were again on food aid, 44% lived in dismal poverty and more than 50% of people remained in the informal economy. The overall growth clearly did not lead to a more inclusive development pattern.

Under the government's current *'agriculture-led industrial development'* model, the services, construction and infrastructure sectors expanded again, financed chiefly by World Bank and through donor country projects and coupled to poverty reduction programmes (e.g., Plan for Accelerated and Sustained Development to End Poverty – PASDEP). Most of the work in these sectors was carried out by EPRDF-affiliated companies and non-party affiliated businesses continued to have difficulty in gaining access.

The overall road network expanded 5%. On 10 September, a new 303-metre bridge across the Blue Nile near Dejen, on the Ethiopia-Sudan route, was opened, financed by Japan. In June, the *World Bank* initiated a new four-year Country Assistance Strategy (CAS), with first-year funding to the tune of $ 635 m. It was aimed at some familiar themes: enhancing governance, service delivery, poverty reduction and building food security. These goals were the same as in previous CAS documents.

Controversy arose over emerging new projects to *lease agricultural land to major foreign investors* from China, South Korea, Saudi Arabia and even Djibouti (its president got 7,000 hectares). This new trend, also evident in other African countries, would see foreigners using the land to produce food for their own domestic markets. As all land is state property, the government could easily appropriate it from local peasants and pastoralists and contract it out on lease, with a promise of financial benefits for the state.

On 7 April, an embarrassing *gold scandal* came to light, when it appeared that the national bank had lost at least $ 17 m due to a fraud involving gold-plated steel bars – an incredible mistake probably due to corruption, and a serious blot on the government's reputation.

On 24 June, the acting auditor general, Assefa Desta, presented a critical report on *excessive government borrowing* in 2006, i.e., Birr 3.3 bn in excess of the amount approved by the legislature. He called the borrowing, with its important subsequent economic effects, 'unlawful'. The report was unfavourably received by the finance minister and the state-appointed governor of the national bank, who disputed the audit, although the auditor general had worked on figures supplied by them. The facts appeared to be correct, because this extra borrowing, combined with at least a 16% increase in the money supply (i.e., printing extra banknotes), partly explained the *accelerating inflation* (15.8% in 2007 and 25.3% in 2008). Furthermore, IMF figures in a report of 31 July appeared to confirm the auditor general's analysis. Later in 2008, it was reported that the money supply had been expanded by 40%, partly due to clients withdrawing money from their bank accounts and leading to a much reduced savings rate. Retrospectively, fiscal prudence appeared to have been abandoned after November 2005. On 1 July, a new auditor general was appointed.

Inflation reached about 40% at year's end, although food price inflation was considerably higher, causing further hardship to the masses of poor people, notably in the cities. In March, the government announced a package of measures to reduce inflation, including monetary intervention, more subsidies, more food imports and cutting import tariffs. All this further dented the already meagre foreign exchange reserves, and the effect was not immediately apparent. The *scarcity of foreign exchange* led to serious balance-of-payments problems. These were partly alleviated by a higher than usual inflow of *remittances*. While the local newspaper 'Fortune' estimated the sum for 2008 to have been in excess of $ 1 bn, it was more likely around $ 850 m, up 25% from 2007. Remittances were mainly spent on family support, housing construction and small-scale business investments.

The government's *budget* (the Ethiopian budget year starts on 7 July) reached Birr 54.2 bn ($ 5.7 bn), and this increase was partly based on an expected revenue increase of 20–25%. The budget deficit was estimated at 4.4% of GDP, but excluding donor grants was 8.4% of GDP. The current account deficit for 2008 was estimated to be about 7–8% of GDP. Foreign debt rose to $ 3.1 bn, despite debt relief. Foreign direct investment was about 2–3% of GDP.

During the year, Ethiopia secured *foreign aid packages* of more than $ 1.3 bn, bringing the total sum of 'development aid' received by the country since 1991 to $ 24 bn. However, Ethiopia still ranked only

169 on UNDP's Human Development Index (of a total of 179 countries), no improvement on last year. Remarkably, on TI's Corruption
Perceptions Index it was ranked 126 out of 180, higher than last year.

Persistent *socioeconomic problems* were unemployment, a low
general level of education and skills in the face of rising education
costs (the illiteracy rate was around 50%), a high number of IDPs
fleeing conflict and natural calamities and a steadily shrinking agricultural resource base due to continuing high population growth.
Any plea for population control was countered by religious authorities, both Muslim and Christian, locked in a competitive 'demographic battle'. This issue too was highly politicised.

The number of *refugees* in the country was estimated by UNHCR
at 59,800. The most recent figure for registered IDPs was more than
200,000, still including tens of thousands in Tigray, a result of the
Ethio-Eritrean border war of 1998–2000. There was also a steady outflow of thousands of *labour migrants* from Ethiopia to Yemen, Saudi
Arabia and Middle Eastern states (many of them being trafficked
women), often via Somaliland and Puntland ports.

The *health* sector expanded in line with population growth but
suffered from a lack of investment and bad facilities. The doctor-
patient ratio rose to 1:37,000. Public health problems such as HIV/
AIDS, infectious diseases, prostitution and maternal and infant mortality remained very serious. In the field of *education*, primary school
expansion continued, with more pupils enrolled and more schools
built in rural areas. The further construction of rural universities was
announced, although the record of the existing ones built over the
last eight years or so was pretty bleak, with bad facilities for teaching
or research, bad living conditions for students, under-stocked libraries and a very weak academic culture. Experts commented that the
aim appeared to be to produce people with certificates, rather than
well-educated or competent people. Some observers spoke of frivo-
lous, non-productive investments in make-believe education. The
old top universities, like in Addis Ababa, were further weakened. In
addition, the high production of BA and MA holders augmented the

problem of massive unemployment among graduates. This problem was also widespread among high school leavers.

Environmental problems remained serious, but while consciousness of these increased they were not seriously or comprehensively tackled, as was evident by the steady expansion of cropland at the expense of forest areas and pasture land, and by the failure to devise and enforce environmental laws on industrial waste, discarded batteries, plastic waste and sewage. In several agricultural areas, tree planting, terracing and irrigation schemes were implemented to reduce erosion. But the uncontrolled pollution by, for instance, the expanding flower industry persisted, blighting the local environment and raising fears among local people over the water supply and the long-term fertility of the land. Only one new flower farm, Fressia Ethiopia, boasted that its production was environmentally friendly. Prime examples of heavily degraded natural resource areas were Lake Koka and the Akaki River, both southeast of Addis Ababa.

Ethiopia in 2009

All public life continued to be strongly dominated by the Ethiopian People's Revolutionary Democratic Front (EPRDF). The country started to gear up for the May 2010 elections, with the government becoming nervous about opposition parties and trying to restrict their expansion. EPRDF party organisation was given priority in an effort to co-opt as many people as possible, particularly those in economic and administrative key positions. This was in line with the EPRDF's mission to prevent a repeat of the 2005 elections, which were nearly lost. Prime Minister Meles Zenawi declared himself ready for another term in office. A new opposition coalition, 'Medrek' or Forum for Democratic Dialogue, was formed by eight parties and gained support by having a broad spectrum of leaders from various backgrounds. The building of their support base in rural areas was hindered by the EPRDF, which was afraid of competition. Overall, there was little evidence of real progress in democratic consolidation. The human rights record was as disappointing as in 2008 – no fundamental improvements were seen with respect to the rights of opposition political activists, journalists and other media agents. Police and army behaviour was unsatisfactory in many cases. Arbitrary arrests, extra-judicial procedures and abuse were regularly reported. Internet access remained restricted, despite a false announcement in March that access was to be free.

The stalemate in relations with Eritrea continued as before, with on-going reciprocal negative propaganda and no dialogue on any subject. No negotiated solution was in sight, mainly due to Eritrea's refusal to enter into any talks before the 2002 Eritrea-Ethiopia Boundary Commission (EEBC) border decision was implemented to the letter, which Ethiopia refused. Ethiopia's armed forces left Somalia in January, with AMISOM troops from Uganda and Burundi being augmented as a stabilisation force in Mogadishu. Ethiopia's relations with other neighbouring countries were uneventful. Meles Zenawi took a prominent role as Africa's representative at the UN climate change conference in Copenhagen.

There was economic growth resulting from infrastructural investment and modest growth in the agrarian sector, apart from coffee. Benefits of growth accrued mostly to the well-established political-economic elite. Substantial uncritical donor-country support was again provided to the tune of almost $ 2 bn. A slight decline in poverty incidence was reported, although the rural masses and urban poor saw little improvement; they remained strongly dependent on government/ruling party inputs and had no access to independent media information. Conditions remained dismal for most rural people and social inequality increased. Again the threat of famine loomed and international humanitarian aid was requested for an estimated 5–6 m people in dire need. The process of concessioning large tracts of allegedly unused or vacant land to foreign investors and governments – without consulting local peasants – continued, with major financial benefits for the federal government, but as yet unforeseen consequences for the local society and economy.

Domestic Politics

The *political scene* was strongly *dominated* as before by the *EPRDF*, the former insurgent movement that came to power in 1991 and proceeded to solidify its autocratic single-party rule under the leadership of *Prime Minister Meles Zenawi* by extending its influence into all spheres of the bureaucracy, administration, press, education system and economic life. *Opposition parties*, while permitted and represented in parliament since the controversial 2005 elections, were repeatedly *obstructed, marginalised and harassed* throughout the year in the context of preparations for parliamentary elections in May 2010. Opposition parties remained divided but succeeded in forming a *new alliance*, the Forum for Democratic Dialogue, or in Amharic 'Medrek', in anticipation of the upcoming elections. The alliance included major political figures from various ethnic backgrounds, including former president Negaso Gidada and former Tigray People's Liberation Front (TPLF) defence minister Siye Abraha, as well as other prominent personalities. Former judge and major opposition leader Birtukan Mideqsa of the United Democratic Justice Party (UDJ) was also a leading member, but she remained in prison. Medrek united eight parties. Apart from the UDJ, which had emerged from the Coalition for Unity and Democracy (CUD) upon its collapse as a result of external interference and internal squabbles after a good showing in the 2005 elections, these were: Arena Tigray for Democracy and Sovereignty (led by former TPLF member Gebru Asrat), the Oromo People's Congress, the Coalition of Somali Democratic Forces, the Ethiopian Social Democratic Party, the Oromo Federalist Democratic Movement, the Southern Ethiopian People's Democratic Coalition, and the Ethiopian Democratic Unity Movement. This coalition represented major groups or parties with an alternative programme for the country, but they were reportedly unable to build up mass support due to harassment of rural activists and frequent party office closures. They also had some internal problems. On 3 November, the opposition parties stated that 450 of their members and candidates had been jailed by the government. The government's message to the public was often voiced in threatening language, perhaps in the belief that a show of force expressed authority; there was little if any appeal to harmony and consensus building.

Opposition politics was generally difficult in a climate of distrust, harassment (especially in rural areas) and complete domination of the state and its resources by the ruling party. Dubious accusations were levelled against opposition figures, including a 'plot to overthrow the government', for which 40 people were arrested on 24 April. They were mostly opposition party members and associates. This 'plot', soon called the 'Ginbot 7' plot after the opposition group in exile led by Berhanu Nega, the Addis Ababa mayor-elect in 2005, allegedly involved a few army officers and opposition party figures, but the octogenarian father of Andargatchew Tsige, an opposition party figure in exile, was also accused. As in previous similar cases in recent years, no credible evidence was presented and, according to many Ethiopians, spite and intimidation by the government seem to have dominated this case. In August, the Federal High Court found 13 of the defendants guilty and one not guilty *in absentia*. In November, the court found another 27 guilty and sought the death penalty for the 40 defendants. It ignored testimonies by some of the accused of abuse and torture in prison and it was hard to conclude that justice was done.

UDJ leader Birtukan Mideqsa had had no trial before being imprisoned again in December 2008 for her alleged 'violation of pardon', and no trial took place during the year. She was held in solitary confinement until June and her health suffered. She remained popular and admired among the Ethiopian public, and the government did not consider legitimate demands, including by donor countries, for her release. Her case remained a point of conflict between the ruling party and the opposition groups, symbolising the lack of progress in democratisation, fair election campaigning, and trust-building in the political process.

On 30 September, an electoral 'code of conduct' for the 2010 elections was signed by the EPRDF and a number of opposition parties (the Ethiopian Democratic Party, the remnant Coalition for Unity and Democracy, and the All-Ethiopia Unity Party), but it had limited value because it did not include the Medrek coalition. No agreement was reached between the government and opposition parties on a reform of the EPRDF-dominated National Electoral Board. Some diaspora-based parties proceeded to voice their opposition to the EPRDF by stating that even armed struggle might perhaps be justified to replace the current government.

On 22 June, in an interview for 'The Times', Meles Zenawi floated the idea that he might step down after the 2010 elections, but this proved to be empty words. It soon appeared that, as all observers and opposition leaders had predicted, he would stand again for election as party leader and prime minister. The *EPRDF* exerted major efforts to extend its *societal hegemony* via the educational and administrative systems. There were reports that people were pressured to become members of the party, and obliged to participate in monthly party meetings to be instructed in the party ideology of 'revolutionary democracy'. Carrying a party card was also a practical necessity for appointment to any public sector job, e.g. for higher education graduates. In addition, the women's and youth wings of the party were expanded, reminiscent of old-style Communist parties. People working in the state administration (from local 'k'ebeles' up to ministries) could not be members of an opposition party, on pain of dismissal. The civil service became even more politicised.

Reports of *corruption* regularly surfaced. The government Ethics Commission arrested 203 suspects for corruption. In some court cases, e.g. on 24 December, officials found guilty of corruption were sentenced to long terms in prison and high fines. On 29 October, an EPRDF member and MP, Bekele Etana, defected to the UK after giving a press release on corruption and unaccounted spending within the federal government, based on his experience as a member of the parliamentary Public Account Standing Committee.

Internal EPRDF party control was maintained by evaluation sessions ('gimgema'). One such a 'fundamental self-evaluation' was announced by the EPRDF on 16 August. An earlier round had already led to the arrest and sentencing (to 10–23 years in prison) of six army officers who had allegedly 'conspired' with and collected arms for the CUD opposition party in 2005.

On 13 February, the House of Peoples' Representatives (parliament) formally approved the new *Charities and Societies (CSO) law*, restricting funding from abroad of any civic organisation to 10% of the budget of local NGOs, limiting the legitimacy of their work in many fields of human rights and social advocacy, and stipulating stiff penalty clauses. It forced many NGOs to scale down or close. On 7 July, the parliament passed a new *'Anti-Terrorism Proclamation'*, with a very broad definition of 'terrorism' that bore no resemblance to its core meaning of armed violence towards non-combatant civilians with the aim of intimidating, creating fear and killing. The new law designated peaceful political demonstrations, property crimes and disruption of public service (and even "intentions to influence the government") as terrorism, in a rather ludicrous extension of the concept. Experts noted that the law, with draconian prison terms and death penalty clauses, appeared to be an effort to outlaw or criminalise any criticism, even peaceful, of the regime. The law was another missed opportunity to build confidence and enhance public security, and while 'innovative' in the judicial sense, observers noted that it left all proportionality behind.

Security problems were evident throughout the year, but remained outside the purview of the national press (silenced by the new Media Law, harassment, newspaper closures and arrest of journalists) and foreign journalists. The main trouble spot was the Somali-inhabited Ogaden, where the government's harsh campaign to suppress the Ogaden National Liberation Front (ONLF), a violent insurgent movement with a similarly bad record, continued. Interviews with local people and eye-witnesses revealed disproportionate violence and gross abuse of civilians in the region and adverse effects on food security. Thousands fled the area. Criticism voiced in human rights reports was, however, dismissed by the government, which said that killings had occurred but were the result of inter-clan fighting. There were also sporadic clashes between government forces and Oromo Liberation Front (OLF) units in the east and west of Oromiya Region.

Several major *'ethnic' clashes* also occurred, e.g. in the south, continuing a recurrent pattern of conflicts about borders, land and water sources between ethno-linguistic groups. They led to hundreds of people being killed and tens of thousands displaced. The two major incidences were the Garri-Boran conflict in the south, in which in February and later in September around 300 people were reported killed and more than 70,000 displaced, and clashes on

20 May between members of the Afar, Oromo and Argobba ethnic groups in northern Ethiopia, which caused the death of 14, with at least 18 seriously injured. Another incident resulting in death was the conflict between the Konso and Dirashe groups on 2–4 January (18 killed). On 24 August, the Federal High Court issued its judgement in a 2008 case of 'ethnic cleansing' which had led to death and destruction in the Oromo-Gumuz area in western Ethiopia, with 101 of the defendants declared guilty. Six were sentenced to death and 95 to prison terms of six years to life.

Religious tensions were recorded between Orthodox Christians and Muslims as well as between Orthodox Christians and Pentecostal-Evangelical Christian groups, which increased in number, but this did not lead to major violent conflicts. Mainstream relations were peaceful. Struggles for influence on the local level were more visible between Orthodox and Pentecostal believers, with many of the latter having entered local administrations in the countryside, which made several of them into arenas of competition. Polemics between Orthodox, Pentecostal and Muslim spokesmen continued in various media but were less confrontational than previously, due to government monitoring. Tensions were, however, always present under the surface. On 2 October, a mob of Muslims reportedly attacked evangelical churches in Western Arsi zone, injuring at least three Christians. On 11 September, the Mulu Wongel Evangelical Church and Qale Hiwot churches in Senbeté town were ransacked and church property burned, due to a false rumour about Christians having 'desecrated' the Qur'an. On 21 January, criminal charges were brought against 18 members of a radical-Islamic Wahhabist group called 'Kwarej' because of their suspected violation of the Ethiopian Penal Code by organising Muslim youths and preparing them to carry out terrorist acts. On 6–10 January, religious clashes between young Christians and Muslims in Dire Dawa resulted in one dead and 20 injured.

Human rights did not substantially improve compared with previous years. Constitutional clauses about civic freedoms and free

expression were 'flexibly interpreted', and were contravened by
recent legislation, as in the new civil society law and in the new
anti-terrorism law. The political system in place was prone to allow
arbitrary and unpredictable repression, although not against all
opponents or opposition spokesmen. There was a trend towards
impunity for the armed forces and police when abuses were committed and reported: only a few perpetrators of misdeeds were apprehended, let alone tried in courts of law, including in respect of
cases related to previous years. Nevertheless, some opposition figures and activists arrested while campaigning were cleared of police
charges in court. Popular singer Teddy Afro, imprisoned in 2008, was
released on 13 August after his sentence was reduced.

In general, the government showed little concern to respond to
criticisms by *human rights organisations* and Western countries,
which called for national dialogue, cooperation and respect for the
constitutional rights of citizens. The independent Ethiopian Human
Rights Commission was thwarted in its fact-finding missions and its
researchers were harassed. Several of its chief officers fled the country in the course of the year. The same applied to the well-respected
Ethiopian Women Lawyers' Association.

In the local (Amharic, Tigrinya, Orominya) press and some diaspora media, discussions emerged on the early history of the
TPLF, the core of the ruling party, with eye witness accounts about
tense internal relations and the violence used by the Front during
its struggle for power. Several books with memoirs of former participants and victims appeared, including sensitive accusations of
abuse and repression. In addition, one former Front member contended that the $ 100 m in Band Aid money given to the TPLF in 1985
to ward off famine in the north was largely used for procuring arms.
This debate continued into 2010.

The *press* and other *media* continued to face serious restrictions,
with arrests and court cases against journalists for alleged defamation. One of the most important independent news magazines,
'Addis Neger', was forced to close in December due to harassment,

and its chief editor fled the country. In June, the private Sheger-FM radio station was also ordered to close. *Internet access* (available to only 0.5% of the population) was not free, with many sites again blocked. Compared with other African countries, Ethiopia had a very low record on numbers of Internet users as well as user freedom, thus slowing down the ITC revolution. Control of the only Internet server, the state-owned ETC, was a prime means of restricting the free flow of information. In smaller towns and rural areas particularly, there was no access to independent information from any source.

Foreign Affairs

The issues of Eritrean-Ethiopian relations, the Somali problem, and Ethiopia's changing place in the global order (relations with donor countries and with new investor countries) remained the primary concern. On the first issue, no progress was registered, with the *stand-off between* Ethiopia *and* Eritrea fully confirmed and no new international initiatives in sight. More young Eritreans, both army personnel and civilians, slipped across the border into Ethiopia. Their number grew by around 900–1,000 per month, and Ethiopia opened several new camps in the north to house them. Propaganda from both sides continued as usual, e.g. via radio and TV programmes aimed at 'the enemy'. In August, the Eritrea-Ethiopia Claims Commission in The Hague published its final rulings on the damage claims by the two countries regarding their 1998–2000 war, with Eritrea having slightly more to pay than Ethiopia. But this did not lead to any rapprochement between the feuding countries; on the contrary, they supported some of each other's opposition groups.

In January, Ethiopia withdrew all of its military forces from Somalia under an agreement negotiated between Somalia's Transitional Federal Government (TFG) and Somali opposition groups. The troops had been there for more than two years in support of the TFG, which made too little headway and exasperated the Ethiopians. The AMISOM forces (reaching 5,200 during the year) partly 'replaced' the Ethiopians in protecting the TFG. However, Ethiopian units stayed close to the border and worked to support the TFG and its allies against the militant Islamist insurgent fronts, which were seen as a security risk to Ethiopia too. Later in the year, there were rumours that Ethiopia made occasional forays into Somalia to support local allies and that it sent them shipments of arms. The new TFG President Sheik Sharif Sheikh Ahmed, a former Islamic Courts Union leader and enemy of Ethiopia, visited Addis Ababa for the AU summit and an IGAD meeting in February, when he also consulted with Ethiopian leaders. He was in Ethiopia again in November to attend the Saudi-East Africa Forum. In the UN and in IGAD, Ethiopia tried to further incriminate and isolate Eritrea, which it accused (with reference to plausible UN evidence) of continuing military support for Islamist radicals in Somalia.

On 1 June, the *Nile riparian countries* reached agreement on many elements of a new treaty on Nile water utilisation and development, despite the persistent refusal of Egypt and Sudan to negotiate any alteration in the status quo, but two controversial key clauses were put in an appendix for a decision to be taken at a later stage, thus keeping the creation of a Nile River Commission on hold.

Ethiopia maintained relatively good relations with the *US* under its new President Obama, who operated cautiously and slowly fell back into the foreign policy pattern of his predecessor towards the Horn of Africa. For Ethiopia, this meant that Washington perceived Ethiopia to be 'stable', a partner in anti-terrorism campaigns, and in need of more foreign development assistance. The US State Department and various US human rights agencies stated that human rights and political conditions were not good in Ethiopia, but this did not prompt the US government to act. For example, the US did not respond to the Ogaden campaign, where no one could deny that gross human rights abuses and cruelty were perpetrated against civilians accused of supporting the ONLF.

The EU played a low-key role in Ethiopia, or at least a rather invisible one, showing a measure of indifference to the country and its people. No EU statements were issued on controversial issues such as the CSO law or the Anti-Terrorism law. Aid funds were kept flowing as usual, with little open critique on the country's record or socio-economic policies. The UK was again an eager contributor, with about $ 180 m of aid provided.

At the UN *climate conference*, on 6–18 December in Copenhagen, Meles Zenawi acted as the main spokesman for Africa, a move strongly criticised by the Ethiopian diaspora. He led a call for hundreds of billions of dollars to be paid to Africa as compensation for the effects of global warming.

Relations with *China* were strengthening and were dominated by economic interests and resource acquisitions by China. Trade soared again and reportedly reached a value of $ 1.376 bn, although with China exporting much more to Ethiopia than it was importing from it, despite China encouraging the latter by special quota and tariff arrangements. The Chinese post-Communist, state-capitalist model and its dominant-party governance system continued to appeal to the Ethiopian leaders, who faced no criticism on politics, governance or human rights issues from the Chinese.

Ethiopia's relations with *neighbours* Kenya, Djibouti, Sudan and Somaliland remained stable and friendly overall. With Kenya, more efforts toward security cooperation were made in view of the southern Somalia problem. With Djibouti, some tension existed over impending price rises for the use of port facilities, on which Ethiopia has been dependent ever since it had made itself landlocked in 1991 by ceding its ports to Eritrea. Sudan and Ethiopia held talks on border issues, with Ethiopia reportedly ceding some contested land to Sudan. Sudan supplied about 80% of Ethiopia's oil needs.

Socioeconomic Developments

Ethiopia registered growth, but poverty characterised the lives of most people and socioeconomic insecurity remained serious. Overall social inequality increased, with a top layer of elite-related business people, officials, cadres and civil servants safe in their jobs and income, and the large mass of peasants and workers in vulnerable, dependent conditions, struggling to make ends meet and retain their dignity.

As usual, there was again controversy, or at least great divergence, over the estimated GDP *growth* figures, based on a variety of divergent figures. The government claimed 10%–11% growth, and more neutral observers some 5%–6.5%. The IMF (in April 2010) gave the 2009 growth rate as 9.9%, in continuance of the solid performance of the last five years. Population growth of about 3%, however, qualified the importance of this GDP growth figure. Ethiopia's per capita GDP was estimated to be ca. $ 330, up slightly compared with 2008. According to official government figures, total GDP rose to an estimated $ 33.9 bn ($ 75.9 bn in PPP terms), as a result of growth in agriculture, infrastructural works and services. While GDP is a limited measure of how the overall economy of a country fares, let alone of well-being or wealth distribution, donor countries, in their often superficial and clueless policies toward African development, were satisfied with the outward picture of growth and kept on disbursing the usual aid flows to Ethiopia. The central government budget reached $ 4.67 bn, but expenditure was $ 5.36 bn. The country's external debt rose to $ 4.2 bn, some 25% higher than in 2008, perhaps due to increased Chinese borrowing.

Despite the GDP growth figures, some 5–6 m people were again in need of *food aid*, and many more (about 7 m) were undernourished or food insecure under the National Productive Safety Net Program. On 22 October, the government officially asked for emergency food aid for 6.2 m people. The reason given was again 'failure of the rains'. While many people died of hunger or hunger-related diseases, a famine disaster was averted by recourse to domestic and foreign food aid supplies.

In agreement with the IMF, a *new macroeconomic package* was drawn up. Domestic borrowing by the government was to be reduced to zero. A first, a 'no strings attached' disbursement of $ 50 m was given in January, after the National Bank of Ethiopia had asked for emergency loans. Thereafter, the government requested a 14-month IMF loan arrangement under the *Exogenous Shocks Facility* (ESF), to "help the country cope with the adverse effects of the global recession" on its balance of payments. Again, on August 26, a loan of $ 240.6 m was granted – 115% of the country's quota. In total, Ethiopia received almost $ 1.8 bn in development aid and loans in 2009, bringing the total sum received since 1991 to just under $ 26 bn.

In February, the Birr (local currency) was *devalued* by 10% and the rate to the dollar was 12.4 in December. *Inflation* went down from a staggering 45.6% in January to about 11% in December. The year's average was about 15%, and was felt notably in the domain of staple food items, weighing heavily on the urban masses. Inflation was fuelled not only by the rising prices of imports (notably fuels), but also by unproductive government spending in the expanding bureaucracy and in party activities (massive membership drives, party cell organisation, propaganda meetings, party and civil service trainings, etc.). The EPRDF claimed to have 5 m members.

Agriculture saw some growth but no major changes, with productivity low, irrigation used on only 3% of the land, and small-scale peasants (numbering about 13.3 m) forced to eke out a living on tiny farm plots, with the government in legal possession of all land. EPRDF-affiliated companies supplied all fertilizers to the peasants. In one respect the land produced a lot – on plots leased by foreign companies and governments, provided by the government with low costs and no legal problems. The phenomenon of *foreign land acquisitions* (critics called it 'land grabbing') gained further momentum during the year, with more land going to these foreign operators. In November, the government announced that it would lease out 3 m hectares of (allegedly unused, empty) land to domestic and especially foreign investors over the next three years, and advertised large tracts on the Ministry of Agriculture website. Controversy emerged among experts over who would gain and whether these schemes

would benefit Ethiopian agrarian producers. While it was too early
to fully evaluate the results, so far few visible benefits that might up-
lift Ethiopian rural producers were seen. Saudi Arabian state media
waxed lyrical about the 'first harvest' of Ethiopian (Saudi-owned)
farms to arrive in the country, while displaced Ethiopian subsistence farmers were less enthusiastic. At $ 0.75–$ 1.0 a day, salaries
of farm workers were very low. Some of the new land exploitation
schemes might also threaten nature reserves or protected areas, as
with plans announced in October that Ethio-Saudi business tycoon
Mohamed al-Amouddin was to build a rice farm inside the Gambella
National Park.

Industry, with a share of 13% of GDP, did show some growth
but saw no major take-off. EPRDF's 'Agricultural Development-Led
Industrialisation' (ADLI) strategy remained in place, despite its lack
of success so far. Mining (gold, salt) remained limited, and natural
gas reserves of an estimated 24.9 bn m3 were known but not taken
into production.

Infrastructural works continued throughout the year, with
major projects in road building and hydro-electricity plants. On 13
November, the new 300 MW Tekkeze Hydropower Plant was officially opened. The Gilgel Gibe II dam on the Omo River also neared
completion. A third Gilgel Gibe dam in the lower Omo was in preparation but was causing uproar due to its foreseen negative effects on
the livelihoods and settlement areas of hundreds of thousands of
people (smaller ethnic groups) living downstream along the Omo
River. The government denied all negative effects and proceeded,
but no adequate impact assessment studies appeared to have been
made, certainly not with the cooperation and input of local people.
Italian firms had a major role in building these dams. Road construction also continued, with Chinese contractors building about
70% of them. *China* also supplied very substantial loans (over $ 1 bn)
to Ethiopia, with about 70% going to state/party-owned companies.
About 120 private Chinese companies were active in Ethiopia, alongside over 800 Chinese projects. A study by the African Economic

Research Consortium published in November showed that many of them were engaged in business and investment ventures for which they were not licensed and that only a few were willing to engage in joint ventures with Ethiopian companies.

Remittances from Ethiopian communities overseas amounted to an estimated $ 970 m and provided a lifeline to many impoverished families, and much was used as start-up capital to form small businesses by people without political connections.

Socioeconomic development was marked by an *increase in social inequality*, showing staggering class differences between the peasants and workers as compared with the business and political elite. People with income and benefits from external aid schemes were popularly known as 'the developmental wealth owners' (in Amharic 'lematawi balehabt'), i.e., a kind of rent-seeking class. They were seen by the population at large as owing their comfortable position to foreign support. *Youth unemployment* remained high (50%–60%).

Other developments in the economy again signalled the efforts of the state/ruling party to expand their power. After warnings were given to *coffee exporters* about 'hoarding' (in the expectation of international price rises), the government in late March revoked the licenses of six main coffee exporters. It then *confiscated* some 17,000 tons of coffee stocks from some 90 traders and began exporting coffee via the state-owned Ethiopian Grain Trade Enterprise. This indicated that the government was ready to intervene in the free operation of the market and also wanted more direct access to export revenue. Coffee accounted for about 10% of GDP and about $ 376 m in sales, down from $ 525 m in 2008, an exceptionally good year. Total exports rose, however, to $ 1.6 bn, while imports were over $ 7 bn with 16.3% of Ethiopia's total imports coming from China, followed by Saudi Arabia at 12%.

According to the UN, Ethiopia's *population* in 2009 reached 82.8 m, indicating that the country was continuing its unprecedented *demographic explosion*. The annual growth rate remained around 2.7%–3%, despite high maternal and disease mortality figures. The infant mortality rate, for instance, was high at about 93 per 1,000 live births, but this still represented a drop over previous years. *Health issues* remained a critical concern. Common diseases were still widespread. In August, there was a cholera outbreak in Addis Ababa (caused by poor sanitation and contaminated food and water), with at least 34 people dead and more than 4,000 hospitalised; in September, 18,000 people were reported infected. The government forbade use of the word 'cholera' ('acute watery diarrhoea' was the approved term), but the UN humanitarian agency sent six mobile cholera treatment centres for training purposes and drugs for treatment. The number of health extension workers expanded to more than 30,000, but the number of physicians was only about 2,100. There was a significant brain drain due to the attractions of jobs abroad.

Several NGOs in the *health sector* were adversely affected by the new NGO law, which restricted their activities. Even those with a programme geared to maternal healthcare or care for the disabled were barred from operating if their income from foreign donations reaching more than 10% of their budget. At a conference on the occasion of World Mental Health Day in Addis Ababa, it was said that several million people in the country suffered from mental health problems, with only 95,000 treated during the year. While the *HIV-AIDS* epidemic still remained a significant public health problem, the number of people dying from the disease dropped by about 20% to an estimated 80,000–90,000. This was due to increased awareness of the disease, more available medication, and behavioural changes, notably among the urban population. Over the past six-seven years, more than half-a-million Ethiopians have probably succumbed to the disease.

Out-migration from Ethiopia to the industrialised world and to Middle Eastern countries continued, both by people seeking employment and by journalists, civil servants, opposition politicians, etc., escaping repression. It was suspected that about 30,000 of these migrants (mostly females) were victims of human trafficking, mainly to Middle Eastern countries. Some 45,000 Ethiopians entered Yemen through Somali ports.

There were about 110,000 *refugees* in Ethiopia, with new influxes continuing to arrive from Eritrea (ca. 11,000) and Somalia (c. 13,000). The UNHCR estimated that the country also had almost 250,000 IDPs, mainly in Oromiya, Gambela and Somali Regions as a result of 'ethnic' clashes and the conflict in the Ogaden. There were also those still displaced by the Ethiopian-Eritrean war of 1998–2000.

Resettlement efforts continued to be made throughout the year, serving the dual purpose of settling populations affected by drought and erosion in new areas, as well as changing the socio-political balance between population groups. Conflicts around *resettlement schemes* occasionally arose, when indigenous people were pushed out or driven from their land by newcomers or disagreed about land and resource use. The attitude of the authorities in such cases was often ambiguous. Locals also regularly refused to accept (large numbers of) resettled immigrants from the north and pressured them to go elsewhere. In one instance in July in the Southern Region, about 5,500 people of northern origin, resettled in the Bench-Maji Zone, were forced from their homes after serious problems between them emerged.

Environmental problems were worrying. Deforestation and land erosion were serious ongoing problems and were combated only in selected areas with tree planting, bunding, etc. Population growth placed continued pressure on the environment, as did pollution in urban industrial areas, including the massive random disposal of plastic bags and batteries from radios, recorders, etc. across the country, visible to any visitor. Environmental awareness increased, especially as a result of NGO reports, government information and academic research, but policies matching this were not making significant headway.

Ethiopia in 2010

The domestic scene was dominated by parliamentary elections in May, which were well-prepared by the ruling Ethiopian Peoples' Revolutionary Democratic Front (EPRDF) government/party, and yielded the universally predicted mass 'victory', allowing the ruling party to scoop all except one of the 547 parliamentary seats. This result was achieved by a smart system of district voting (based on the principle of 'first past the post'), an intimidating presence of armed guards and soldiers at many (rural) voting stations, the prevention of effective opposition campaigning in the months before the election, and effective control of the vote-counting process by the EPRDF-controlled Electoral Board. This outcome followed the directives given to party cadres in meetings with the political leadership after the 2005 elections, which had produced a strong showing for the opposition and neglected the 'organisation of the vote' by the ruling party. The 2010 election results led most observers to talk of the further closure of political space and, in effect, of establishing a one-party system. A noticeable deterioration in the political atmosphere and growing intolerance of critical debate on any issue were seen. Feelings of fear and insecurity increased. Some observers even spoke of an 'Eritrea-scenario' unfolding in Ethiopia: consolidation of an unquestioned autocracy. Army and internal security forces were kept on alert throughout the year.

Ethiopia's international position remained relatively unchanged in that foreign donor countries/institutions were again forthcoming with substantial funds and did not engage in any fundamental debates on the EPRDF's governance practices and policies, captivated as they were by the discourse of 'development' and 'economic growth' within which the government presented all its initiatives and policies. Criticism of the political closure, the shut-down of freedom, rights abuses and the skewed business climate from the press, social scientists, civil society groups and international human

© KONINKLIJKE BRILL NV, LEIDEN, 2017 | DOI 10.1163/9789004346826_009

rights organisations were brushed off by donors without discussion of the points made. Relations with neighbours showed little substantive change: stalemate with Eritrea on the border issue and generally cooperative relations with other neighbouring countries. The process of leasing huge tracts of land to foreign investors continued. Benefits from these ventures accrued for the government and foreign companies, but not for displaced local people. Dependency on foreign aid remained high. Communal relations between religious groups showed occasional signs of tension, resulting in various violent clashes and religious polemics. Ethnic confrontations receded, but tensions were still present below the surface.

Domestic Politics

The scene was dominated by the *elections for parliament and regional assemblies* on 23 May. As expected, these elections led to an unprecedented 'victory' for the ruling party in all domains on a playing field that was not remotely level. The campaign phase was marred by many incidents of harassment, intimidation and arrests. Reports from the opposition Forum (*Medrek* in Amharic) group, an alliance of eight opposition parties, referred to many cases of members being threatened at gunpoint to prevent their putting themselves up as candidates or registering for the vote. In addition, opposition candidates and supporters were reportedly killed in Harar, Ambo, Dire Dawa, Jijiga and Shire towns. The Ethiopian Electoral Code thus did not have much effect in the field.

The elections for the national parliament ('House of People's Representatives') gave 546 of the 547 seats to the ruling EPRDF and its allied parties (EPRDF 499, six smaller allied parties 46 seats, one independent who later declared for EPRDF) and one Forum as the only opposition seat. Of the 1,904 seats in the regional state councils, 1,900 were taken by the EPRDF and its allies. This picture confirmed the trend towards the monopolisation of political space already

seen in the 2008 local elections, 100% of which had been won by the
EPRDF. These figures were improbable and would even have made
the Soviet Union blush. However, independent observers did not see
the elections as an exercise in democracy: external election observers were highly critical and unanimous in judging the elections not
free and fair, although 'technically' well run and disciplined on the
part of the voters. Only the AU declared the elections credible, but
this statement did not surprise anyone. The results were contested
by opposition groups, but they received no hearing in any forum.
Knowing the violent reputation of the incumbent government and
with the memory of the 2005 street massacres perpetrated by police
and special army units still fresh, the opposition parties refrained
from calling for public demonstrations in order to protect the public. This election consolidated the *hegemony of the EPRDF*, which
went on to consolidate the unity of party, state and government
institutions. But the political and social atmosphere in the country
deteriorated, as was evident in the continuous use of threatening
language towards non-EPRDF people, post-election harassment
of opposition parties and activists – although the national leaders
were usually left unmolested – and discrimination in terms of access to basic resources for ordinary voters in districts where the opposition had made some showing (according to official figures of
the National Electoral Board 21% had voted for opposition parties).
Many observers were puzzled by this authoritarian and intolerant
approach by the ruling party, but it went to show again that the concept of a 'loyal opposition' was foreign to it. Fear and resentment
among the public grew as heavy-handed intimidation and suppression of debate about policy alternatives increased.

The EPRDF went on to recruit ever more party members, and
in practice party membership became a precondition for employment in the public sector and government bodies, and for
gaining access to state support for basic goods, food aid, etc. The
EPRDF stuck to its *ideological formula* of 'revolutionary democracy', firmly rejecting the model of mainstream liberal democracy.

This was again made clear during its 8th Organizational Congress, held on 15–17 September in Adama (Nazret) under the slogan "The Ethiopian Renaissance will reach an irreversible stage by realizing the Growth and Transformation Plan". This congress was preceded by the 10th regular congress of the *Tigray People's Liberation Front* (*TPLF*), the core party of the EPRDF, on 6–9 September in Meqele. In the same month, the other three constituent parties of the EPRDF (the Amhara National Democratic Movement, the Oromo People's Democratic Organisation and the Southern Ethiopian Peoples' Democratic Front) also held party conventions and made some changes in their leadership. A new national cabinet was only announced on 5 October (after some 'leadership struggles' within the four EPRDF parties), with *Prime Minister Meles Zenawi* confirmed as leader and the Southerner Haile-Mariam Dessalegn as vice premier and minister of foreign affairs.

The popular *opposition leader Birtukan Mideqsa*, of the United Democratic Justice Party (UDJ) and Forum, remained in prison during the elections but was finally released in October. Thoroughly intimidated by her solitary confinement and disappointed by the divided opposition, she announced later that she was to step back and not return to active politics in the foreseeable future. The opposition parties, although they had capable members and some important names, such as a former TPLF defence minister and a former Ethiopian president, did not organise themselves effectively – not least because constant surveillance and obstruction by the ruling party/government prevented them from building up a well-rooted and accepted support base in the country – and could not therefore impress. They disagreed on the basis of their programmes, as well as over ethnic allegiances, and were excluded from parliament by the May elections.

On 25 December a number of people were convicted on allegations of *conspiracy to overthrow the government* by force of arms in April; 33 individuals were sentenced to life imprisonment and five received the death penalty. Several of the accused were allegedly tortured while in custody. One of the defendants was the 80-year-old father of opposition party leader Andargatchew Tsige (who himself had fled the country) of the former Coalition for Unity and Democracy party. The charges seemed very improbable and the trial biased. In the Oromiya region numerous arrests of suspected government opponents were made, always on the charge of being members of the Oromo Liberation Front (OLF).

In May there was a riot at Addis Ababa University, reportedly between Tigray and Oromo students. This followed the pattern of the 'campus wars' of the previous few years which proceeded along 'ethnic lines' and had fragmented the once-powerful Ethiopian student population. *Ethnic group tensions* remained visible but did not produce major clashes as in previous years. However, many problems concerning communal relations, district borders and land access remained unresolved. Tensions also occurred between Orthodox and Pentecostal Christians and Muslims, resulting in occasional violent clashes and *religious polemics*. Only in a few cases arising from earlier deadly conflicts and property destruction were court sentences handed down: e.g., on 2 September the Federal High Court condemned 103 people (six received the death penalty) on charges of 'genocide' in a case of 'ethnic' clashes between groups in the Benishangul Gumuz and Oromia border area in 2008, when hundreds of people were killed. During the year, there were reports of several massacres (in June in the Afar Region with 30 people killed and 50 wounded and in Benishangul-Gumuz Region on 21 May with 23 people killed), but whether they were 'ethnically motivated' was not clear. In a bizarre incident in October, soldiers entered an Orthodox monastery to arrest a monk who had prophesied a "government change". Some people in the monastery were allegedly killed during this action.

Armed resistance movements existed in several areas: in the east the Ogaden National Liberation Front (ONLF) among Ethiopia's ethnic Somali population and in the south and southeast the OLF, an Oromo movement. Both called for autonomy if not secession from the current 'federal' Ethiopian state. Not much was heard of the Ethiopian Peoples Patriotic Front, a previously active rebel front in northern Ethiopia, and they made the mistake of allying themselves with Ethiopia's enemy Eritrea, which lost them support in the country. The government continued its military campaign against the ONLF and was accused by human rights groups of violent abuses against the civilian population in the Somali Region.

The public sector was in the grip of the government-introduced five-year *'Growth and Transformation Plan' (GTP)*, launched at a time when the population had barely recovered from the 'Business Process Re-engineering Plan' (BPR). The results of this latter plan were not entirely clear, but were much influenced by the political agenda of the EPRDF. The GTP aimed at, among other goals, 11% annual GDP growth and a phenomenal rise in export earnings from $ 1.3 bn in 2010 to $ 8–10 bn in 2015. It also included plans to build a railway system and new mega-dams for energy production and export, and to have industry take the lead in development – a quiet abandonment of the previous 'Agricultural Development-Led Industrialisation' policy. On 12 August, Prime Minister Meles Zenawi told reporters that Ethiopia would probably be food self-sufficient in about five years under the GTP. On democracy and governance, nothing new was heard. Local observers and participants noted that 'management-speak' schemes like BPR and GTP were effectively used to bring the entire civil service and all government-dependent institutions (such as universities) into line with the dominant ideology of governance, create dependency, and flout autonomous, merit-based action. Remarkably, the IMF's country office stated on 27 December that "... the Fund is ready to back Ethiopia's five-year strategic plan in anyway the government wants" – a clearly political statement.

The effects of the *restrictive NGO law* (Charities and Societies Proclamation or CSO Law), passed in 2009 and effective as of January, were felt increasingly strongly in that many local and foreign-supported or civic organisations saw their work thwarted and had to close. This only left scope for religious organisations and community-level savings clubs and burial societies. The neutral civic space was again seriously limited, as was most evident in the closure of civic groups before the May elections. During 2010, the number of civil society organisations was reduced from about 4,500 (in early 2009) to about 1,400, and 90% of the staff lost their jobs. After the EPRDF victory, no breathing space was given to civic and associational life; on the contrary, ruling party recruitment drives and revenge measures against those who had dared to vote for the opposition were reported. Other laws, such as the new media law and the anti-terrorism law, also made their overall restrictive effect more felt, as most generally accepted political opposition and demonstrations could be labelled as 'anti-constitution' or 'anti government', etc., and be prosecuted.

The *independent media* suffered from close monitoring and repression. The printed weekly 'Addis Neger' was forced to close in December, the editor-in-chief of the weekly 'Awramba Times' resigned on 14 May after government threats, and the paper's office was attacked on 18 August. The Ethiopian broadcasts by 'Voice of America' and 'Deutsche Welle' were frequently jammed by order of the government. Several journalists, including Tsegaye Tiku of Ethiopian state television, defected, bringing the total number of journalists who had fled abroad since the 2005 elections to 155. None of the 13 independent newspapers that had been closed since the May 2005 election crisis were allowed back into business.

In October, an important *report* on the alleged *deleterious effects of foreign aid* and uncritical donor support on Ethiopia's political climate was published. The HRW study 'Development without Freedom', a critical, field-based study on the policies of repression and intimidation by Ethiopia's government in the wake of donor support and aid programmes, claimed that the latter were manipulated to deny perceived opposition supporters, or anyone who thought differently, material support (even food aid), training, agricultural inputs and legal aid. HRW also claimed that many laws and practices introduced by the government and the ruling party went against Ethiopia's 1995 constitution. The report, illustrated by numerous telling quotations, was immediately condemned by the government and ambivalently received by the donor countries united in the 'Development Assistance Group'. But neither government nor donors could offer strong arguments or facts to refute the report's observations and conclusions. The enduring puzzle for donors, observers and the Ethiopian public alike, much discussed in the press and the critical literature, was why the government and the EPRDF – in view of the evident achievements already made – still felt the need to keep up the repression, intimidation and biases in its policies and allowed all this to become progressively worse. Other independent reporting from both urban and rural areas alleged a disturbing atmosphere of fear, deception and distrust that seemed to corrode the social and political fabric of society. In December, a disturbing *report on conditions in the notorious Ma'ekelawi prison* in Addis Ababa and the highly abusive treatment of its (political) prisoners appeared on Ethiopian diaspora websites. The text was in Amharic and apparently based on information and testimony from within the prison system.

Foreign Affairs

Relations with *neighbouring countries* showed continuity and little change: stalemate with *Eritrea* on the border issue – with neither side giving in or advancing new ideas on demarcation or the normalisation of relations – and stability and overall cooperative relations with Somaliland, Kenya, Djibouti and Sudan. But there was continued tension with *Southern Somalia* because of the ongoing civil war and the terror threat from radical Islamist fronts, instability and piracy. Ethiopia, as a land-locked country since 1993, remained dependent on the ports of Djibouti (for the use of which Ethiopia reportedly paid about $ 70 m annually) and Berbera in Somaliland.

International support for the government was forthcoming from the USA, the EU, the UK and China. Ethiopia was seen as a key player in the so-called 'war on terror' in the wider region of the Horn of Africa and the nearby Middle East, where threats from Islamist terrorism were seen in Yemen and Somalia. While these threats were certainly real, as evident in the bloody al-Shabaab terrorist attack in Kampala in July, which killed more than 70 civilians, the foreign and economic policy of 'donor countries' was too much shaped by it, as if no alternatives were available and as if domestic repression had to be part of anti-terror policy.

Ethiopia remained intricately involved in *Somalia*, where the civil war raged on between radical Islamist insurgents (al-Shabaab, Hizbul-Islam) and Somalia's transitional federal government (TFG) in Mogadishu and its allied militias. But Ethiopia kept a low profile. By end-January, it had withdrawn virtually all of its remaining troops from Somalia under a 2009 deal with the expanded TFG, but it provided training and arms to some TFG-allied forces in the border areas. Ethiopia also made occasional brief forays into Somalia (e.g. in the Beledweyn region) to support forces loyal to the ill-performing TFG. In July, it also briefly intervened in the Ayn area of the disputed region of Sool, on the border between Puntland and Somaliland, against a local D'ulbahante clan militia. Ethiopia maintained working relations with Somaliland and the government of the autonomous Puntland region. With Kenya, joint action was undertaken to rein in remnants of the armed OLF insurgents operating in the southern border areas.

New tensions emerged with Egypt over the *Nile question*, when five riparian countries led by Ethiopia signed a 'Nile Common Framework Agreement' on 14 May. It was aimed at a new water-sharing pact to replace the 1929 and 1959 agreements that favoured Egypt. Ethiopia wanted to make a start on utilising more of the Blue Nile waters for agrarian projects and hydropower (ca. 82% of Nile waters originate from the Blue Nile, or Abbay, whose sources are in Ethiopia). A dam project on the Blue Nile was in preparation. These initiatives led to concerned responses from Sudan and Egypt. In November, Meles Zenawi suddenly made a statement that Egypt was backing rebel groups in Ethiopia because of the Nile dispute and said that "if Egypt went to war with upstream countries over this issue it would lose". Egypt reacted with puzzlement to these remarks.

Based on the very critical June EU Election Observer Mission report, *international and Western donors* (USA, EU) voiced some criticism of the conduct of the elections and called for more openness and fairness in the political process. But by and large they kept their relations with the Addis Ababa regime on the same level. EU foreign relations coordinator Catherine Ashton said on 25 May: "The legislative elections in Ethiopia were an important moment in the democratic process in the country." The meaning of this statement was unclear. The US criticised Ethiopia's human rights record and poor performance in democracy indicators in its annual State Department Human Rights survey, which was, predictably, as in all previous years, rejected point-blank by the Ethiopian government, although the substance of the reported facts was not refuted.

Nevertheless, Ethiopia collaborated with the US, EU, and Asian and African countries (such as Kenya and Uganda) in security matters, including combating international Islamist terrorism. China capitalised on its 'apolitical' business relations with Ethiopia and was praised by the ruling government as a 'dependable friend'.

In December, Meles Zenawi attended the G-20 summit in South Korea. Also in December, he presented himself as Africa's spokesman on the Global Climate Change summit in Cancún, Mexico. On 22 September, Meles was invited to give a speech on economic issues at Columbia University in New York, an event to which much of the Ethiopian community in the US objected. In June, Meles visited France. Ethiopia was in turn visited by a number of ministers from EU countries (e.g., Norway, Ireland, France) and others throughout the year. Ethiopia also continued to exert an important influence in the sub-regional organisation IGAD.

Socioeconomic Developments

Demographic and economic data were not fully accurate, with most international sources giving estimates dependent on Ethiopian government ministries and the Central Statistical Authority's data. Ethiopia's population reached an estimated 84 m people, a reflection of continued *high population growth* (2.7%–3% a year), straining resources, the environment and the economy. The median age was 16.8 years and 46.3% of the population were under 14. The public health sector made some progress with extensions of clinics and prevention programmes for HIV-AIDS and malaria, but there was no major success with regard to family planning, which was also actively opposed by religious spokesmen, locked in a battle about religious demography.

Ethiopia experienced economic growth while at the same time a high proportion of the population were *food-aid* dependent: in February, the government requested food aid for 5.2 m people, and in addition about 7.5 m were in the Productive Safety Net schemes (food-for-work projects). Later in the year, these figures fell. The US provided $ 330 m in humanitarian and food aid.

Income inequality remained stark and did not diminish, with a small group of exceedingly rich people in the political and economic elite, and a large mass of relatively immobile peasants, pastoralists and urban poor on the bottom rungs of society. The population below the 'poverty line' was estimated at 38% (a slight decline), but in the new Oxford University Multidimensional Poverty Index, which realistically weighed a country's whole gamut of criteria of human (under)development, not just income, Ethiopia was ranked last but one (before Niger) of the 104 countries covered.

Ethiopia's *state budget* was an estimated $ 4.36 bn (revenues), with expenditure of about $ 5.098 bn. The current-account balance deteriorated from an estimated –$ 2 bn in 2009 to –$ 2.2 bn. The country's GDP reached $ 30.94 bn. The 2010 *GDP growth* was estimated at *8%*, and per capita GDP was about $ 365, in PPP terms about $ 1,014. The general government gross debt was estimated as

35.3% of GDP. The foreign debt sum reached c. $ 4.28 bn, up $ 620 m from 2009.

The economy as measured in GDP showed *donor-driven growth*, mainly due to infrastructure projects, food aid, health-care investment, and land lease fees. There was limited endogenous productive growth in agriculture and industry. Agriculture constituted 43.5% of GDP, industrial production 13.4%, and services 43.1%. Agricultural production benefited from favourable weather conditions. Exports rose by $ 100 m to $ 1.729 bn, and consisted largely of coffee, gold, flowers, qat, leather products, live animals, and oilseeds (e.g., sesame). About 15% of all imported goods came from China as the country's largest partner, followed by Saudi Arabia with 8.5% (petroleum). China was also the largest export destination (11%), followed by Germany (9.75%).

Despite growth and dynamics in several sectors, as a whole the *economy was still on life support.* In 2010, it received an estimated *$ 3 bn in foreign aid*, bringing the total received by the government since 1991 to some $ 26 bn. The largest donors were the US, the EU, the UK and several other European countries, with China coming up rapidly as well. Among the Western donors, the most loyal and uncritical fan of the Ethiopian government was the UK's Department for International Development, which was impervious to calls for critical distance and did not have an agenda of furthering accountability and democratisation in the country.

In the context of long-term development programmes, the government followed the 'Plan for Accelerated and Sustainable Development to End Poverty' (PASDEP II), covering the period 2005–2010. Half of its target aim to increase major food crop production via smallholder stimulation and expanding commercial farming was reached. In 2010, 19 m tons of major crops were produced, below the aim of 38 m tons, as a result partly of lack of rain, and partly of policy failures.

Donor country institutions claimed that Ethiopia made progress on several of the *MDGs*, which was no doubt true: there was higher

educational enrolment, poverty reduction, child mortality reduction and HIV-AIDS decline. The fixation on the MDGs nonetheless
tended to constrain the outlook on requirements for progress on the
legal system, inclusive growth, equity, rule-of-law and democratisation issues. According to some critical but muted donor community
voices, the large volumes of aid money given to Ethiopia showed
high inefficiency and were not sustainable. The Ethiopian model
of continued reliance and dependence on massive foreign aid was
seen as insufficient for durable growth, also bearing in mind declining support for development aid in the heavily-indebted Western
donor nations.

Another crucial lifeline was the large sum in *remittances* sent by
overseas Ethiopians to their families, mostly via (in)formal chan-
nels. The official figure (National Bank of Ethiopia) was $ 780 m,
but informally transferred sums were likely to be similar, making
the more than 1 m Ethiopians abroad the most valuable foreign-
exchange earners for the country, exceeding export earnings. These
remittances were used largely for survival and for small business
and construction investment.

China remained a crucial partner, mainly for the government. It
greatly appreciated that investments and business ventures were
undertaken without conditions being imposed in the domains of
human rights, transparency or 'good governance'. It also gave occasional grants and projects 'for free'.

While Ethiopia invested heavily – with donor-country money
– in new mega-dams to produce *electricity*, recent figures revealed
that current energy consumption (3.15 bn kWh) was still below actual energy production (3.46 bn kWh). The proven large natural gas
reserves of 25 bn m3 (notably in the Ogaden region) were not taken
into production. The government also signed a deal with a French
company to build a wind generator park in Tigray, able to generate
120 MW electricity from 2012 onwards. The government announced
its aim to eventually produce 10,000 MW annually.

Poverty rates declined slightly, but an estimated 70%–75% of the
population still lived below the $ 2-a-day line. There were no official

figures on unemployment, but youth and urban unemployment were notably claimed to be high (40%–50%). The steady flow of impoverished rural people to the towns, notably Addis Ababa, continued. An estimated 50,000–70,000 children, youths and beggars lived on the streets of the capital. Gender inequality remained a marked feature of (rural) Ethiopian life, with low representation of women in public functions, and many women experienced abduction for forced marriage associated with local customs, and various specific health problems.

As in previous years, the economy was dominated by two *big conglomerates*: the EPRDF-linked Endowment Fund for the Rehabilitation of Tigray (EFFORT), a group of at least a dozen large companies controlling construction, infrastructure-outlay, publishing and export trade (and led by EPRDF party stalwart Abadi Zemu), and MIDROC, led by the Ethio-Saudi tycoon Mohamed al-Amoudi, who again moved closer to the government and became more active as investor in large land investment schemes. Al-Amoudi adopted a more aggressive stance toward any civil society organisation or expert or press articles that criticised his plans for massive agro-farms in vulnerable areas. Together, the two big conglomerates undoubtedly controlled the major part of the official national economy and were seen to strongly restrict the access of newcomers by various formal and informal means. Also remarkable was the increased public role of Azeb Mesfin Gola, the wife of the prime minister, who alongside her role as MP ran a number of companies (including Mega Publishing).

Two highly visible and controversial socioeconomic developments were *construction of mega-dams*, with work on the third Ghibe (Omo River) dam started and work on a new Blue Nile dam in preparation, and the *giving out of even larger tracts of land* by the government to mostly foreign investors. The main regions affected were Oromia, Gambella, Afar, Amhara and the Southern Region. This was easily done because all land was state property, and farmers and pastoralists were just users, never owners. Foreign governments, presidents and companies, and even groups of farmers (e.g. from Punjab, India), were allowed to start ventures on Ethiopian state land. Whatever the motives and justifications given by the government for what some called this 'sell-out policy', the venture was to the immediate disadvantage of smallholders, who were removed with little or no compensation and had to choose between leaving or becoming (underpaid) day labourers on the new mega-farms (for up to $ 1 a day). Legislation supportive of local inhabitants and (former) cultivators was not in place. The government stood to profit from substantial lease fees, which would amount to hundreds of millions of dollars in a couple of years. Concerned experts were of the opinion that the *long-term ecological and food security effects* of these schemes were uncertain at best. In addition, the beneficial effects for Ethiopian farmers and entrepreneurs were not yet evident, as most if not all produce could be 'repatriated' to the investor countries, and little technology and management knowledge transfer was visible. Additional effects – regarded as negligible by the government – were the displacement of people, the impending demise of local societies and agronomical systems, and the damage to existing flora and fauna and the ecological balance. Despite global concerns with biodiversity loss, ecological sustainability and respect for the rights of local people, these issues were usually declared unimportant and marginal in the face of 'development'. There were reports of people being forcibly removed from their land and protesters being arrested and some killed. As such local protests were quickly suppressed, only Ethiopian diaspora activists and various experts could mount public criticism. Donor countries, gullible and fixated only on 'development' in terms of GDP growth and 'poverty reduction', did not say much and went on spending funds to support doubtful schemes initiated without much debate or negotiation on alternatives.

The economy also suffered from the *global economic crisis*, but not severely. In November, the IMF again bailed out the cash-strapped government by providing the second instalment ($ 62.67 m) under the Exogenous Shocks Facility, bringing disbursements to the total sum available under the arrangement (\$ 240 m supplied over 14 months).

A major *devaluation of the currencybirr* by 16.7% vis-à-vis the dollar occurred on 1 September, and consumer price rises (food items, fuel, transport, construction materials, other import commodities) soon followed. Predictably, the measure was welcomed by the IMF. At the end of the year the *birr* stood at 16.4 to the dollar and 21.7 to the euro. It was problematic that export growth, despite stimulus measures, did not catch up sufficiently with the rise in imports, resulting in a balance of trade deficit larger than in 2009. Food and non-food *inflation* went down significantly from 2009 (8%–10%) to an estimated 7%, but rose again towards the end of the year. As interest rates were low (several percentage points below inflation), there was little national saving.

In the Wall Street Journal's 2010 *Index of Economic Freedom Score*, Ethiopia was ranked 144th, six places down from 2009, and 30th of 46 sub-Saharan African countries. Lack of investment freedom, labour freedom, property rights enforcement and monetary freedom, and serious corruption were outlined as key problems.

Independent *labour unions* did not exist. The only existing union, the Confederation of Ethiopian Trade Unions (CETU), remained in the hands of regime loyalists. This explained why the CETU was hardly present in public debates and did not put forward or achieve any major workers' demands.

Regarding the *education sector*, both primary and secondary education facilities were extended, as was evident in higher numbers of enrolment. Overall government spending on education increased. Higher education also saw quantitative expansion. On 13 April, the government announced the construction of ten new universities, in addition to 13 already built during the last decade. Reasons for this investment primarily in quantity instead of quality (most new universities were seriously undersupplied with qualified staff and facilities, and more than 50% of graduates were unemployed) remained unclear, but it may have had to do with politics, with every (ethnic) region or district wanting its own university. Academic culture was, however, under high pressure resulting from lack of openness, self-censorship, heavy teaching loads and little room for research. In April, independent Ethiopian academics set up the first Ethiopian Academy of Sciences, as yet without government funding.

The problem of the *'brain drain'* was again evident: World Bank figures for 2010 suggested that the migration rate of the tertiary-educated population was 10.1%, that 29.7% of physicians born in the country and 16.8% of nurses left Ethiopia. This was a general problem and put the perennial programmes for 'capacity building' into perspective: an unfavourable working atmosphere, lack of free-doms, and low pay made people leave and thus perpetuated the need for continuous capacity training.

In *telecommunications*, a steady growth of cell phone use was seen, now with more than 4 m users (1 in every 20 Ethiopians: still much below the African average). The only provider, Ethiopian Telecommunications Corporation (ETC), kept strict control. Public television and radio were also state-controlled, with a few private pro-government stations (e.g., Radio Fana). Community radio stations in the regions were similarly controlled. Only 0.57% of the popula-tion had access to the Internet, a low in Africa, and lines were often over-stretched, slow and unreliable. Many foreign-based Ethiopian diaspora websites were blocked and electronic traffic was said to be routinely monitored by the state via the ETC and with the help of Chinese experts. But on 2 December it was announced that Orange-France Télécom would take over the management of ETC (renamed Ethio-Telecom). Liberalisation of the telecom sector (like the banking sector) was again refused by the government, although it solicited for membership in the WTO. Overseas Ethiopians took the initiative to launch a news satellite, the ESAT, but it was often successfully jammed by the Information Network Security Agency, allegedly with material and technical assistance from the Chinese government.

Environmental problems saw no solutions and no large-scale re-medial policies. Irrigation, terracing and bunding were stimulated in the intensively cultivated highlands, but deforestation and erosion continued. In some pastoralist areas overgrazing occurred, leading to competition and conflicts between cultivators and herders in some areas (e.g., Afar vs. Somali, Boran vs. Somali). The new policy of large land leases to foreign companies and investors led to a growing rush on land, without proper planning for local people or environmental consequences. The long-term disadvantages of large-scale flower farms for the local water systems and ecology of the Addis Ababa-Nazret and Addis Ababa-Shashemenne corridors became increasingly clear. Nature reserves and wetlands important for wider regional ecological systems were under threat from new 'investments'. Several legal requirements related to land use and exploitation by investors, often somewhat different in regional states, were promulgated but were not strictly implemented and were subject to informal negotiation.

Ethiopia continued to host large numbers of *refugees* from Somalia (about 65,000) and Eritrea (about 45,000), with both numbers growing every month, as well as a steadily shrinking number of Sudanese refugees (about 25,000), many of whom returned to (Southern) Sudan. Ethiopia also had about 200,000 *IDPs*, including refugees from internal conflicts in the Ogaden, non-resettled displaced people from the Ethio-Eritrean border war of 1998–2000, and victims of various local ethnic group conflicts (e.g., in Gambella). People displaced as a result of large land acquisitions by foreigners may add thousands to the pool of IDPs in the near future. Many people also escaped Ethiopia for various political reasons, like the thousands who went to Kenya, or, even more, for socio-economic reasons, like the thousands more who tried to get to Yemen via ports in Somaliland and Puntland.

Ethiopia in 2011

Ethiopia saw an intriguing combination of economic growth (although uneven and full of uncertainties), progress on MDGs, and a harsh and repressive political climate. De facto power in all political, economic and social domains was in the hands of the sole party in government and in parliament, the Ethiopian Peoples' Revolutionary Democratic Front, now in its twentieth year in power, and still led by Prime Minister Meles Zenawi. Independent private media, NGO activities, open political debate, academic freedom, respect for human rights and economic freedoms were under pressure. Many opposition politicians and independent journalists were put behind bars on charges that were difficult to take seriously. Nevertheless, Ethiopia's prominence, regionally in the Horn of Africa and on the wider world scene, increased. It was courted by traditional donors (the EU and USA), as well as by new emerging powers, such as India and especially China, both major investors in the country. Ethiopia's leaders, notably the prime minister, were present at major world forums. Incidents of religious and ethnic violence occurred, reflecting deep divisions in the population, and several low-key armed rebellions also continued in peripheral areas. No consultative political processes with opposition forces of any kind were in evidence.

Economic dynamism and growth were substantial, leading to continued high GDP growth, advances in health and education coverage, and substantial infrastructure investment, sustained by international aid flows. Domestic and international controversy over large-scale commercial land acquisitions by foreigners and mega-dam construction grew in intensity, as their social and environmental costs were denied by the government and debates about these schemes were criminalised. Ethiopia suffered from a huge budget deficit, excessive government spending and high inflation, and there was little critical scrutiny of its non-economic record. A serious drought in the south and east caused pockets of famine and malnutrition, which led to several thousand deaths and was combated with the help of humanitarian aid from Western donors and UN agencies.

Domestic Politics

Ethiopia remained a *highly constrained political environment*, marked by entrenched authoritarianism and one-party rule dominating all sectors of society, from political processes to economic life and civic and social structures. The country scored low on all available indexes of governance and freedoms. Its redeeming features in the eyes of Western donors and Asian investors, however, were its economic growth, openness to foreign investment and general improvement on MDG criteria. Ethiopia was notable both for its relatively high GDP growth rate, public spending in education, infrastructure outlay and healthcare, and its investments, notably in extractive industries and land commercialisation. The growing economic confidence of the regime was not, however, reflected in political or social confidence; the lack of political and socioeconomic freedoms, the stifling public space and the serious lack of trust in the solidity, legitimacy and performance of governmental institutions remained a hindrance to inclusive development and sustained the high level of distrust and dissatisfaction felt towards the government by the general population.

The *ruling party*, the *Ethiopian Peoples' Revolutionary Democratic Front (EPRDF)*, led by Prime Minister Meles Zenawi, who entered his twenty-first year in power, governed with the support of 546 of the 547 MPs in the House of People's Representatives and thus faced *no parliamentary opposition*. The ruling party's virtual monopoly meant there could be no serious public debates, and virtually all the executive's proposals were unanimously approved.

Extremely *restrictive laws* regarding NGO activities, civic political activity, media freedom and public order had their effect and, combined with the intimidating behaviour of police and special forces, bred distrust, fear and self-censorship among citizens. They affected the media, business life, civil society activities and even university research and teaching programmes. Political parties were recognised in law, but existed only outside the parliament (apart from a single non-EPRDF member, from the Medrek party) and were under constant pressure. They were thus marginalised and had no impact on policy formulation.

The *independent press* – or what was left of it – was the only place where some shades of debates on national policy were reflected and some cautious criticisms appeared, but in the course of the year several of these publications were harassed and closed, among them the weeklies 'Addis Neger' and 'Awramba Times'. A shrinking number of non-governmental journals remained, including 'The Reporter' and 'Fitih', and some economic weeklies. Journalists were hindered and threatened and a number of them again left the country, alleging intimidation and threats to their safety.

The ruling party seemed to fear all criticism, divergent opinion and policy debate, and increased its grip on the country by implementing close surveillance and widespread party recruitment drives. A continued process of *fusion of state administration* with the EPRDF and its cadres thus occurred at the national, regional and local levels and it became difficult to see any distinction between the state and the party. The combined police, army and security services backed up this authority structure with surveillance and selective coercion. A process of 'democratisation' (already nominally on-going for more than 20 years and with no end in sight) was evident only in government rhetoric and hardly at all in reality. The government saw its record on economic growth indicators as sufficient ground for its legitimacy, and regarded itself as indispensable and irreplaceable. This was the reason for a redefinition of national policy aims whereby the 'developmental state' model advocated by the ruling party and Zenawi marginalised any political democracy, freedoms and human rights discourse.

The EPRDF also wielded power by keeping office holders on their toes with demotions, sudden dismissals and 'evaluation sessions' (called *gimgema*). For example: in February, Tamiru Ambelo, chairman of the local administration in Gambella Region, was fired for protesting against foreign land acquisition schemes in his area; on 12 November it was announced that the minister and state minister of trade had been dismissed; on 13 November the Addis Ababa land administration deputy-manager was sacked. Deviation from the party line was the usual cause of such dismissals and demotions, which were daily political practice throughout the country, as were regular EPRDF training sessions for public servants, teachers, etc., to keep them ideologically in line with the party's developmental model. In June, seven army generals, 240 colonels and nearly 500 commissioned officers were removed. In January, the long-serving former foreign minister Seyoum Mesfin took up a new post as ambassador to China. On 28 May, the *EPRDF marked its twentieth year in power*, with public celebrations.

Domestic peace was still not achieved, with on-going armed rebel movements defying the government. Examples were the tenacious Ogaden National Liberation Front (ONLF) in the Somali-inhabited Ogaden area, and actions in parts of the Oromo areas, where remnant Oromo Liberation Front units were active, and in Gambela, where the Anywa people were hard hit by displacement due to externally-driven land lease schemes and the expansion of neighbouring groups, and suffered on-going precarious living conditions, and there were rumours that some Anywa youngsters had taken up arms. Army units also clashed with Afar rebels in November, near the village of Derrab and local conflicts about territorial borders continued to occur between certain ethnic-based communities. For example, on 2 January, five people were killed and 11 injured in clashes between Guji Oromo and Sidama people in the southern Wondo Genet district, and in December the Borana and Gabbra peoples in the Ethio-Kenyan border area fought several battles over pasture and water resources, resulting in 15 people killed and more than 6,000 displaced.

The government kept the lid on the escalating *religious tensions*, which nevertheless led in some places to clashes and attacks, notably between Christians and Muslims, and between Pentecostal-Evangelical groups and traditional believers, as well as internally between denominations within the Christian and Muslim communities. On 29 November, hundreds of Muslim students, aided by Muslim police officers, burned down an Orthodox church in the village of Qoto Baloso, in the predominantly Muslim Silte zone, after a controversial court ruling that it had been built without legal authorisation. In the Muslim town of Besheno (in Alaba district) in January, Evangelical Christians were harassed after Muslims posted notices on the doors of Christian homes saying they should convert, leave the city or face death. In March, there were reports that radical Muslims had killed one Christian and burned down eight churches, a Bible school and 17 Christian homes in the town of Asendabo after a false rumour that Christians had "desecrated the Qur'an". In the same month, Muslims in the Goda district of Jimma were reported to have burned down ten Christian homes, leaving 80 Christians homeless. In several places in the south, Evangelical or Pentecostal Christians were reported to have destroyed places of worship belonging to traditional religions.

On the national level, some disquiet emerged within Ethiopia's Muslim community in response to attempts by the government, in an apparent effort to discourage 'Wahhabist extremism', to impose a particular form of Islam (i.e., that of the 'al-Ahbash' movement, seen as non-political and non-Wahhabist). On 8 October, Minister of Federal Affairs Shiferaw Teklemariam issued credible warnings about illegal underground activities of 'Wahhabists', but Ethiopian Muslims were, on principle, loath to accept any government imposition in matters of faith.

Some internal political *controversy* emerged on the nature and scope of the *massive land acquisitions* by foreign and domestic investors, as many of these commercial schemes appeared to damage the interests of local communities, causing alarm among local farmers and the public at large. In February, it became known that even Ethiopia's (ceremonial) President Girma Wolde-Giorgis had expressed sympathy for some of these concerns, agreeing with a delegation of the Majangir people who pleaded for a halt to the lease of an extensive part of their area to an Indian company. However, even support for this call from the state's Environmental Protection Agency (EPA) produced no result. In November, the newly-installed sultan of the Afar people, Hanfareh Ali Mirah, son of Sultan Ali Mirah, who died on 25 April, indirectly referred to the potentially harmful effects of foreign land leases and major industrial developments in Afar territory, which would consume huge amounts of water to the detriment of local people. The government held no consultations with local stakeholders and gained substantial revenue from land lease fees, declaring that the benefits in terms of food security, knowledge transfer and agrarian development would become obvious. It acted against the local protesters who opposed these deals and arrested hundreds of people. In addition, the government pursued its *resettlement schemes*, moving people from allegedly overpopulated, drought-stricken areas to new sites, which regularly led to clashes with local people, many of whom were injured and killed by the police and security forces. State *villagisation* programmes, notably in Gambela Region, also met with resistance. In August, the BBC screened an impactful, critical documentary on the political use the government was allegedly making of foreign aid packages, penalising citizens perceived as critical of government policies. As usual, the British government and its aid agencies, like other Western donors, did not want to know and were dismissive of these findings.

Domestic repression of free debate and media continued, including the arrest of, among many others, journalists Reeyot Alemu and Woubshet Taye (of the 'Awramba Times') in early June, Sileshi Hagos in early September, and Eskinder Nega, a popular blogger, on 11 September. There were many other examples. In March, more than 200 members of the Medrek opposition party were arrested in the Oromiya region. On 29 August, Legesse Deti Dhaba, former secretary-general of (Oromo) Mecha-Tulama Self-Help Association, was put in prison. On 8 September, the popular actor Debebe Eshetu was detained for alleged contacts with an exiled opposition party, and members of opposition parties, such as Unity for Democracy and Justice executive members Andualem Arage, Natnael Mekonen and Asaminew Berhanu, and the All-Ethiopia Democratic Party's secretary-general Zemenu Mola were also arrested. No credible charges were produced against them, but the 2009 'Anti-Terrorism' law allowed virtually any critic of government policy to be charged and tried by state prosecutors. On 11 November, 24 people, among them six journalists, were charged with'terrorism'. Some of the accused stated before the court that they had been abused and tortured in custody.

There were *no public protests* in Ethiopia, apart from occasional university student demonstrations. On 25–28 November, students at Gondar University protested over badly spoilt food that had caused health problems for many students. This turned into a wider demonstration for academic rights and freedom in general. It was suppressed by federal police, with one student killed and others arrested. In January, some 340 Addis Ababa University Oromo students were arrested and abused for protesting against the Oromia regional government's decision to move its capital from Addis Ababa to Adama (Nazreth).

The government tried to prevent news about the 'Arab Spring' from reaching mass audiences in Ethiopia and none of the state media reported on it in any detail. Occasional acts of protest occurred, but did not spark mass movements. On 11 November, Yenesew Gebre, a 29-year-old school teacher from the southern town of Waka, set himself on fire, apparently in protest against Ethiopia's repressive politics. Proper medical care was not given and he died of his injuries. This was not reported by any media except opposition diaspora websites (difficult to access in Ethiopia).

Local human rights organisations could no longer operate, their accounts being frozen and their field investigators harassed. Only a government-instituted human rights council was tolerated but it produced no reports during the year. The annual reports of HRW, AI, the Committee for the Protection of Journalists, Reporters without Borders, etc., were highly critical of the regime's overall record, registering no improvement over previous years. The 2011 US State Department's annual human rights report also referred to a depressing catalogue of serious human rights problems.

Foreign Affairs

Foreign policy was the sole prerogative of the top echelons of the EPRDF, which rejected all other opinions or debates questioning the party's approach. Opposition parties, civic groups and the media had no impact on policy, and even ran the risk of being prosecuted for expressing their criticism.

In the *Horn of Africa region*, Ethiopia maintained cooperative relations with Kenya, Djibouti, Somaliland and Puntland, including in the fields of security, regional policy and economic relations, but these relations were characterised by an underlying fragility and volatility. Sudan was important as a growing oil supplier. There was some tension with *Egypt* over the implications of the Blue Nile dam, constructed by Ethiopia without any prior consultation with Egypt. In a surprising comment to parliament, Meles said on 4 April that Ethiopia should build a defence capacity to repel any "Egyptian threat". During the 35th session of UNESCO's World Heritage Committee in June in Paris, a call was made on Ethiopia to "immediately halt all construction" of a second mega-dam, Gibe-3, due to its potential damage to world heritage sites and to Lake Turkana.

Ethiopia continued to support *Somalia*'s transitional federal government (TFG) in Mogadishu against the radical insurgency of the Islamist al-Shabaab movement and cooperated with some local Somali militias allied with the TFG. In December, Ethiopia carried out military operations near its border with northern Somalia to back efforts by the TFG and the AU Mission in Somalia (AMISOM) to combat al-Shabaab, which was on the retreat after the Kenyan military invasion in October. Ethiopia continued to play an important role in *IGAD*, the *AU*, and various international donor forums.

In July, Ethiopia deployed troops to the contested *Abyei* area in *Sudan*, as major part of the UN Interim Security Force for Abyei.

Relations with *Eritrea* remained as tense as ever. There were no signs of a solution to the border dispute, and the government kept a large military force in place near the border. Economic links were also absent. Government rhetoric against the Eritrean leadership and plans for its removal continued. In his performance report to parliament in April, Meles announced a more assertive policy towards Eritrea, abandoning the so-called "passive defensive attitude". In addition to diplomatic pressure, support for Eritrean opposition groups in exile was also stepped up. In April, the completion was announced of the installation of power transmission lines to Sudan and Djibouti, intended for the future export of energy from the mega-dam hydropower stations.

Internationally, relations with *China* and *India* (the largest foreign investors in Ethiopia) as well as other Asian countries grew in intensity, driven by the economic logic of easier loans, investments and the absence of any political conditions. The government also strengthened its relations with emerging countries such as Turkey and Malaysia. On 23 August, Turkish Foreign Minister Ahmet Davutoglu visited Addis Ababa for economic cooperation talks and a visit to the AU.

Ethiopia also continued to enjoy the economic support of the *traditional donor countries* – mainly the EU and the USA – who had no qualms about the political stagnation and repression in the country and did not insist on respect for constitutional rights and accepted political and media freedoms. Ethiopia continued to be perceived as a *security partner* of Western and Middle Eastern countries in the wider Horn of Africa against Islamist terrorism in Somalia and the spread of al-Qaida-like groups from Yemen and other areas. This largely 'immunised' it from serious criticism of its domestic political record.

During the year, a large number of confidential US embassy cables (from the Addis Ababa embassy and covering the years 2006–2010) was released by *Wikileaks* and revealed *strongly critical views* on the Ethiopian government, often in stark contrast to official US State Department policy.

In July, *two Swedish journalists* were *arrested* in the Ogaden area and charged with "illegal entry" (via Somaliland) and "*support to a terrorist organization*" – the rebel ONLF on which they were making a news report. They were charged and faced the prospect of long prison sentences. International journalist associations, the Swedish and other foreign governments and the Ethiopian opposition called for their release. In an unprecedented trial in December, they were sentenced to 11 years in prison, although negotiations on their release started soon afterwards.

Ethiopia was *visited* by a number of *world leaders*. On 13–14 June, US Secretary of State Hillary Clinton attended for talks with the government and at the AU. Egypt's new Prime Minister Essam Sharaf visited in May, former US President George Bush, whose humanitarian charity ran a health programme in the country, in December, and UN Secretary-General Ban Ki-moon on 25–27 May to attend the AU summit and visit some health extension projects in northern Ethiopia. In January, French President Nicolas Sarkozy visited at the head of a business delegation for talks with the government and to attend an AU summit. Even Bill Gates, as philanthropist and head of his Gates Foundation, visited the country on 27–28 March for talks with the government on health policy and agriculture. Various high-level politicians from the UK (Ethiopia's major European donor) also visited, including: in July, Minister for Africa Henry Bellingham; in August, *Mark Lowcock*, Permanent Secretary of DFID (this institution was a major Ethiopia cheerleader); and in June, Simon Fraser, a permanent under-secretary at the Foreign and Commonwealth Office.

Prime Minister Meles made several *foreign diplomatic trips.* On 27 January, he was at the World Economic Forum in Davos, Switzerland; on 30 June, he attended the 17th AU summit in Malabo, Equatorial Guinea, giving a keynote speech on 'youth empowerment'. He also chaired meetings of the Committee of Heads of State and Government on Climate Change, held at the Malabo summit, and, on 16 November, at the AU in Addis Ababa. In May, he attended the G-8 summit in Deauville, France. In September, he went to the US, where he was invited by Columbia University to give a speech on his "developmental state model", and was there met with vociferous objections from the large Ethiopian diaspora audience present. On 10–11 October, he attended the large international 'Energy for All' conference in Oslo, Norway. He also paid a visit to Cairo for talks with the Egyptian government in September, where an agreement for a 'trilateral committee' (Egypt, Sudan and Ethiopia) to manage the Nile issue was signed.

Relations with *Egypt* thus seemed to be improving slightly after an earlier row over the planned building of the Blue Nile Dam, when Ethiopia's minister for water resources had in April even ruled out granting permission for an Egyptian representative to visit the site of the dam. On 12 November, a 25–member Egyptian delegation arrived in Addis Ababa on a working visit to discuss economic cooperation and the dam issue, which remained a delicate subject.

Cross-border migration of people and goods across Ethiopia's rather porous frontiers continued, and there were also substantial flows of *contraband goods* into the country, both with and without bribes, from Djibouti, Somaliland, Puntland and Kenya.

Socioeconomic Developments

The year was marked by another very serious *drought* and food shortages in southern and eastern Ethiopia – extending to south-central

Somalia, and particularly evident in the Oromo, Afar and Somali-inhabited areas. While Ethiopia needed regular additional food aid for some 3–4 m people, as in previous years, this year's drought presented an added emergency, although not an acute famine endangering the lives of millions, as some media and NGO reports claimed. The severe drought, said to be "the worst in 60 years", demanded extra relief food assistance for some 4.5 m people (or $ 398 m). Several thousands died but a major famine disaster was averted via domestic and especially international resources (from the USA, WFP and UNHCR).

Ethiopia made some progress in *increasing food production* through incentives, new land exploitation and more use of fertilisers. The absolute number of those in need remained more or less constant, despite the 3% annual population growth rate. The economy overall maintained a *high rate of growth*, although skewed toward donor-funded infrastructure outlay and growth in services, rather than in productive capacity.

Ethiopia's *population* increased this year by almost 2 m people, reaching an estimated 85 m. Population density thus increased, impacting strongly on resource use and complicating livelihoods, access to land, food security and ecological sustainability. In *urban areas*, notably the capital, Addis Ababa, urban 'renewal' went ahead full-speed, with the destruction and replacement of old, popular neighbourhoods in the city centre and the transfer of the population to the outskirts of town, into new three- and four-storey 'condominium housing' complexes. The plan was to turn Addis Ababa's city centre into a massive business district without "slum neighbourhoods". Many complaints were heard among displaced persons about the new, substandard facilities, the delays in delivery, the disruption of solid social networks, and the loss of employment and income. On 28 November, a controversial new 'Urban Lands Lease Holding Proclamation' was gazetted, which in effect nationalised urban land and eliminated all remaining forms of transferable and inheritable urban private property: such property would have to be held on lease so that everything could eventually be redistributed and expropriated at will by the authorities.

The *environmental impact* of large-scale land acquisitions and investments – many of them monocultures of sugar cane, rice, maize or bio-fuels over vast areas, destined for export – was not seen as an issue of concern in government policy.

The economy of *pastoral societies* on the southern and eastern fringes of the Ethiopian highlands was again under pressure from government sedentarisation and land alienation policies that privileged cultivators over herders, accompanied by a civilisational discourse labelling pastoral people as "primitive" and "backward" (e.g., in a speech by Meles on 25 January). There were no successful compensation schemes for displaced or dispossessed pastoralists – who were without territory rights as they formally lived on state land and whose customary rights were rarely recognised – making these people increasingly vulnerable and marginalised.

More land was cultivated for agrarian production by both smallholders and new investors, and the government seemed to step up the incentivisation of the country's farmers. However, parts of existing national parks were also handed over to domestic and foreign agrarian investors. The enforcement of existing environmental laws was lax, and the EPA was notable for its lack of impact and activity; it usually supported all government measures. The EPA did not pursue its role of demanding environmental impact assessments and implementation clauses from new agrarian investors. Neither national policies on ecological sustainability nor meaningful respect for the customary use rights of locals – notably pastoralists – were in evidence, as the gospel of quantifiable economic growth was put above all.

Some *mining* companies, both foreign and domestic, started up new mining exploration ventures (prospecting for potash, gold, tantalum, nickel) in eastern and southern Ethiopia.

The economy showed a *GDP growth* of 7.5% to a total volume of $ 95 bn. The *per capita GDP* rose to $ 380. Government spending made up some 20% of GDP. Domestic tax revenue grew by almost 20%, most of it from dues on imported goods. *Export* proceeds increased by an estimated 30% to about $ 2.5 bn, and growth was chiefly in newer sectors such as gold mining, flowers, horticulture, hides, skins and leather products, and *ch'at* (the stimulant Catha edulis), while income from the country's traditional export product, coffee, stagnated. The main export destinations were China and Germany. Imports came primarily from China, the US and Saudi Arabia.

Manufacturing growth occurred (in textiles and leather), but was limited and below potential, as overall investments went mostly into infrastructure (particularly dams and road building) and services. Job growth occurred notably in the service sector, which yielded 43% of GDP. Agriculture contributed 44% to the national GDP and grew in absolute terms but hardly in relative size. Some 80% of Ethiopia's working population were engaged in agriculture, and 6% in industry. The *private business sector* remained weak, with state and party-affiliated businesses (notably the ruling party-linked EFFORT business empire) taking the lion's share of economic activity and protecting their access and interests. The major private player (although closely linked to the government) was multi-billionaire Saudi-Ethiopian tycoon al-Amoudi, who made many new investments in commercial agriculture. *Unemployment* remained very high, although exact figures were not available and calculations differed. Estimates varied from 24% to 50%. Youth unemployment remained alarming, with estimates as high as 60%–70%. The higher education institutions kept on expanding and producing graduates, but they found no jobs.

Economic growth did little to alleviate the employment and poverty problems. With regard to ICT, the *mobile phone market* expanded in tandem with population growth, but lagged behind growth rates and coverage in most other African countries. The *sole Internet provider* remained the Ethiopian Telecommunications Corporation, which, despite technical innovations and extension of services and coverage, did not allow full demand-driven expansion and information

freedom. The state also maintained its *ban on foreign banks* entering the domestic market, but this was a move widely supported by
the population. Ethiopia continued its membership negotiations
with the WTO. The country maintained its huge *trade balance deficit*, with imports exceeding exports by $ 5 bn, or 250%. *Remittances*
from Ethiopians abroad to relatives and friends in the country were
only partly registered, but reached an estimated $ 1.5 bn.

Another worrying sign amidst the news of economic growth was
the jump in *foreign debt*: although Ethiopia had significantly reduced
its debt in 2008 under the HIPC initiative, when it fell to $ 2.7 bn, it
reached $ 12 bn (or ETB (birr) 200 bn) in December. Most of this
was due to huge loans and investments in infrastructural schemes,
including the Renaissance Dam, Gibe-3 Dam, new railway plans and
agrarian state plantation outlays. Some 47% of the foreign debt was
now owed to China (which in 2011 lent the state-owned Commercial
Bank of Ethiopia $ 300 m in one go); other substantial lenders were
India and the Kuwait Fund. Although figures differed with regard
to their source and calculation method, the public debt reached
an amount between 29% and 42% of GDP; foreign debt was half of
this sum. Total international aid to the country (including loans and
grants) amounted to about $ 3 bn, the largest in Africa. According
to UNCTAD's Investment Report, however, *foreign direct investment*
had declined compared with the previous year to $ 184 m.

The national *budget* for the budget year July 2011–June 2012 was
ETB 117.8 (or $ 6.8 bn), a 39% rise compared with 2010. Some 59%
of government spending was on capital expenditure, i.e., on infrastructure, energy supply, state housing complexes, state companies,
education, health facilities, etc. About 39% was allocated to the regional governments.

The economy was marked by *very high inflation*, which hit the
middle classes and the poor very hard: the annual rate computed in
December was 35%, with food inflation reaching 46%, the highest
in Africa. Non-food inflation was 21% on an annual basis. This high
rate – also reflected in the higher state budget – was explained by the

government's expansionist monetary policy, and, as the government emphasised in order to shift the blame, by external, world market factors. The IMF and World Bank contended that, at the most, only 15% of the 35% rate could be explained by such external factors. In January, the government tried to combat inflation with enforced price controls and threats to the nation's traders, but this was a total failure, as the policy did not address the root causes of the problem.

The *very ambitious investment programmes* under the 2010 Growth and Transformation Plan caused the World Bank head in Ethiopia in July to issue warnings that these plans were unrealistic, unsustainable, and far beyond Ethiopia's means. A row between the government and the World Bank followed. The underlying assumption of the regime appeared to be that the global donor community would again in due course have to cough up the costs or issue debt forgiveness, as a 'reward' for its economic growth policy. For the 5,250–MW Renaissance Dam, under construction since early 2011 in a gorge 40 km from the Sudanese border, the government raised ETB 7 bn ($ 408 m) domestically via government bonds, with the general public constantly urged to buy them. Civil servants were forced to acquire them 'voluntarily' by handing in one month's salary.

According to the World Bank's Global Business Report, the *business climate deteriorated* somewhat, despite all the news about growth figures. Ethiopia dropped seven places on the 'Doing Business' index, mainly due to additional restrictive regulations, bureaucratic complexity, lack of trust, judicial insecurity and corruption. *Corruption*, however, was still significantly lower than the African average. On TI's global 'Corruption Perception Index', Ethiopia was ranked 116th out of a total of 178 countries, but its ranking did not fall either, despite judicial action against dozens of officials. Notably problematic were the top levels of government, regional governments and parastatal entities. Anti-corruption drives were selective and often seemed politically motivated. The growing restrictions on doing business also showed the naivety of foreign investors and company owners, who did not count on the ultimately

politically conditioned business environment, where state directives could suddenly change the rules of the game and force those
who had already invested a lot to just go away and take the losses.

An estimated 29% of the population remained below the *poverty
line*, which was nevertheless a reduction of 5%, and on this score,
as on health, child mortality and education enrolment indicators,
Ethiopia performed comparatively well on the UN MDGs. Life ex-
pectancy and the general educational level (and literacy) rose. On
other world indexes measuring wider human development, such
as the Multidimensional Poverty Index or the Legatum Prosperity
Index, Ethiopia did not do well.

In 2011, Ethiopia hosted more than 290,000 *refugees* from
neighbouring Eritrea, Sudan and Somalia. Up to 55,000 *Eritreans*,
mainly young males, continued to flee to Ethiopia to escape national (army) service, unemployment and repression in Eritrea.
The drought and famine in south-central Somalia caused an estimated 130,000 *Somalis* to enter UNHCR camps in Ethiopia (mainly
Dolo Ado). More than 27,000 *Sudanese* refugees from the Blue Nile
Region entered Ethiopia in September-October after violent clashes
that began on 1 September between the Sudanese army and rebels
from the Sudan People's Liberation Movement North, later followed
by another 19,000. On 8 December, Ethiopia became a member of
the International Organization for Migration, which allowed it to
seek more international assistance and cooperation on migration
and refugee issues.

Out-migration roughly comprised two groups: poorer migrants
in search of work in neighbouring countries and the Middle East
(via Djibouti, Kenya and Bosaasso port in Puntland), and the more
educated – often professionals, intellectuals and political dissidents.
Figures for both remained relatively high, running into many thousands. The first group also comprised the many hundreds of children
given for adoption and the victims of child and woman trafficking.
The latter out-migration, of educated people, put Ethiopia among
the global top-20 of countries affected by 'brain drain'. A special

group of migrants were the about 3,000 'Falash Mura' people, descendants of Ethiopian Jews or Beta Israel, who were able to move to Israel, their preferred destination.

Wood being the chief source of household energy in the countryside, *deforestation* went on unabated in the wake of high population growth. The problems of *pollution* by industry, horticulture (flower industry chemicals) and consumer waste (e.g. huge amounts of batteries and plastic bags scattered in the landscape) was not addressed. Environmental sustainability was a remote ideal. The government announced plans to invest in solar and wind energy with the help of donor country funding. The construction of mega-dams for hydro-energy was also claimed to contribute to solving Ethiopia's long-term energy supply problems, but the possible local environmental and economic damage caused by these mega-schemes (also intended for future 'energy export' to Sudan, Djibouti and Kenya), in contrast to that of existing micro-dams, loomed large.

Ethiopia in 2012

Ethiopia's political system suffered a blow when its dominant prime minister and architect of the authoritarian one-party state, Meles Zenawi (born 1955), died in August from an undisclosed illness, after 21 years in power. His position fell to his deputy, the southerner Hailemariam Desalegn, as confirmed by the central committee of the Ethiopian Peoples' Revolutionary Democratic Front (EPRDF). Hailemariam, one of the most loyal non-Tigrayan followers of Meles and groomed by him for a high position, remained very dependent on the dominant party elite, notably the TPLF party within the EPRDF. No policy changes or overtures were announced toward civil society or other political parties (represented in the 547-member parliament with just one seat) and political repression seemed to continue after Meles' death. Opposition parties and other critics had practically no space in which to act.

Economic policies continued to emphasise infrastructure development with the support of foreign capital, large-scale agrarian investment schemes on land leased to foreigners and party–linked business people, and efforts to increase the export base beyond coffee. There was again noticeable economic growth, but dependence on donor grants and loans remained very strong. Social and class inequality continued to increase. No changes were registered with respect to the problematic land policy, with the state as sole owner. Economic growth figures were, as usual, enough to mute any kind of criticism from 'donor' countries, the World Bank and the IMF, who again demonstrated their utter indifference toward the social, political and human costs of Ethiopia's coerced and biased growth model. Investments by India, China, Turkey and other 'emerging countries' were maintained. Foreign policy was marked by continuity: Ethiopia remained a partner of the USA in security operations in the wider region, was kept in an ongoing stalemate with Eritrea, maintained an armed covert political presence in southern Somalia to contain an expansion of the civil conflict into Ethiopia, and followed a policy of cooperation, intensification of economic relations, and intelligence exchange with its neighbours, Somaliland, Djibouti and Kenya. Relations with South Sudan also expanded. Tensions remained with Egypt about Ethiopia's mega-dam being built on the Blue Nile. Alongside local protests, some misgivings were also expressed in Kenya about expected negative impacts of the large Gibe-3 dam on the Omo River on the environment and on economic activities dependent on Lake Turkana.

Domestic Politics

The *government* and the *ruling party*, the *EPRDF*, further *increased their hold on state and society*, with more local-level party recruitment, restriction of the political process to the party only, and more control of all important business sectors and state institutions. The formal boundary between party and state institutions was not respected. No visible changes occurred in the political and governance system or the media landscape, and state-dirigist economic policies continued as before. Ethiopian society was thus characterised by a continuing *repressive atmosphere* and a political system in the grip of the ruling party. The authorities, in line with what they regarded as necessary for a 'developmental state', used heavy-handed tactics against perceived opponents and non-party members. In the Freedom House ratings, Ethiopia was ranked low on 'political rights' and on 'civil liberties': scoring 6 on a scale of 7 – one of the lowest scores in Africa. A pluralist polity was therefore conspicuously absent, and 'democracy' – while a popular slogan on state television and in policy speeches – stayed in the wings. The political elite, a complex conglomerate of dependent ruling party constituencies of ethno-regional elites in the Regional States, circled around the top ruling party leadership of the EPRDF, built around the core Tigray People's Liberation Front (*TPLF*), the central movement. Some emerging new middle-class groups that owed much of their rise to their appendage to and protection by the dominant EPRDF were important as a support constituency. Membership of the party was also seen as an informal prerequisite for gaining access to jobs, financial benefits, certain educational programmes and favourable court decisions. There was thus a powerful incentive to become a party member in a country where the labour market was non-transparent, the unemployment rate high (notably youth unemployment at an estimated 40%–45%), and access to a secure job often predicated on nepotism or corruption. Accountability and transparency mechanisms were not in place – unless the in-party political evaluation sessions (*gim gema*) on individual performance were seen as such. But these did not take place under legal or parliamentary scrutiny.

The shock event of the year was the unexpected *death of Prime Minister Meles Zenawi* in a Brussels hospital, after an undisclosed illness that had kept him incommunicado since 26 June. Weeks of speculation and mystery ended when his death was finally announced on 21 August, although the actual date of his death and the nature of his fatal illness were not disclosed. A remarkable effort to 'canonise' his record almost immediately commenced, whereby any public expression of scepticism about his achievements and legacy was penalised. All public offices and government institutions were obliged to mourn and there were cases of people being accused for not having shown the required amount of grief. City authorities, notably in Addis Ababa, displayed mass produced portraits and sayings of the late national leader along all major roads. Leading party circles and the government hastened to endorse the full continuity of Ethiopia's policies in all fields and a redoubled effort to "realise Meles Zenawi's vision for Ethiopia". Deputy Prime Minister *Hailemariam Desalegn*, a southerner and member of the Southern Ethiopian Peoples' Democratic Front (SEPDF), one of the four constituent ethnic-based units of the EPRDF, was named as the new prime minister a week after the announcement of Meles' death. On

August 23, he had immediately declared that *Meles' policies would be continued without change*, including his economic policies, and proceeded to imitate the former leader's style and rhetoric in his public appearances and statements. This was confirmed in his speech on 21 September to the House of People's Representatives. All was part of a strenuous effort to maintain unity and ensure continuity of the EPRDF party regime. On 29 November, Hailemariam appointed two additional deputy premiers (in addition to one already in his place), an unconstitutional move allegedly at the instigation of the TPLF leadership to 'balance' power and ethnicity in the EPRDF leadership: each of the four constituent ethnic-based parties within the EPRDF was now represented.

Debates about national policy were little in evidence in the *media*. The independent press was further reduced, with only a handful of weeklies (such as 'The Reporter' and 'The Monitor') perilously surviving amidst government pressure and threats, and at risk of the government challenging or even ruining the reputation of those who tried to question its policies and modes of operation. The few economics weeklies (such as 'Addis Fortune' and 'Capital') rarely wrote about political and social matters.

A number of *court cases against journalists* and *civil society figures* revealed that the judicial system was unable to deliver what would be commonly accepted as proper justice: relevant evidence and credible witnesses did not play a role and all cases were based upon the highly controversial anti-terrorism proclamation of 2009, although it contradicted the 1995 Ethiopian Constitution. For example: Woubshet Taye, former deputy editor of the defunct weekly 'Awramba Times', was given a 14-year prison sentence in January on charges under the anti-terrorism law after publishing a critical assessment of the ruling party's performance over its 20-year rule; Yusuf Getachew, editor of the Muslim weekly 'YeMuslimoch Gudday', was arrested after a raid on his house because he had expressed support for large Muslim demonstrations (and his two chief journalists went into hiding); the journalist Re'eyot Alemu was detained in prison and given an additional penalty in August, when she did not show the 'required' grief on the death of Meles Zenawi; journalist and blogger Eskinder Nega was also kept in prison on a dubious verdict. In July, an entire edition of the weekly 'Fitih' was impounded, and it was closed down later in the year under government pressure, as were 'Ethio-Channel', 'Negadras' and 'YeMuslimoch Gudday'.

Two Swedish journalists, J. Persson and M. Schibbye, who had been arrested and jailed in 2011 for moving around in the Somali (Ogaden) Region without the required papers and for attempting to talk to local people and Ogaden National Liberation Front (ONLF) members about the armed conflict in the Somali Region, *were released* in September, after continued pressure from the EU and Sweden.

Political opposition was given little space and less prominent leaders faced harassment. For instance, in June, two members of the opposition All Ethiopia Unity Party (AUEF) in North Gondar Zone were arrested and disappeared. On June 27, Andualem Arage, vice chairman of the opposition front 'Medrek', and Unity for Democracy and Justice Party official Natnael Mekonnen were declared guilty of 'terrorism and treason' – charges it is difficult to accept. The sentences (life and 18 years, respectively) were seen as absurd and abusive. Human rights organisations, as well as the annual US government report on human rights in Africa, stated that torture was regularly used in Ethiopian prisons. Police and security forces largely operated with impunity. Despite social and political developments within Ethiopia being well-documented by (local) journalists, researchers, travellers, and NGO staff, policy-making bodies within and outside the country showed little inclination to accept evidence-based analyses, let alone fresh thinking in the domains of political organisation, socioeconomic policy or law.

Various *armed resistance movements* remained active but kept a *low profile*: the ONLF in the Somali Region 5, the Oromo Liberation Front in the west and east of the country, and a few smaller groups in the north, e.g. the Ethiopian Peoples Patriotic Front and the

Ethiopian Unity and Freedom Force. There were some reports that they carried out hit-and-run attacks on prisons in the towns of Adigrat and Debre Marqos, and burned down business premises of ruling party adherents in Metemma, on the Sudan border. The government routinely accused them of being 'Eritrean agents'.

Religious tensions were frequent, illustrating the ongoing dynamics of the competition in evidence for a number of decades, between Muslims and Christians, Protestants and Orthodox, and Protestants vs. traditional believers, especially in the south. Within the Muslim community, there were also disputes and clashes over different versions of Islam, and its doctrines and public role. Salafist and Wahhabi-inspired 'reformist' groups regularly attacked Sufi Muslim communities, mosques and sheikhs. The Protestant and Evangelical communities continued to grow, reaching an estimated 20% of the total population. There were no reported lethal clashes between believers of different faiths.

In June, the head of the *Ethiopian Orthodox Church* (EOC), the controversial Patriarch *Abune* P'aulos died unexpectedly after a brief illness. Disunity in the EOC and demands voiced in the large Ethiopian Christian diaspora in the USA, where the previous (deposed) patriarch, *Abune* Merkorios, resided, meant that no successor had been chosen by December.

The continued *stand-off between the government and the Muslim community*, notably in Addis Ababa, was significant. Muslim civil protest was huge and persistent throughout the year. While fears of radicalisation and possible violent action by certain radical Islamists in the country were by no means imaginary, the government aggravated things with its heavy-handedness and policy of repression, and especially by its imposition of what was called 'Ahbashism' on the Muslim Supreme Councils in the country – appointing members of the *al-Ahbash* Muslim organisation, based in Lebanon and with a small number of followers in Ethiopia, as custodians and teachers of the constitutional precepts on religion and state, and of a more moderate Islam. This was to counteract the perceived growth of Wahhabist and Salafist radical versions of Islam. Since late 2011, the government, in an effort to instil what it regarded as a moderate, non-Salafist version of Islam in the state-supported Muslim Supreme Councils in the country, had employed Sufi-leaning al-Ahbash teachers and this continued through the year, generating opposition. Large-scale demonstrations regularly took place after Friday prayers at the premises of the Aweliya School and Mission Centre, a stronghold of orthodox, scriptural Islam (long financed by Saudi Arabia), and later also at the capital's Anwar Mosque. They stayed peaceful, but various Muslim diaspora websites made calls for more radical action and violent jihad. Demonstrations in other cities and in the countryside followed. In April, five Muslims were killed by police during demonstrations in the town of Asassa, in July clashes with police near a mosque in the capital resulted in four dead and many wounded, and in October four people were killed in Gerba, a small town in the north. Members of an action committee formed at the Aweliya Centre in the capital were arrested in October. In December, 29 prominent Muslims (mostly members of the action committee) were charged with 'terrorism' offences and were to stand trial in 2013. Weekly Muslim demonstrations continued throughout the year, and drew support from the Christian, notably Orthodox, community. This also led to a decline in communal clashes between the two faith communities.

Foreign Affairs

Ethiopia became *more assertive* in its *foreign policy* and regarded itself as the undisputed hegemon in the Horn of Africa region, in line with its growing economic role and its investments in trans-frontier infrastructure investments (the Blue Nile and Gibe-3 dams, a new railway to Djibouti, electricity cables to Kenya, plans for an oil pipeline from South Sudan across Ethiopian territory to either Kenya or Somaliland), and its role in IGAD and the AU and at the UN climate and other conferences. Ethiopia supplied troops for the Abyei and Darfur peace-keeping forces in Sudan and elsewhere. In total, it had more than 5,000 troops in various African trouble spots.

Good relations with *Kenya* were maintained, and military action in Somalia against the al-Shabaab movement was gradually coordinated, although Kenya's invasion of Somalia in October 2011 had taken Ethiopia by surprise. *Djibouti* lived mainly on Ethiopian port fee charges and transit trade and remained a stable partner, as did *Somaliland*, with Ethiopia keeping an eye on the port of Berbera for future use. Ethiopia kept troops along the *South Somalia* border buffer zone, and still had troops in Somalia's Beledweyn-Baidoa area in December, assisting the Somali government militarily. It continued to support the Transitional Federal Government in Mogadishu and, after 20 August, the newly installed successor federal government under President Hassan Mohamud.

Relations with *Sudan* were kept business-like, but there was an element of tension due to the large Blue Nile dam, built only some 45 km from the Sudan border. Relations with *South Sudan* expanded, with Ethiopia seeing it as a potential supporter/client state. Many Ethiopian private investors and traders moved to open businesses in Juba. Ethiopia's relations with *Saudi Arabia* were superficially amicable but experienced tensions below the surface. The Saudis were weary of the Renaissance Dam, and there were also regular cases of Ethiopian maids and migrant labourers being abused in Saudi Arabia, as well as apprehensions about the export of radical Islamism.

Relations with *Eritrea* continued in stalemate. There was no movement regarding the border dispute, and both governments kept substantial armed forces near the frontline. Ethiopia admitted making two forays into Eritrean territory in March to hit Ethiopian rebel group hideouts. Eritrean opposition groups in exile received continued support from the government.

Ethiopia kept its international position as an important player in *north-east Africa*. It was a prominent member in the AU, IGAD and other international forums. On 27 January, Meles chaired IGAD's 20th Extraordinary Summit Meeting in Addis Ababa. Just before his death, he participated in the 22nd World Economic Forum on Africa, held on 9–11 May in Addis Ababa under the theme 'Shaping Africa's Transformation'. On May 18, he was one of four African leaders to attend a high-level meeting on global agriculture and food security in Camp David (USA), held on the margin of the *G8 summit*. Shortly afterwards, he left for Brussels (Belgium), where he would enter hospital. The new prime minister, Hailemariam Dessalegn attended the inauguration of Somalia's new premier, Hassan Sheikh Mohamud, on 16 September in Mogadishu, and on 28 September addressed the UN General Assembly in New York. In December he made a state visit to Kenya.

Ethiopia maintained its *economic and development aid links with Western donor countries* (the EU and the USA) and continued its role as a partner in regional security matters (and anti-terrorism campaigns) in the Horn of Africa and wider Red Sea region. Little if any criticism of its domestic political record was expressed by its Western or Asian international partners.

During the year, Ethiopia was *visited by many foreign dignitaries and policy makers*. From 23 to 30 January, many African leaders assembled in Addis Ababa for the 18th AU summit. Also in January, Jia Qinglin, a high-ranking Chinese official, held talks with Zenawi. On 1–3 March, IMF Deputy Managing Director Naoyuki Shinohara visited Ethiopia. On 17 April, South African Minister for International Relations and Cooperation Ms Maite Nkoana-Mashabane attended the 2nd Joint Ministerial Meeting between South Africa and Ethiopia. Also in April, the World Bank's new president-elect, Jim Yong Kim, visited. In July, Egypt's President Mohammed Morsi was in Addis Ababa for an AU summit and for talks on a Nile waters agreement. In July too, International Organisation for Migration Director General William L. Swing and UNHCR High Commissioner António Guterres visited for talks and to visit a refugee camp in western Ethiopia.

Socioeconomic Developments

Economic growth was again registered in agriculture, services and industry, but somewhat below target. While overall production increased in the agrarian sector due to good weather, expansion of areas under cultivation and productivity increases, it was not sufficient to attain food self-sufficiency. The food security situation remained precarious, and while there was no famine, in August about 3.7 m people were estimated to be in need of *food aid* and humanitarian assistance. Some 6–8 m food-insecure people were under the Productive Safety Net Programme. The paradox of GDP economic growth concurrent with conditions of mass food insecurity was not solved, because these two processes ran on separate tracks: development via massive donor funding of infrastructure projects and (land) investments, and failing support and opportunity for the roughly 13 m smallholders, because investments by foreigners, state/party-affiliated persons and rich domestic investors were made in large-scale commercial ventures, not in smallholder activities. This fitted the new government aim of national food security, not individual or household food security on the local or regional levels. The number of landless people thus increased by tens of thousands. Ethiopia was ranked 100th in the list of 105 countries in the Global Food Security Index: a disappointing result after 21 years of ruling party policy aimed at food self-sufficiency and security.

While economic data varied widely, as usual, according to the sources used (even the World Bank and UN agencies gave different figures), Ethiopia registered an estimated real *GDP growth* of about 6%–7%, still one of the fastest growing non-oil economies in Africa. Total GDP was in the range of $ 41 bn. An important contributor to growth was the good harvest: according to the Central Statistical Agency, food output was 21.9 m tonnes, 7.4% more than in 2011, due to better weather conditions and a 2.2% expansion of cultivated land. According to government figures, there was also significant growth in industry (17.9%), and services (11.5%). Employment patterns did not change much: agriculture employed an estimated 80% of the work force, industry 6% and services 14%. Industry saw the gradual expansion of cement, textile and leather production.

Official *unemployment* figures were not provided, but it was estimated that at least 29% of the working-age population of about 39 m did not have a job. Population growth was about 2.7%. Some 29% of the population remained below the official UN poverty line. An underestimated factor adding to GDP was the growing inclusion or 'capture' of the informal economy in the state's registration frameworks, in which the government invested much effort. The government continued strenuously with the implementation of its 'Growth and Transformation Plan' (2010), an almost sacred, non-negotiable economic blueprint for the development of infrastructure and a commercial agrarian economy.

Foreign *donor funds* kept flowing in as usual. For example, the UK providing close to $ 400 m, the US more than $ 600 m, and various EU countries followed suit. The British DFID, true to its reputation, saw no problem in assisting the government in its policies, including helping with the mitigating effects of the forced relocation of peoples in the south to make way for dam construction, mega-plantations and resettlement schemes. This Western donor support was in addition to World Bank and IMF funding, much of which went to support the PBS ('Protection of Basic Services') programme, a positive-sounding scheme but one that reinforced the political grip of the government on local society, supported the (forced) relocation and villagisation of people across Ethiopia, and undermined local livelihoods.

The *state budget* was $ 6.1 bn, while expenditure amounted to $ 7.2 bn. The published budget deficit figure was –2.7% of GDP. According to the government's own figures in July (for budget year July 2012–July 2013), the total budget was to be nearly $ 8 bn. The current-account balance deficit was –$ 2.95 bn, up almost $ 1 bn from the previous year. Taxes and other domestic revenue supplied 14.5% of the state budget. Some $ 1 bn in the state budget was expected to come from external sources. Public (government) debt was about 44% of GDP, no different from last year. In December, *external debt* was estimated at $ 10.0 bn, up $ 1.5 bn from 2011. Total international aid to the country (including loans and grants) reached more than $ 3 bn, but foreign direct investment remained modest at an estimated $ 105 m–$ 110 m.

Most *government spending* was on infrastructure, mega-dams, education and health coverage, defence and security, cadre training, and commercial agriculture projects. Emerging countries active in Ethiopia, such as India and China, concentrated on infrastructure outlay, agricultural commodities, business investments and trade. In July, the French company Alstom signed a € 250 m contract with Metals & Engineering Corporation of Ethiopia to supply turbines and generators for the hydroelectric power plant of the Grand Renaissance dam. In January, it was revealed that the UK government was ready to provide € 15 m to € 17 m funding for Ethiopia's controversial 'special police' in the Ogaden region.

Annual *inflation* was 23%: beginning at around 33% at the beginning of the year but going down to 17% in December. This high rate – although much lower than in 2011 – caused economic instability and ate away at the earnings of the lower-middle and working classes. The IMF repeatedly expressed caution regarding inflation-related risks, and worries were also expressed concerning the unreasonable expansion of credit to public (i.e., state) enterprises and the restrictions on private banks and on lending to private businesses. The World Bank, although generally supporting government policies, issued some statements about the lack of benefits of growth felt by low-income and poor groups (20%–30% of the population).

Preparations were made to construct a power transmission line from the Gibe-3 dam to Kenya, for the future export of 400 MW of electric power, a $ 1.2 bn project to be funded by the World Bank, the French Development Agency and the AfDB. As in previous years, Ethiopia received most of its income from abroad in the form of *remittances* by migrants. The total sum was unknown, due to the largely unregistered transfer of funds, but was again estimated at $ 1.5 bn. Apart from this contribution, the Ethiopian diaspora – notably in the US – remained staunchly critical of the Ethiopian regime.

Exports of gold, leather products, flowers and khat were all up, while coffee exports – still the largest foreign exchange earner – were stable and somewhat disappointing. Export earnings were dented, however, by the undiminished high port fees of about $ 1 bn that Ethiopia had to pay to Djibouti, a country effectively existing as a service centre for the Ethiopian state and business classes. *Imports* amounted to $ 10.6 bn, up almost $ 1 bn from 2011, and consisted notably of petroleum and petroleum products, chemicals, machinery, consumer and luxury items, and textiles. The trade deficit remained high at about $ 7 bn. Ethiopia's main trading partners were Saudi Arabia (10%), China (9.9% and growing fast), the US (7.6%) and India (4.6%).

As in previous years, Ethiopia continued negotiations on membership with the *WTO*, but the process dragged on and was not concluded.

Urban areas saw more in-migration from the countryside. Urbanisation reached 18% and kept growing fast. The building boom in most major cities continued, but the urban masses suffered from high food price inflation, unemployment and poverty, leading to several desperate deeds, as on 24 April when a man set himself on fire on Menelik Square in central Addis Ababa, shouting: "I have nothing to eat." He later died of his injuries. Enduring poverty and bad governance in many rural areas led to a significant outflow of tens of thousands of people to the cities and abroad. Some 150,000 children lived on the streets.

Investment in the *education sector* was maintained and quantity-wise the sector saw more growth. The literacy rate in urban areas was alleged to have increased to 78%, and in rural areas to almost 40%, although these seemed optimistic figures. Universities again took in large numbers of students, but almost 50% of graduates could not find work and had to enter the informal sector (street trade, day labour, petty crime, etc.). Persistent calls for more quality instead of quantity and more freedom in education were heard. The top people in the educational institutions were virtually all party members. The government put more emphasis on technical and vocational education training, to which 80% of high school graduates were to be directed, with the rest going to higher education. Cell phone penetration reached 18% of the population, but Internet penetration was only 1.7%. National *health expenditure* amounted to about 4.9% of GDP.

The construction of the two *mega-dams*, the $ 5 bn 'Renaissance' dam on the Blue Nile and the Gibe-3 dam on the lower Omo River, continued, and the Ethiopian public continued to pay their obligatory 'voluntary' contributions, deducted from state employees' salaries, to finance them. This was because international (World Bank, AfDB) funding had been refused or fell short, in part due to doubts about the ecological, political and social feasibility of these ambitious schemes. The Blue Nile dam was turning out to be very expensive, now estimated to cost ca. $ 5 bn, and the Gibe-3 dam was seen to be causing ecological and social damage to local populations of cultivators and agro-pastoralists, labelled "primitive and backward" by the government. Many of them lost their land, homes and herds, and saw their cultures denigrated and assaulted. Dozens of local people from the Mursi, Nyangatom, Kara and Bodi ethnic groups and others also died, allegedly due to poisonings, shootings and livelihood destruction. Local people were sometimes told to give up herding and cultivation and to settle down in newly designated villages. The government said it "… would give them food aid for the coming years". Plans to herd the local people into such resettlement villages and to prohibit pastoralism were underway, with the international 'donor' community, as usual, dogmatically concentrating only on GDP growth and nothing else, and keeping quiet. However, FDI remained modest at an estimated $ 206 m, with Turkey and India accounting for 59%.

The *leasing* of *large tracts of agricultural land* to foreign and domestic investors continued. The state-owned Sugar Corporation also went ahead, taking over huge areas in the south-west for its own mega sugar plantations, removing local people in the process, and forcing them into new villages. Some of these schemes were led by TPLF-affiliated ex-generals. The whole effort was accompanied with much military action and intimidation, and thousands of agro-pastoralists were threatened. Government plans to concentrate them in a limited number of villages were deeply resented locally and were resisted. The entire process remained very controversial and abusive, and there were many reports of violent incidents – difficult to check in detail due to government intimidation and suppression of independent newsgathering and the penalising of local people, but no doubt with a strong basis in fact. Local journalists and researchers were also pressurised to tell only 'good news', and some internalised the message and went so far as to deny any abuses on the ground. On 28 April, gunmen in the western Gambella region *attacked a large commercial farm* owned by Ethiopian-born Saudi businessman Mohammed Al-Amoudi and killed five workers, among them a Pakistani, and injured nine. In southern Ethiopia, there were regular skirmishes between government armed forces and local people whose livelihoods were threatened, with hundreds of victims. Several massacres were reported by human rights monitoring groups. For example, in October in the south-west, government troops expelled about 130 people from their villages to claim the land, which was to be allocated to others for gold prospecting. No international news agency picked up such stories. In January–February, in the Gurafarda area, west of the southern town of Mizan, local communities of previously resettled people from the drought-stricken Amhara Region were violently expelled at the instigation of the local state administration. These *tens of thousands of displaced people* did not receive adequate compensation or alternative housing, and lived as IDPs somewhere in the south. This and similar incidents went uninvestigated, with donor country embassies unaware of, or indifferent about, the veracity of the allegations of abuse. 'Ethnic' clashes led to some 100–150 deaths and the displacement of thousands, e.g., in Moyale town, in Gambela region, and in the Borana-Gabra area.

In various *global rankings of governance and business freedoms*, Ethiopia fared little better than in previous years, but its image improved due to its economic dynamics and upbeat business spirit in the growing metropolis of Addis Ababa and a few other cities, such as Awasa, Meqelle and Bahir Dar. Although these rankings and the data sources on which they were based needed to be viewed with caution, they indicated changes. On the Legatum 'Prosperity Index', measuring wealth and well-being, Ethiopia was placed only 133rd (of a global total of 142 countries). On TI's corruption perception index, however, it did better, ranked 113th (out of 176), moving up from last year – a result that might come as a surprise, especially to rural Ethiopians, who complained constantly about bribery and nepotism. On the influential HDI for 2012, however, Ethiopia was only 171st (out of 176 countries), despite its much touted progress on the MDGs. On the 'Index of Economic Freedom', the country also fell several places and was in the (lowest) category of 'repressed' economies.

Ethiopia's 'developmental model' gave no evidence of a rights-based approach, although this was to be discerned in nominal form in the constitution and was still a preference of both its citizens and various UN agencies. Ethiopia's peasants were on the receiving end of the 'Growth and Transformation Plan' of September 2010, with the possible exception of a minority of richer 'model famers' who got some material support and other benefits, though at the cost of their independence and with obligatory membership of the ruling party.

Population growth showed few signs of slowing down and, with an extra 2 m added each year, the country maintained its growth rate of 2.7%. The total population reached about 88.5 m, compared with 35.4 m in 1980. The *pastoralist sector* felt the continued onslaught of government policy, directed at its gradual 'transformation' – read: termination – as an economically viable way of life. The government's

aim, as hinted at in the 'Growth and Transformation Plan', was to
sedentarise pastoralists and turn them into controllable cultivators.
Various statements by Ministry of Agriculture officials underlined this
aim. No consideration was given to the fact that most pastoralist habi-
tats were utilised effectively for livestock-raising and were unsuitable
for long-term permanent agriculture, or would require disproportionate investment in irrigation, roads and other facilities.

An apparently puzzling aspect of Ethiopia's 'growth economy'
was the steadily increasing number of *people trying to leave the
country*: political refugees and economic migrants seeking green-
er pastures in neighbouring countries or preferably further afield.
Apart from the regular number of politically harassed people, many
of the unregistered economic migrants complained of high tax bur-
dens, poverty, unemployment, job discrimination, or inability to pay
their debts for fertilisers and other inputs. Tens of thousands of impoverished and desperate Ethiopians went to Yemen, Saudi Arabia
and other Middle Eastern destinations. According to new reports
from international organisations and NGOs, *organised human trafficking* also increased, which led to criminal gangs taking a stronger
hold on these migratory flows. On the route to Yemen via Puntland
or Djibouti, this led to regular excesses such as hostage taking, kid-
napping, blackmail, and even deliberate drowning and killing of
migrants near the shore. The Ethiopian *'maid trade'* to the Middle
East, as well as the offering of ever-growing numbers of children for
adoption, also continued, with as yet unproven but persistent allegations that the Ethiopian government and ruling party agents ben-
efitted from this financially (via licensing offices and other shady
'services'). As in previous years, the perilous journey across the Red
Sea to Yemen led to hundreds of people drowning or dying in other
ways during or after the crossing.

The number of *refugees from neighbouring countries* reached
376,410, with an estimated 225,000 Somalis, 86,000 Sudanese, 4,000
from Kenya, and 63,000 from Eritrea, a country from which 700 to
800 mainly young people entered Ethiopia every month.

Ethiopia in 2013

Ethiopia maintained strong economic growth and received increased foreign investment, but remained one of the most authoritarian and repressive regimes in Africa, with government control extended over the economy, political life and cyber-space, and the containment of private business and overall human development. Political pluralism was officially tolerated but denied in practice. Media freedom was strongly curtailed and human rights problems remained serious. A new opposition party, the Semayawi (or Blue) Party, consisting mainly of young people, was closely monitored and disrupted at strategic moments. Mass Muslim protests against "state interference in religious life" continued on a regular basis, but were repressed. Muslim grievances were not addressed and no dialogue was held.

Economic growth was evident in increased GDP, infrastructural expansion and continuing investment in the health and energy sectors, but benefits were distributed very unevenly. The construction of two large river dams (on the Blue Nile and the Gibe-Omo) went ahead despite local and international objections, lack of scientific studies and a significant rise in the national debt. More FDI, including in industrial production, was visible. Sharp nationwide inequalities became further entrenched, with a party 'nomenklatura' and a new state-supported, co-opted middle-class on the one hand, and the large mass of the population still at the margins on the other. Agrarian area extension and large-scale land leases continued, while the pastoralist sector was further discouraged and repressed to make room for commercial plantation agriculture. Some schemes did not deliver and others provoked a regular stream of criticisms from local people, NGOs and human rights organisations, whose analyses were categorically rejected by the government. No inclusive options or adequate compensations for land loss were offered. Several million people were in need of emergency (donor) food aid throughout the year. Religious communal tensions were less prominent than in previous years, but several clashes between ethnic communities still occurred. The low-key armed conflict in the Ogaden (Somali) region continued.

Ethiopia confirmed its dominant role in the Horn of Africa, IGAD and the AU. Its military and diplomatic efforts in Somalia continued, with its forces nominally placed under the AU Mission to Somalia. Rivalry between Ethiopia and Kenya persisted with regard to the future scenario for Somalia, although both countries supported the federal government in Mogadishu. Ethio-Egyptian tensions over the impact of the huge 'Renaissance' dam under construction on the Blue Nile, which was expected to severely reduce Nile water levels in Egypt, were not resolved. Neither was there progress in settling the 'border conflict' with Eritrea. Northern Ethiopia received a continuous stream of thousands of young people fleeing from Eritrea.

Domestic Politics

Political life remained fully controlled under the heavy authoritarian hand of the ruling *Ethiopian People's Revolutionary Democratic Party (EPRDF)*, the sole ruling party for 22 years. No development towards a democratic system or democratic public debate could be discerned, although new terms such as 'developmental democracy' occasionally surfaced. State and party remained closely intertwined, and all higher-ranking government personnel had to be party members or were pressurised to join. Opposition party members were not allowed to be appointed to any important positions in the politico-economic system. Party members were regularly briefed and 'educated' on party programmes and policy in training sessions and meetings. Party membership increasingly became a prerequisite on the job market, e.g., for college graduates. *Prime Minister Hailemariam Dessalegn* appeared to be unchallenged at the helm of government.

There was no scope for the *political opposition* to exert any influence. The government could not handle policy criticism and tended to react to it in bad faith. The activities of a new opposition *Semayawi Party* (Blue Party), a moderate democratic movement with broad support and a youthful constituency, built upon the experience of previous democratic parties, but it was obstructed and kept under constant surveillance. The opposition party 'Medrek' ('Forum') also complained of constant intimidation and harassment. Several opposition party leaders, among them Adualem Arage, remained in prison on a dubious charge of 'terrorism and treason'. The parliament (with only one of opposition member among the 547 MPs) showed few signs of life and was used by the executive to rubberstamp its decisions. On 14 and 21 April, *local and city council 'elections'* were held, with the bizarre result that of the 3.6 m seats (!) only five went to opposition or independent candidates. On 7 October, the parliament elected a new president (a merely ceremonial function) for a six-year term: Mulatu Teshome, of Oromo background and educated at a Chinese university.

A tenacious feature of Ethiopia's politico-economic system was *corruption*, although it was generally felt to be less serious than the average for Africa, except at the elite level and in fast growing sectors such as mining, land acquisition, infrastructure investment, etc. During the year a number of officials were arrested on corruption charges, including, on 10 May, the head and deputy-head of the Ethiopian Revenue and Customs Authority, Melaku Fanta and Gebrewahid Woldegiorgis, together with several businessmen. High Court judge Zerihun Assefa was also detained on 21 January, accused of accepting bribes. In the course of the year, the Oromia State authorities dismissed 82 employees for corruption in connection with land management. However, the anti-corruption drive was quite selective and made no dent in the web of nepotism and bribery as a whole, and only some cases were reported. Many complaints were registered – even in a World Bank report – about the Ethiopian Telecommunications Authority as a hotbed of corruption. However,

Ethiopia held a surprising 111th place (of 177) on TI's Corruption Perceptions Index. On various other indexes prepared by global institutions, Ethiopia's rankings remained roughly unchanged, with slight improvements in economic freedom. Serious deterioration was seen in Internet freedom, press freedom and human rights.

The government's *tense relationship with the Muslim community* was not resolved, although increased scrutiny and repression muted the protests. The trial of Muslim community leaders arrested in 2012 made little progress. Regular peaceful Muslim demonstrations continued, calling for the government to respect the constitutional provision of 'non-interference of the state in religious affairs' and the release of those arrested On 12 December, 12 of the 29 Muslim leaders in custody were released and their charges dropped. On 4 August, at least 14 Muslims were killed by security forces in Kofele and Totolamo villages during an attempt to arrest a 'suspected' local imam. During the 8 August 'Id al-Fitr' celebrations over 1,000 Muslims were arrested and detained. On 13 October, two Somalis were killed in Addis Ababa, apparently when they were preparing a bomb. The government kept up its rhetoric against Muslim extremism, including in the state press and through a new TV documentary on the risks from religious fanatics.

Media suppression continued, with the few remaining independent newspapers closely monitored. Two of them, 'Addis Times' and 'Le-Hilina', were closed down. Journalists Eskinder Nega, Woubshet Taye Yusuf Getachew, Solomon Kebede, Bekele Gerba, Olbana Lelisa, and Ms. Reeyot Alemu (recipient of a UNESCO 'world press freedom prize') remained in prison, often serving disproportionately heavy sentences, and with some being refused urgent medical attention. In February, the noted journalist Temesgen Dessalegn, of the closed-down weekly 'Feteh', was charged with 'defaming the government' in connection with articles about the late prime minister, Meles Zenawi. On 25 December, a court in Awassa condemned journalist Asfaw Berhanu to two years in prison for an article on dismissed government officials. The authorities also regularly took other journalists and editors in for questioning and short periods of detention.

Telephone services and the *Internet* were continuously *censored*, with most diaspora and opposition sites blocked. The state-owned Ethio-Telecom Corporation remained the sole provider. The government, with the help of Chinese technology and experts, continued to perfect Internet and e-mail surveillance with DPI ('deep packet inspection') programs and FinFisher Trojan tools, going well beyond any security concerns and with reference to the controversial 'anti-Terrorism' proclamation of 2009. This drive toward surveillance led to a lack of independent information exchange and self-censorship across the board. Throughout the year, public activism by opposition party members or civil society activists in Addis Ababa, Gondar, Dessie, Alamata, and other towns was also met with arrests and dispersal.

As in previous years, *ethnic conflict* was a source of underlying countrywide tension, which sometimes came out in the open. On 23 September, severe inter-communal clashes between Oromo and Somali communities in the Meyu and Kumbi districts in East Hararghe Zone of Oromiya Region resulted in some 90,000 people being displaced by the violence.

The armed *conflict in the Ogaden* Somali region also continued. The Ogaden National Liberation Front (ONLF), the main insurgent group fighting for justice and autonomy for the Somalis, was weakened but not defeated. The Region 5 authorities remained quite unpopular with the ethnic Somali population, as incumbent Regional president Abdi Mohammed Umar, a former security man and staunch EPRDF loyalist, ruled with a heavy hand via his 'Liyyu Police' (special forces) and was regularly accused of human rights abuses and corruption. In October, government talks with the ONLF in Nairobi (Kenya) failed because of the government's precondition that the rebels accept the Ethiopian constitution.

Religious tensions between the three main blocks of believers – Orthodox Christian, Muslim and Evangelical/Pentecostal – were limited, but caused regular problems at the local level and within communities. Traditional believers, especially in the South, were regularly targeted and ostracised, notably by Evangelical/ Pentecostal believers, who rarely tolerated them. Within the Muslim community, there were ongoing tensions between so-called 'reformists' and radicals and the mainstream, more Sufi-leaning groups. On 28 February, the 71-year-old 'Abunä' Matthias, originally from Tigray, was elected by the synod of the Ethiopian Orthodox Church as the new patriarch after a six-month interregnum. In December, he was unexpectedly placed under house arrest and interrogated, after allegedly criticising the EPRDF.

Human rights concerns continued to be invoked by observers, noting illegal detention, disappearances, extra-judicial killings, and prison torture, notably of political opponents and protesters. There were also indications of substantial human trafficking. Facts were difficult to check due to the non-cooperation of the authorities.

Persistent *human rights transgressions* were also noted in the wake of the regime's frantic *developmental efforts* regarding *dam building* and *large-scale commercial agricultural ventures*. The appropriation and clearing of large tracts of land to make room for new plantations raised continuous problems, e.g., in Gambela, Afar, and the Omo Valley. No respect was given to local customary or land use rights. Reports by human rights organisations and journalists confirmed that people were often forcibly displaced, with frequent use of violence and intimidation. Cases of arbitrary arrests and killings, even by army snipers, were cited. In the case of some smaller ethnic groups, virtually all land was confiscated, endangering their livelihood system and causing food scarcity and poverty. Local inhabitants alleged that no consultations were held and no compensatory mechanisms of any substance were in place. *Evictions from the land* and *forced villagisation*, notably in Gambela, led to despair and protest, notably among Anywa (one-third of whom – about 40,000 people – were already displaced). In October, local residents set fire to an Indian-owned farm. In other places, locals threw rocks at security guards, cars and agricultural machinery. The government, instead of opening up the issues to public scrutiny or improving its procedures, denied everything. No charges were brought in cases of army or police abuse of citizens. Donor agencies such as the UK's Department for International Development (DfID) and USAID said that "no abuses" were evident, and denied the local evidence.

The *judiciary* functioned in ways that usually supported the political stance and policies of the government and could only be called independent in name, despite the professionalism and sincerity of many judges, who often had to bend to political pressure. Pro-government bias was visible in political and media freedom cases, as well as in business disputes. In the eyes of law experts, access to fair and timely justice for citizens could not be said to exist. Constitutional provisions were often 'pragmatically' interpreted and overruled by additional, restrictive laws. This was especially evident in the field of human and civil rights. The *Freedom House Index* put Ethiopia in the problematic category of *'not free' countries*, and rated the quality of its legal environment as very low. The country's Internet freedom ranking was fifth from bottom, and the worst in Africa. Several reports published during the year by international organisations, including HRW, alleged the systemic use of *torture* in Ethiopian prisons, as well as appalling prison conditions for the approximately 80,000 inmates.

Despite *donor countries* refusing to investigate or act on possible *misuse of aid money* or human rights problems, reports of rights abuse under donor-funded schemes were serious enough to urge the African Commission on Human and Peoples' Rights to call for a halt to the forced relocation of thousands of local people in the South in connection with 'resettlement' and 'villagisation'. The World Bank finally put its Inspection Panel to work to investigate some complaints, among them one of an Anywa farmer forcibly displaced from his land in the Gambela region. Evidence was available from local people that money received by the government under

the 'Protection of Basic Services' (PBS) programme was used to
fund forced displacements and evictions from the land. The World
Bank appeared to follow up on its November 2012 statement that a
"plausible link" existed between the PBS programme, partly funded
by the Bank, and the (forced) resettlement process and dispossession in Gambela. But the Bank appeared slow in acting on this: by
year's end no field investigation had been carried out and nothing
was heard of the case. The government adamantly refused to coop-
erate with the investigation. On 12 October, Ethiopian-Americans
held a demonstration outside the World Bank offices in Washington,
DC, accusing it and the IMF of "financing tyranny in Ethiopia". The
US State Department's annual report on Ethiopia was also very critical of repressive politics and human rights abuses.

Foreign Affairs

Ethiopia cultivated *good neighbourly relations* in the *Horn of Africa
region* with Kenya, South Sudan, Somaliland, the Somali federal government and Puntland. Djibouti was needed for its vital port services. Ethiopia paid Djibouti an annual total of $ 722.5 m in port
duties – apart from the additional costs incurred by Ethiopian traders. In December, new conditions were imposed by Djibouti regarding advance payment for goods to be transferred to Ethiopia. There
were some *tensions with Kenya over Somalia*, where both countries
had troops – and some differences in strategic aims and support for
various parties. For instance, in the southern autonomous Jubaland
region, Ethiopia and Kenya supported opposing clan-group militia
leaders for the regional 'presidency'. Ethiopia remained prominent
in *IGAD* and in the *AU*. From 27 January to 3 February, the 20th AU
summit was held in the new AU building in Addis Ababa, during
which Prime Minister Hailemariam Dessalegn was elected as AU
chairman for a one-year term.

 Tensions with Egypt over the *Nile issue* were not resolved. In fact,
an on-going dispute was the controversy over the massive $ 4.2 bn

hydro-electric 'Grand Ethiopian Renaissance Dam' on the Blue Nile, a national prestige project for Ethiopia and a bone of contention in its relations with Egypt due to the drop in the Nile water flow that was expected during and after construction. Egyptian Foreign Minister Mohamed Kamel Amr and his Ethiopian counterpart Tedros Adhanom met on 18 June in Addis Ababa to defuse tensions over the dam, which had intensified after Ethiopia began to divert the river waters to form the 70 bn m3 reservoir in April. They reached no agreement, however, either in June or in followup discussions later in the year. Ethiopia denied that the construction of the dam would have any negative effect on Egypt's use of the Nile. On 20 June, the member states of the *Nile Basin Initiative* met in Juba (South Sudan), to discuss future Nile water cooperation. Ethiopia urged other riparian states to ratify a controversial water deal, the Cooperative Framework Agreement, proposing that upstream countries be allowed to implement irrigation and hydropower projects without first seeking Egypt's approval. This was opposed by Egypt and Sudan. No clear results came out of the meeting, apart from normative resolutions about the desirability of 'cooperation'. On 26 February, Saudi Arabia's Deputy Defence Minister Khalid bin Sultan spoke fiercely of the Renaissance Dam constituting a threat to Egyptian and Sudanese security, but the Saudi government later distanced itself from this statement.

In the global context, the *us* remained a *staunch ally* of Ethiopia, as did the *UK* and *China*. The country's apparent stability in the volatile and terror-prone Horn of Africa region induced these donor countries and economic partners to continue to support the regime with few questions asked and to treat reports of human rights abuses, domestic repression and displacements with benign neglect. Apart from regional security agenda priorities, the developmental discourse and economic dynamics of Ethiopia also remained unreservedly popular among donor countries, who often disregarded wider issues of local people's rights and livelihoods as well as environmental problems in the wake of rural 'development'. 'Abuse-free development' was not a donor interest.

Ethiopian leaders undertook a fair number of *international visits*, and in turn the country, as a key state hosting the AU headquarter, was visited by several world dignitaries and politicians. Hailemariam Dessalegn visited China on 14–19 June, and Sudan on 3 December, for high-level talks. As AU chairperson, he was at the Climate Change conference in Denmark on 28 October, and met with Egypt's interim president Adly Mansour during the African-Arab summit in Kuwait on 19–20 November to discuss the Nile water issue. On 15 December, the prime minister gave a speech at Nelson Mandela's funeral. Foreign Minister Teodros Adhanom paid many foreign visits, among them to the UK in January, the US in May, and South Sudan in February.

Visits to Ethiopia included one by a UK parliamentary delegation on 18–22 February to explore health policy issues. On 24–27 February, US Deputy-Assistant Secretary of State for Democracy, Human Rights and Labor Karen Hanrahan visited for talks on economic, political and human rights issues. US Secretary of State John Kerry was in Addis Ababa on 25–26 May for high-level meetings and to attend the AU 50th anniversary celebrations, while on 23–24 July US Deputy-Secretary of Defense Ashton Carter came to meet with senior government and military leaders on the "U.S.-Ethiopia security partnership" and to attend an AU meeting. Ethiopia was also visited by UK Deputy Prime Minister Nick Clegg on 15 February. During a 17 July visit, an EU parliamentary delegation urged Ethiopia to release journalists and opposition politicians jailed under the 'anti-terror' law. On 23–26 November, Chinese Vice-Premier Ms. Liu Yandong was in Addis Ababa to meet Hailemariam and other leaders for talks on bilateral relations. In November, Thailand's prime minister visited Ethiopia and, on 9 December, Queen Máxima of the Netherlands, in her capacity as the UN Secretary-General's special advisor on 'inclusive finance', was in Ethiopia to promote the UN's programme for improving financial services to the poor.

In early July, a delegation from Ethiopia's Somali Region visited the government of neighbouring *Puntland* in Garowe for political and business talks, with a return visit in late August by a delegation from Somalia's Puntland to Region 5 (Somali) of Ethiopia. On 2–3 September, the president of Puntland, Abdirahman M. 'Farole', visited Addis Ababa for talks in connection with Ethiopian mediation in the dispute between the autonomous Somali region of Jubaland and Somalia's federal government in Mogadishu. *Somaliland*'s President Ahmed Mohamud 'Silaanyo' and several of his cabinet members were in Ethiopia on 8 December for talks and to attend the 8th Ethiopian 'Nations, Nationalities and Peoples' Day, an official state "celebration of ethnic diversity", held in Jijiga, capital of Ethiopia's Somali Region.

No rapprochement between Ethiopia and *Eritrea* over their border dispute and other bilateral tensions was achieved. On 29 April, at a meeting in New York with UN Secretary General Ban Ki-moon, Ethiopian Foreign Minister Teodros Adhanom repeated an earlier offer by his prime minister to open direct talks with Eritrea, but no response was forthcoming. A mediation effort by Qatar – aimed partly at reasserting its presence in the Horn of Africa to counteract Turkey's growing influence – did not see progress either.

Socioeconomic Developments

Ethiopia's economy, measured in GDP terms – and infrastructural investment, minerals exploitation and food production – continued to grow, although figures were approximate due to inconsistent records and exchange rate fluctuations. The country's *total GDP* was estimated at *$ 46 bn* (or ETB (birr) 877.5 bn), a *7%–8% increase* for the year. The World Bank and IMF saw the year's GDP growth rate as 7%–7.5%, while the government spoke of 11%. Some 46.5% of GDP was generated by agriculture (of which 19% by the livestock sector), 14.5% by industry, and the rest (38%) by services and donor funds and loans. *Inflation* remained high, at about 10% over the year, reflected in the commercial banks' prime lending rate of 14.5%, but was 10%–13% lower than in the previous year.

The *state budget* announced on 7 July (start of the budget year) amounted to *almost $ 8.3 bn*, 10% higher than the previous year, of which some 20% was foreign-sourced. Defence spending was increased to 15%, and agriculture took 10%. The current-account balance was $ −3.484 bn, or minus 7.5% of GDP. Government revenues, although expanding as a result of better tax collection, remained below target, reaching ca. $ 5.8 bn. These data made the financing of all developmental aims in the 2010 Growth and Transformation Plan (GTP) improbable, even with all the external funding.

Total *international aid* to the country (including loans and grants) was *more than $ 3.3 bn*, almost 40% of the national budget, meaning that the pace of growth was quite heavily dependent on external input. The UK and the USA were the largest donors. China, India and Brazil were the fastest growing business investors, also partly providing loans (e.g., for infrastructure and new manufacturing outlays). Turkish and Saudi investments also increased. The UK's DfID again became the target of criticism due to its disregard for human rights aspects of its aid programmes, including its apparent financing of part of the training for the 'Special Forces' in Somali Region 5, and its denial of human rights abuse in developmental schemes in the South, even after sending a delegation to 'investigate' the issue. Other Western embassies rhetorically committed to respect for 'inclusive development', 'human rights' and 'rule of law promotion', were equally indifferent, primarily focusing instead on doing business in the shadow of expanding Chinese and other international competition.

FDI inflow was estimated at $ 970 m, significantly higher than in 2012. *Remittances* by Ethiopian migrant communities abroad were not all registered but again were massive, *estimated at $ 1.3 bn*; they were an essential lifeline for many families and provided start-up capital for small private businesses. The combined external financial resources (at least $ 4 bn) offset the big import-export imbalance and the relatively low domestic revenues.

The *economy* remained *heavily centralised* and *dominated by the state*, in particular by the sole ruling party, the EPRDF, which aimed for total 'institutional capture'. It owned all large corporations, e.g., building materials and transport providers, export/import business-es, the media, infrastructure projects, etc. The military nature of the development process was striking: for instance, most of the sugar plantation projects in Southern Ethiopia were run by the state-owned Metals and Engineering Corporation, led by (ex-)military personnel, all party members. Also the Gibe-3 and Blue Nile hydro-dam construction sites were run like military camps, with multiple perimeter fences and a heavy security presence. No foreign banks were allowed to operate in the country. Long on-going discussions about accession to the WTO were again not concluded.

On the *economic freedom index*, Ethiopia was ranked 151th of 178 listed countries, meaning 'mostly unfree' and showing only slight improvement. Ethiopia further solidified its typical top-down state/party economy, with all leading positions held by party members, who received regular ideological training to keep them in line with the official growth and development plans and the party manage-ment system.

Agriculture continued to be the most important economic sec-tor, employing 70%-80% of the work force. Production output in-creased, notably as a result of the efforts of smallholders, and not from large-scale plantations or state farms. In a surprise move, the government revoked the land-lease allocations of around 3,000 in-vestors for their alleged "failure of developing the land". They includ-ed the Indian entrepreneur Karuturi, who saw his allotted area of 300,000 ha. significantly reduced.

The *food security situation* generally improved during the year, as average June-to-September rains in most areas were favourable. However, the June-to-August main harvest was below average in parts of Amhara, Tigray, and Oromiya. Weather hazards, including floods, hail storms and landslides, destroyed property, damaged crops, displaced populations and resulted in the death of livestock in Amhara Region and the Southern Nations, Nationalities and Peoples Region. A major economic setback in August was caused by *flooding* in parts of the Somali Region and Amhara Region, notably

North and South Wollo zones and in North and South Gondar, Oromiya, and West Gojjam zones. Nearly 40,000 households were affected and some 33,000 ha of crops were badly damaged.

Despite ongoing investment in healthcare and education, *human development*, measured on the basis of the HDI, was slow in improving and the country was still ranked 173rd (of 187 countries). The HDI differed markedly between regions and urban areas.

The *import bill* was almost $ 11 bn, while *export earnings* were estimated to total $ 2.8 bn to $ 3 bn, almost equal to the previous year. The *trade deficit* was therefore about $ 7.5 bn. The slight export growth was partly due to global market price fluctuations. The number 1 crop remained *coffee*, producing 26% or $ 747 m, down from $ 832 m the previous year (global price decline). Other exports were khat, bringing in $ 271.5 m (up 13%), leather products ($ 121.9 m, an increase of 10%), and textiles ($ 97.9 m; up 16%). This showed the same sectors predominating, as before, and also growing. Flower exports yielded ca. $ 246 m, but this sector showed signs of stagnation, if not slight decline. An underestimated currency earner, because largely unregistered, was *livestock*: much of it was traded cross-border to Sudan, Somalia, Djibouti, or Kenya, and was estimated to bring in at least $ 300 m. *Gold*, however, was the second (and growing) foreign currency earner, representing $ 570 m of a total of ca. $ 600 m revenue for minerals export. Artisanal miners produced 8.3 tonnes of placer gold, valued by the National Bank at $ 420 m. MIDROC, the only Ethiopian company involved in gold-mining, produced ca. 4 tonnes. In line with its monopolistic, state-capitalist policies, the state continued to force out local artisanal miners from their mining areas, to be transferred to companies (MIDROC, Ezana Mining). A few international companies were given prospecting rights for gold and base metals, e.g., the British firm Nyota Minerals in Wollega Zone and the Egyptian company Ascom Precious Metals Mining in western Ethiopia.

Oil and gas exploration continued, but an eagerly anticipated oil find in the South Omo block did not materialise. On 6 March, the

UK-based Tullow Oil company announced that no commercial-grade oil deposits had been discovered in the area. With the aim of starting to *export hydro-electricity* to neighbouring countries, Ethiopia worked on the construction of power transmission lines, expected to be functional in 2015, from the Gibe-3 hydro-electric dam site to Djibouti and Kenya. The 2,000 MW line to Suswa in Kenya was financed with loans worth $ 1.2 bn, mainly from the World Bank and the AfDB.

There was a gradual *expansion of industrial production*, leading to an estimated 9% growth rate, as foreign partners/companies, alongside domestic investors, were allowed to set up production lines, Ethiopia being attractive as a (very) low-wage country. A new industrial zone for export-oriented manufacturers was set up in Addis Ababa. China intensified its plans for industries, and more licences were also granted to (state) companies from India, Turkey and South Korea, for leather and shoe production, textiles, car assembly, etc. Without it being admitted openly, the dogmas of "Agricultural development-led industrialisation" advocated by the late prime minister, Meles Zenawi were being abandoned or 'adjusted' in favour of a more direct, autonomous path to industrial investment.

In the course of the year, Ethiopia concluded deals on *railway construction projects* – e.g., to Awasa in the South and to the port of Djibouti – with Turkish and Chinese companies, to be financed partly with foreign investor capital. In June, China's Exim Bank announced a loan $ 475 m for the railway. As part of its extension of *urban* transport facilities, the government commenced the construction of an *Addis Ababa Light Rail Transit*, an electrified light-rail system with a total length of 34 km. It was planned to be completed in 2014 and to have capacity to transit 80,000 passengers per hour. Other state-led development projects in infrastructure (especially roads), large-scale commercial agriculture, educational and health outlets and state enterprises went ahead during the year, following an almost unchanged course since the 2012 death of Meles Zenawi and his GTP of 2010.

All this was, however, accompanied by a rapidly *growing national debt*, estimated at $ 16.11 bn, according to data from the Ministry of Finance and Economic Development. In 2008, it had been only $ 4.35 bn. The debt-to-GDP ratio reached an all-time high of 36%. There was a gradual shift from concessional loans to market-based loans. The high debt and the growing repayment burden (debt servicing cost ca. $ 440 m) made the country vulnerable to falls in the price of its export products, such as coffee. The government made no effort to establish a needed local secondary market for both government and private debt issuance, where bonds could be traded. There was only a primary bond market, specially for bonds to finance the construction of the (not yet fully cost-covered) Renaissance Dam. Of the total debt, the domestic public debt stood at $ 4.9 bn. High inflation (currently at ca. 12% and in previous years 20%–30%) reduced the attractiveness of domestic bonds.

No reliable figures were released on *unemployment*, but in view of the massive rates of outmigration of young jobless people, including college graduates, it was estimated to be very high (some 40%). Official figures indicated that ca. 29% of the population lived below the 'poverty line', especially lower-class and rural families with many children, but the real number was probably higher. There continued to be large numbers, estimated at around 150,000, of *street children*, often orphans, of whom there were about 90,000 in Addis Ababa alone. No adequate social support structure existed to alleviate this problem, although a number of foreign and local NGOs tried to address it. In urban areas, thousands of 'illegal' houses were demolished without proper replacement or compensation, victimising large numbers of the poorer urban population.

Despite the much vaunted economic growth, investment, political 'stability', etc., the Ethiopian authorities issued *two humanitarian aid appeals* to the donor community, one for January–June and one for July–December. The first cited 2.4 m people in need of food relief, with a gross emergency food and non-food requirement of $ 258.9 m. After deducting the then available resources of

$ 83.2 m, a total $ 175.7 m was required for the first half of the year (including 165,751.7 tonnes of food, at an estimated cost of around $ 132.4 m). In July, the appeal for the rest of the year was made to the tune of $ 285.3 m to meet emergency requirements for ca. 2.7 m people. Thus, the situation of *constant food emergency* for millions of people continued. These figures were nevertheless considered as 'progress', because with a fast growing population (reaching about 90 m) the number of needy was not much higher than in previous years. According to several observers, the figures for food aid may have been an underestimate, because requirements for pastoral areas in the south, east and southwest were often not fully assessed. As usual, the government counted on (Western) donor countries to pay for most of the food aid. And again, they did: the US government alone had already provided more than $ 212 m. In fact, by 30 September, donor countries had committed nearly $ 484 m to humanitarian relief operations.

Ethiopia thus remained one of the *largest aid and development assistance recipients* in Africa. Most of it went straight to the central government and was spent according to its wishes. No evidence of donors seriously monitoring the conditionalities of aid was visible. Few of the funds and projects went into peripheral areas such as the Afar Region or the Ogaden, where the ONLF insurgency continued and where facilities for the civilian population remained seriously underdeveloped. Pastoralist peoples in general received little support. Only one initiative was noted: an $ 85 m loan provided by IFAD for 'pastoral community development'.

A major dramatic event was the (*forced*) *return of at least 140,000 Ethiopian workers* and domestic servants from *Saudi-Arabia* (ILO figures), after a number of violent incidents in which Ethiopians were humiliated or killed by Saudis in the streets. A stream of 'return migrants' started in November. This sudden exodus was the culmination of years of Saudi anti-foreigner (especially anti-Ethiopian) sentiment and abuse by the public and police. Both Muslim and Christian Ethiopians were hit by this. Most, though not all, returnees came back to Ethiopia as 'failures', with little capital and limited prospects of finding work or state support. Even their relatives in Ethiopia were ambivalent about their return, because of the extra burden of having to maintain them. The stream of out-migrants to Yemen and Saudi Arabia from Ethiopia via Somalia (Puntland's port of Bossaso), normally up to 80,000 to 90,000 per year, continued but dropped by one-third.

The number of *IDPs* within Ethiopia due to flooding, drought (as in Afar Region), or conflict was estimated at 370,000, with many being seen as 'protracted' cases with no return or resettlement in sight. The UNHCR estimated in August that Ethiopia also had 420,579 refugees from neighbouring countries, including about 240,000 from Somalia.

Ethiopia in 2014
(*by Jean-Nicolas Bach*)

Politically, the year was marked by preparations for the fifth general elections, scheduled for May 2015. So-called 'right-wing multinational' groups failed to create a broad coalition to counter the ruling EPRDF and appeared weakened by internal struggles (doubtless exploited by the EPRDF) in the run-up to the elections. A four-party front of ethnic and multinational parties nevertheless maintained its candidacy and thus represented the first coalition to contest two successive general elections. The young Blue Party, created in January 2012, was to take part in its first election.

The end of 2014 brought an opportunity for evaluation of the EPRDF's performance. Economically, it was the moment to present visible results of the first Growth and Transformation Plan (2010–15). Prime Minister Hailemariam Desalegn announced the achievements made in terms of infrastructures. The drafting of the next five-year plan began. Although the first versions were not made public, the government continued to pursue the objective of furthering the industrial transition of the country through major infrastructural projects, large-scale agricultural schemes and the development of a narrowly controlled private sector. But the relatively positive economic situation could not hide a dramatically deteriorating sociopolitical situation: as many inhabitants said, "one cannot eat rails" and there was social discontent over persistent poverty, the high cost of living, recurring water and electricity shortages, and what many denounced as increasing corruption. The tense relationship between the EPRDF and parts of the Muslim community eased, but problems were 'solved' by threats and imprisonments rather than by negotiation. Demonstrations in the Oromo region were harshly repressed by the security services. Demonstrations organised by political opposition parties multiplied throughout the year; most were

© KONINKLIJKE BRILL NV, LEIDEN, 2017 | DOI 10.1163/9789004346826_013

peaceful, but some were marked by imprisonments of party activists and leaders, and sometimes by violence. The macroeconomic growth rate remained strong, officially at 11.4%, largely attributed to the government's spending on infrastructure and various mega projects, substantial remittances, FDI (mainly from China, India and Turkey) and agricultural schemes.

The government maintained the long pursued strategy concerning its regional policies, intervening diplomatically and militarily in order to prevent conflicts spilling over and affecting Ethiopia's economic gains. It thus maintained a strong diplomatic involvement in the resolution of the crisis between Sudan and South Sudan, and also with regard to South Sudan's civil war. About 4,000 Ethiopian troops officially joined the AU Mission in Somalia. The tense relationship with Egypt over the construction of the massive dam on the Blue Nile showed signs of improvement. Relations with Eritrea were still blocked by both sides due to a lack of political will to negotiate.

Domestic Politics

The political sphere remained fully under the undisputed hegemony of the *Ethiopian People's Revolutionary Democratic Front* (EPRDF), and had a good chance of remaining so after the 2015 elections. However, deep tensions existed within the Front. Relations between its four constituent components (the *Tigray People's Liberation Front* [*TPLF*], the Amhara National Democratic Movement [ANDM], the Oromo People's Democratic Organization [OPDO], and the Southern Ethiopian Peoples' Democratic Movement [SEPDM]) and within the dominant TPLF itself were likely to need redefinition after the elections. In fact, although the TPLF still controlled the economic, security and military apparatus, tensions had been increasing since the death of the dominant prime minister Meles Zenawi in 2012. An '11-day tour' organised by some veteran TPLF figures in May in Tigray found evidence of discontent among local population and elites, who accused the current regional and national leadership of 'bad governance' and 'corruption'. It also revealed increasing tensions between older members of the TPLF and younger cadres. In addition, tensions increased between the leaders in Addis Ababa and in the Tigray region, the former fiefdom of the TPLF, where demands for more autonomy were emerging.

Further intensification of such competition within the TPLF had the potential to endanger the *balance of power within the* EPRDF, where relations between the various political groups also became more tense during the year; this was described by one observer as a "leadership in disarray". As the TPLF remained dominant, the ANDM was claiming a greater share of power, partly citing its support of Meles' group during the 2001 TPLF crisis. While the SEPDM remained relatively weak within the EPRDF and supportive of its head and prime minister Hailemariam Desalegn, the OPDO was shaken by the EPRDF's repressive response to demonstrations in the Oromo region in May.

The story began with the new '*Addis Ababa and the Surrounding Oromo Special Zone Integrated Development Plan*' (known as the 2014 '*Masterplan*'), made public by the Addis Ababa City Administration in May. As its administration expanded into the surrounding Oromo territories, many Oromos feared that the fast development of the capital would prevent them from accessing their land or even force them to move, as had been the case in the Western Gambella region. (Addis Ababa, itself a city-state within the federal system, is situated in the middle of the Oromo region, which is the biggest region and is home to the largest ethnic group, the Oromo, representing about 35% of Ethiopia's population.) By integrating eight towns administered by the Oromo region, the 2014 Masterplan was denounced as expanding Addis Ababa illegally. Many Oromos took to the streets in various regions, and especially on university campus (as in Ambo and Weda Walabu). The reaction of the security services was very harsh, as *dozens of demonstrators were jailed* and 11 were officially acknowledged to have been killed by security agents (30 according to AI, up to 65 according to Oromo political leaders). This reaction had a profound impact within the ruling OPDO, as many members contested the policy of the EPRDF. OPDO members and TV journalists lost their jobs because of their 'narrow political views'. What happened in the Oromo region during the spring not only illustrated the tensions within the ruling EPRDF, but was also indicative of the readiness of the government to use violence to deal with discontent. It marked a turning point in the year, as the government attitude towards opponents clearly hardened from then on.

This development could be observed in the government's attitude toward *opposition parties*. The political opposition had been permitted to organise peaceful demonstrations since 2013. In February, Unity for Democracy and Justice (UDJ) and the All-Ethiopia Unity Party (AEUP/'Mähihad'), two of the largest opposition parties, organised a major demonstration in Bahir Dar in Amhara Region to denounce the 'insulting' declaration of the region's vice president, a member of the ANDM, concerning displaced Amhara peoples in the Beni Shangul region. Peaceful demonstrations were held by the AEUP in Sewela (Southern Region), and the Blue Party, notably in the capital city and in Gonder (Amhara region). The Ethiopian Federal Democratic Unity Forum ('Medrek') also held markedly successful demonstrations in Addis Ababa and Hawassa. However, the last *demonstrations turned violent*: in December, the Blue Party called for a demonstration in the capital, where UDJ and the AEUP also took part. Many members were arrested and spent several days in jail, including the Blue Party leader, Yilkal Getent. With the election date drawing closer, pressure on opposition activists increased and they were regularly detained for a few hours, a few days or a few weeks. Others, accused of being linked with foreign-based terrorist groups such as 'Ginbot 7' or the Oromo Liberation Front (OLF), remained in jail.

The year was also characterised by the *failed merger between* UDJ and the AEUP. In an attempt to recreate a united 'right-wing multinational' opposition similar to the 'kinijit' coalition in 2005, UDJ and the AEUP signed a 'pre-merging agreement' in June – by so doing, UDJ de facto left the 'Medrek' coalition with which it had gained one parliamentary seat in the 2010 election. But irregularities were soon exposed by internal dissent in the AEUP, and the National Electoral Board (NEBE) eventually rejected the legality of the merger. This left both political formations deeply divided by internal factionalism. Unexpectedly, dissident groups within each party overthrew their respective presidents and assumed the leadership in October–November, but the NEBE once again rejected the legality of these changes; by year's end no decision had been taken on the status of the previous leaderships. Many UDJ dissidents decided to join the Blue Party to campaign as its candidates, but this was once again rejected by the NEBE. The entire opposition suffered from this failed merger and entered the electoral campaign in a clearly weakened position. UDJ and the AEUP were now isolated and could not properly register their candidates. 'Medrek' lost a strong member with deep roots in the strategic Amhara region. The Blue Party remained stable for its first participation in an election, although many of its candidates had been rejected by the NEBE.

Press freedom also suffered dramatically during the year. Six private media outlets were closed, and many journalists were arrested or forced to flee the country. According to HRW, during the year "22 journalists, bloggers, and publishers were criminally charged, and more than 30 journalists fled the country in fear of being arrested under repressive laws". Among the cases that received most international attention, Eskinder Nega and Reyot Alemu (both arrested in 2011 and remaining in jail) were representative of many journalists who were forced to self-censor out of fear of being charged. In October, Temesgen Desalegn was sentenced to three years in jail for his articles published two years before in 'Feteh'. Still waiting to be judged, the *Zone9 bloggers* were representative of the closing space of the press in 2014, symptomatic of the application of the Anti-Terrorism Proclamation, and illustrative of the increasing fear among the EPRDF leadership of infiltration into Ethiopia by 'Ginbot 7'.

The blog, founded in 2012 with the motto "we blog because we care", published challenging critical views of EPRDF policies. Of the nine bloggers, six were arrested in April, along with three journalists who were close relatives. They were later charged with terrorism, and more specifically with being 'Ginbot 7' agents in Ethiopia. The other three bloggers escaped and were now operating from abroad (USA and Sweden). These recent measures against journalists explained why Reporters Without Borders' 2015 World Press Freedom Index ranked Ethiopia 133rd out of 179 countries.

The *human rights situation* also generally worsened. A Freedom House summary published in February 2015 said: "Ethiopia is rated Not Free in Freedom of the World 2014, Not Free in Freedom of the Press 2014, Not Free on the Net 2014." AI also contributed to the growing international concern and criticism of the Ethiopian government by publishing a report in October that referred to the arbitrary detention in Addis Ababa and in the provinces of several tens of thousands of activists, journalists and opponents; according to the report, some 5,000 Oromos had been arrested between 2011 and 2014. Local activists were arrested in the regions: the Oromo Federal Congress, for instance, denounced the arbitrary detention of several hundred of its activists since the demonstrations in the Oromo region in spring. Blue Party members also became victims of repeated harassment, as in March, when ten members were detained for up to ten days for shouting political slogans on the occasion of International Women's Day in Addis Ababa. Preventive arrests of activists took place to thwart demonstrations and deter opponents from informing the public about future gatherings. Weynshet Molla, head of financial affairs of the Blue Party, was detained for about a month during the summer for her participation in a Muslim protest in Addis Ababa. Muslim demonstrations continued during the year, but the situation was less tense than previously – although jailed Muslim leaders remained in prison, charged with terrorism. In sum, local activists as well as leaders of the Oromo Federalist Congress, the AEUP, UDJ, the Blue Party, the Ethiopian Democratic Party and

Arena Tigray (a member of 'Medrek') were repeatedly arrested and some of them charged, along with journalists, under the 2009 Anti-Terrorism Proclamation.

One of the most widely reported and debated political events of the year was the arrest of *Andargachew Tsige*. He had British citizenship and was the general secretary of 'Ginbot 7', which was labelled a terrorist organisation by the government and led by a former prominent politician, Berhanu Nega. The movement was operating partly from the USA – through its media outlet, ESAT – and partly militarily from Eritrea. The Eritrean government offered sanctuary and allowed the armed wing of 'Ginbot 7' to train – the movement claimed to have about 18,000 trained soldiers. Andergatchew was arrested in Yemen in June while in transit to Eritrea. He was then extradited to Ethiopia, where he remained detained at an unknown location. This was not an isolated case: in January, two representatives of the Ogaden National Liberation Front (ONLF; another armed group based in the Somali Region in eastern Ethiopia) were arrested in Nairobi (Kenya) and handed over to Ethiopia. The Andargachew case provoked many reactions within Ethiopia and in Ethiopian social media networks abroad, where he was often considered a 'hero', but it was also a reminder of the reality of the 'terrorist' threat in the region, its support by the Eritrean government and its regional ramifications. Relations between Western countries and Ethiopia became quite ambiguous. The British government – which was denied access to Andargachew several times – cancelled a fund previously directed to supporting the formation of police forces. Relations with the USA also became tense as Washington hosted 'Ginbot 7' leaders and Ethiopian political exiles. US Secretary of State John Kerry found himself in an uncomfortable position when it emerged that a young student he had met and congratulated publicly was arrested a few months later as one of the Zone 9 bloggers. However, the apparent absence of any strong international criticism of the Ethiopian government during 2014 was striking. The EU, silently, did not plan to send an election observation mission for the 2015 election. This eloquent diplomatic silence was clearly due to the fact that Ethiopia still represented a pivotal ally in one of the world's most unstable regions.

Foreign Affairs

The projects implemented by the Ethiopian 'Democratic Developmental State' extended far beyond the national borders: hydroelectric dams, irrigation schemes, roads and railways were drawing new economic boundaries. The EPRDF was well aware that any lasting national development within Ethiopia depended on a minimal degree of regional stability. As Defence Chief of Staff Samora Yenus noted, Ethiopia had to remain involved militarily in order to defend its development. The Ethiopian leadership thus continued to pursue its agenda of working hard militarily and diplomatically to stabilise its borders.

In April, Global Firepower ranked Ethiopia as the third-strongest *military power* in Africa. Ethiopia in effect allocated $ 7.5 bn of its budget to defence – a sector that was becoming a powerful branch within the Ethiopian economy. Ethiopia had for a number of years maintained strong involvement in a very unstable region targeted by heavy terrorist attacks. Militarily, it continued its involvement in operations under international mandates in the Horn of Africa: in *Darfur* (Sudan) in the hybrid UN-AU mission (UNAMID) to which Ethiopia contributed around 2,400 soldiers, and in *South Sudan* under the UN Interim Security Force in Abyei (UNISFA), in which it was practically the sole troop-contributing country, having sent around 4,500 soldiers since 2011. Ethiopia became the fourth-largest contributor to UN missions in 2014.

In January–February, Ethiopia's regional security policy took a dramatic turn as Prime Minister Hailemariam Desalegn announced the integration of Ethiopian troops into the AU mission in Somalia (AMISOM). Ethiopia had been intervening regularly in Somalia since the fall of the Barre regime in 1991, most heavily between 2006

and 2009 against the Union of Islamic Courts, and since then inter-
mittently in support of AMISOM. But Addis Ababa's interventions
in Somalia had been conducted without an international mandate.
The new move thus represented a radical change for Ethiopia's regional involvement in Somalia, at least officially – as the country
remained de facto quite independent with regard to its operations
in the field. Furthermore, by contributing to AMISOM, Ethiopia had
now become a leading troop-contributor to internationally mandat-
ed missions worldwide. Ethiopia's participation in AMISOM could
be seen as partially motivated by financial considerations, since
AMISOM was financially and logistically supported by the UN and
the EU, but this would be too simplistic an explanation. Being part
of the mission allowed the government to obtain a perspective from
within. In this regard, Nairobi's decision to contribute Kenyan troops
to AMISOM in 2012 may have been decisive. Tensions remained between Addis Ababa and Nairobi in 2014 concerning the fate and
management of the borderland region of Jubaland in south-west
Somalia. Joining AMISOM may also have helped the Ethiopian regime in terms of building a positive international image, especially
in the context of the coming election and the dramatic narrowing
of political space.

The difficult relations with *Eritrea*, Ethiopia's northern neigh-
bour, did not improve. The UN Border Commission's 2002 decision
to recognise disputed territories (including the town of Badme) as
part of Eritrea had made the withdrawal of Ethiopian troops from
'its' territory a precondition for negotiations. The UN Monitoring
Group on Somalia and Eritrea accused Eritrea of hosting armed
groups opposed to Ethiopia ('Ginbot 7' and the Tigray People's
Democratic Movement), and of supporting others within Ethiopia
(the ONLF and the OLF), while Addis Ababa hosted Eritrean opposition parties (the most important being the Eritrea National Council
for Democratic Change and the recently founded Eritrean Youth
Solidarity for National Salvation) and provided them with offices,
conference venues, and some funding.

Addis Ababa was also deeply involved diplomatically in the *Sudanese peace processes*, hosting many peace conferences in the Ethiopian capital, notably under the auspices of IGAD. As tensions between Khartoum and Juba eased, armed conflict had erupted within South Sudan in December 2013. Within *South Sudan*, the opposing camps, the SPLM and SPLM-In-Opposition, signed several ceasefires that were never adhered to and conducted peace talks almost throughout the year in Addis Ababa, with IGAD as the forum for mediation. But the mediating team, led by the veteran Ethiopian TPLF leader Seyoum Mesfin (Ethiopia's ambassador to China), failed to persuade the belligerents to accept a minimum compromise by the end of the year and no solution was in sight.

Due to these ongoing conflicts in neighbouring countries, Ethiopia became the leading refugee-hosting country in Africa. In collaboration with international humanitarian agencies, Ethiopia offered assistance and protection on its territory to more than *600,000 refugees*, mainly originating from South Sudan, Eritrea and Somalia. The vicious conflict in South Sudan that broke out in December 2013 had displaced more than 1.5 m people and, according to UNHCR, around *190,000 South Sudanese* refugees were hosted by Ethiopia in 2014; the same source indicated that there were about 100 new arrivals from South Sudan every day. The expanding camps for South Sudanese refugees in Gambella Region in western Ethiopia, already facing tensions due to land grabbing and local population displacements, threatened to further increase socioeconomic problems there.

The antagonism between Ethiopia and *Egypt* over the Grand Ethiopian Renaissance Dam on the Blue Nile was not yet finally resolved, but seemed to be drawing closer to an amicable agreement. The situation between the two countries remained stalled, as Egypt still feared the negative impact of the dam on the downstream flow of water. But in contrast to earlier open threats, the new Egyptian government of President al-Sisi adopted an increasingly pragmatic approach to negotiations. In October, both countries agreed to commission further independent studies to assess all direct and indirect consequences of the dam and to prepare a trilateral memorandum of understanding between Egypt, Ethiopia and Sudan. Ethiopia left no doubt about its resolve to complete the building of the dam, as it had become a matter of national pride and was considered essential for providing electricity to other infrastructural and development projects.

Socioeconomic Developments

Ethiopia's *population* officially reached 89.7 m according to the Central Statistical Agency, and around 95 m according to international financial institutions (IMF, World Bank). Population growth rate continued to be high, as the last census, in 2007, had estimated a population of about 74 m. According to the World Bank, *poverty* had been reduced by 33% during the previous decade – although it estimated that 37 m Ethiopians were still poor or vulnerable to falling into poverty. This contrasted with a recent study by the Oxford Poverty and Human Development Initiative (OPHI), which ranked Ethiopia among the poorest countries in the world. OPHI's Multidimensional Poverty Index categorised 87.3% of the population as "poor", 58.1% as "poor and destitute" and 36.8% as poor with less than $ 1.5 per day. Ethiopia's *Gini* coefficient was 0.336 and the HDI 0.435. Poverty thus remained hard to fight, although 60% of government expenditure in recent years had been oriented toward pro-poor economic growth (agriculture, education, health and road development), and despite an impressive sustained GDP growth rate.

Prime Minister Hailemariam Desalegn officially announced an 11.4% *economic growth rate* for the fiscal year (clearly outpacing the SSA average). International institutions also estimated that real GDP growth had remained very solid in 2014, but nevertheless considered the Ethiopian figures to be overestimates. The IMF, for instance, gave a growth rate of 10.3%. The official GDP per capita in 2014 was about $ 630.

The service sectors and remittances were estimated to contribute about 9% and 10% of GDP, respectively, but *key drivers of growth* remained national investments in transport infrastructure (roads, rail), energy (hydroelectric power generation through dams) and agriculture. *Agriculture* officially grew by 8.5%, taking advantage of the transformation of subsistence smallholders into commercial farmers, helped by the development of roads, power supplies and market networks. However, the agricultural sector's development was constrained by unfavourable international commodity prices for important cash crops (such as coffee).

Manufacturing industries (23% of GDP) continued to benefit from public investment. Rumour had it that the government would invest $ 20 bn in the power-generating sector for the second *Growth and Transformation Plan* (2015–20). The Plan had not yet been made public, but was expected to follow the path of the previous plan, with massive investment in infrastructure and a strong state-led economic policy. Finance Minister Sufian Ahmed told Reuters in December that "without investing in infrastructure, it is now abundantly clear that Africa cannot sustain growth".

The pace of *infrastructural 'mega-projects'* continued, although not quite as fast as the initial ambitious schedules had foreseen. These projects included 159,000 condominium houses that Hailemariam said were under construction. The road network expanded further (road-building accounted for almost one-third of the national budget). The government officially announced the start of construction of a 220 km road linking the north-east of the country to the port of Djibouti. China consolidated its predominance in financing these roads, as well as the impressive new Addis Ababa Light Railway, one line of which was expected to be tested in February 2015; 87% of the Light Railway project was already completed, as well as 80% of the Addis Ababa-Dewole railway. India also increased its involvement in the construction of infrastructural projects, notably in the field of railway construction. The government announced ambitious plans for the construction of 5,000 km of railway lines in the coming years, and also the expansion of Addis Ababa's international airport.

Among key infrastructural works, the construction of *dams for hydroelectric power generation* continued to be pursued with impressive speed. Electricity was expected to partly support domestic economic development and infrastructure projects (such as electric trains), but was also foreseen to be exported to neighbouring countries. In 2014, Djibouti was already benefitting from Ethiopian hydroelectricity. Construction of the Gibe III dam was 89% completed, and of the Genale dam 66% completed. But the most impressive project under construction remained the *Grand Ethiopian Renaissance Dam*, 43% of which was already completed. Started in 2013, the construction of the $ 4.2 bn dam was planned to finish in 2017 and was expected to then produce 6,000 MW (the government announced that 700 MW would be produced as early as 2015). The Ethiopian Electric Power Corporation issued Millennium Bonds to finance the project to enable the Ethiopian populace to remain the sole financier of the dam, which had become a symbol of national pride. The issue of more bonds by the government in December was intended to raise finance for infrastructural projects for which sufficient funding seemed to be lacking.

The government further confirmed its gradual turn towards market-oriented economic policies, issuing its first *Eurobond* in December after an international investors roadshow. The 'B1' or 'B' assigned to Ethiopia by rating agencies Moody's and Standard & Poor's, respectively, in their short-term and long-term financial risk assessment, combined with the IMF's September declaration that the risk of debt distress was low, enabled the government to issue securities for the first time. Ethiopia had till then been shut out of the international bond market. In this respect, 2014 represented a radical turn that should be seen as the culmination of constant government attempts to enter the global financial markets, as Hailemariam declared in December that this was not a new government policy. He said that international institutions had not previously allowed Ethiopia to apply for commercial loans in the capital market, but this had now changed. The $ 1 bn loan would run over a period of ten years at an interest rate of 6.625–6.675%. By issuing a debut international bond, Ethiopia confirmed its economic improvement and gained recognition of its ongoing success by international public and private institutions. Nevertheless, many socioeconomic challenges still remained.

Inflation was further controlled and was brought down to a low 5.6% in September. The government was thus able to confirm the substantial reduction of inflation that had been accomplished in 2013 (8.1%) as compared with 22.9% in 2012 (with average inflation of 16.1% over the previous five years). This reduction was due to the pursuance of a tight monetary policy and the positive effect of a good primary harvest on domestic food prices. However, the continuing drop in global raw material prices, the fiscal deficit (about 3% of GDP) and a falling exchange rate, still threatened to keep inflationary pressure high. The government also used the exchange rate as a policy tool, seeking to devalue the national currency (birr; ETB) with the aim of maintaining export competitiveness. This supported sustained economic growth, but kept the risk of inflation high (the average exchange rate in 2014 was ETB 21.1:$ 1). Furthermore, export growth was still outstripped by that of imports and the current-account deficit was projected to have widened to 7.3% of GDP in 2014. The fall in key commodity prices (e.g. coffee, horticulture) led to a drop in Ethiopian export revenue of an estimated $ 60 m. The volatility of agriculture, which still represented almost half of the economy's gross value added, and the sector's exposure to climatic hazards (drought, flooding) also remained as restraining elements.

Another challenge for the Ethiopian authorities was the stable and pervasive level of *corruption* in the country, as documented by TI's Corruption Perceptions Index. Ethiopia had been ranked 111th out of 177 countries in 2013, and was ranked 110th out of 175 countries in 2014. Even more critically, Ethiopia was ranked ninth of the ten African countries with the highest illicit financial outflows (between 1970 and 2008), as documented by the AU High-Level Panel on Illicit Flows led by South Africa's former president Thabo Mbeki. The panel reported that Ethiopia could have lost about $ 16.5 bn in this way in the period 1970–2008, substantiating IMF and World Bank reports that estimated Ethiopia to have lost more than $ 11 bn in illicit outflows during the 2000s.

Ethiopia in 2015

The main political events of the year were the May national parliamentary elections and the massive Oromo revolt against the
Addis Ababa Masterplan, which had aimed to incorporate Oromo
farmlands. The elections were won, as expected, by the ruling
EPRDF, with none of the 547 seats conceded to the opposition. It
was a lacklustre and subdued event, with little international press
coverage, and was regarded with deep scepticism and scorn by
Ethiopian opposition parties, independent observers and most of
the international community. The Oromo revolt led to major upheaval, with some 400 people killed and the government's land
policy at risk.Controversies over the closed political process, the
impunity of the security forces, media repression, land issues and
large-scale land investment schemes continued, turning violent in
some places.There were visits by some prominent world leaders and
ministers, among them US President Barack Obama, who also attended a meeting at the AU headquarters in Addis Ababa.Ethiopia
received tens of thousands of refugees from surrounding countries
– Somalia, Eritrea and South Sudan (in the wake of the civil war
there) – cared for mostly by UNHCR, and saw an almost equal number of out-migrants.Relations with its neighbours, except Eritrea,
were stable and rather cooperative, with a closer bond emerging
with Djibouti. The Nile issue was unresolved, however, despite some
signs of more cooperation between the Nile Basin countries. In the
economic domain, GDP growth and massive infrastructure growth
proceeded, with the Gibe III hydro-power dam lake starting to fill
up, amidst ongoing controversy over its negative effects on the environment and the livelihoods of downstream peoples. The second
Growth and Transformation Plan (GTP) for 2015–20 was promulgated in September, but was not published, still being fine-tuned by
policymakers. In effect, it meant continuity with GTP I, with no policy changes. Donor countries and the IMF and World Bank had no

qualms about keeping donor funds flowing, despite serious repression of human rights, a restrictive private business environment, growing environmental problems and unsolved food security issues.

Domestic Affairs

Domestically, two events stood out: the May parliamentary elections and the Oromo farmers' revolt around Addis Ababa, resulting in death and destruction.

The *elections* for the Ethiopian House of People's Representatives took place on 24 May. They were preceded by a subdued and very lacklustre electoral campaign, in which the ruling Ethiopian Peoples' Revolutionary Democratic Front (EPRDF), in power since 1991, held all the trump cards. Many opposition party candidates were forbidden from running by the National Electoral Board. There were a few debates on national television, but campaigning by opposition groups was severely curtailed and hindered, notably outside the capital. Several opposition demonstrations were violently put down, as on 18 January in Addis Ababa, with dozens or people seriously injured. No foreign observers attended on election day, apart from an AU delegation, and a sense of competition was absent. Several prominent opposition leaders, including of the Unity for Democracy and Justice (UDJ) party, were jailed before the elections.

The elections themselves were well organised and largely peaceful, with voters having been urged if not compelled to vote by the authorities. Although a significant part of the population voted out of conviction, many others had no trust in the secrecy of the ballot and voted for the ruling party, unwilling to take a risk. Still, more than 500 members of the Ethiopian Federal Democratic Unity Forum or *Medreq* coalition were arrested at polling stations in Oromia region before and on election day, and 46 people were beaten and injured during the elections; six people sustained gunshot wounds and two were reported killed. The report by the AU group praised the "peaceful and orderly" conduct of the elections but fell short of endorsing them as democratic or competitive.

The elections led to *a win of all the 547 seats for the* EPRDF and its various constituent (ethnic) parts, and they also took 100% of the seats in the 108-member *House of Federation* and the nine state regional assemblies. This result, declared on 22 June, was received with suspicion and scepticism across the board. Not all voters had voted for the ruling party, but the 'first-past-the-post' system meant that representation of opposition voices was impossible. Election Board officials and local authorities were anxious to prevent an opposition party win in their constituency and used all means to prevent it. The main opposition parties, the Medreq coalition (consisting of the Oromo Federalist Congress [OFC], Oromo National Congress, Arena-Tigray, the Ethiopian Social Democratic Party-Southern Ethiopia Unity Party, the All-Ethiopia Unity Party, and the Unity for Democracy and Justice [UDJ]), plus the independent 'Semayawi' (Blue) Party (mainly with a younger constituency), were disappointed if not appalled, although they had seen it coming. Neither of them secured a seat. The result had little credibility and effectively made the political process, let alone 'democracy', in Ethiopia irrelevant, with the ruling party positioning itself, in the words of opposition, for "continued eating" and "perpetual" power. The EPRDF showed no desire to engage in any national dialogue or debate about policy alternatives and the parliamentary sessions after May reflected this. A further post-election media crackdown also followed, with critical or independent journalists not tolerated and the Internet seriously censored. On global indexes, Ethiopia scored worst in Africa for Internet use and freedom.

Internationally, the response to the elections was muted. The US government and the EU showed no interest and issued cautious statements that they, respectively, "... remain committed to working with the Ethiopian Government" and "... look forward to continuing and deepening ... partnership".

Opposition politicians continued to be intimidated and targeted by the regime. Four opposition party members were reportedly killed in the post-election months. OFC leader Beqele Gerba, who was released in March after serving a four-year jail term, was arrested again on 25 December in connection with his alleged role in the Oromo protests against the land confiscation around Addis Ababa. Again, the charges had little evidence to stand on.

In the post-election consolidation of the regime, Prime Minister Hailemariam Dessalegn, seen as a transitional figure after the death of former prime minister Meles Zenawi in 2012, was able to consolidate his position and was re-elected as leader of the EPRDF and as prime minister. He went through a severe internal party grilling (performance evaluation session, or *gimgema*) on 11 May, but survived it. After an EPRDF congress in August, consolidating the policies followed thus far, a new cabinet was installed in October, with a reshuffle of some personnel and many new state ministers positions (bringing the total to about 80), with their own lavish budgets for new four-wheel drive cars and office furniture.

A major crisis was precipitated by *mass Oromo protests* in November–December against 'land development' and investments around the capital in connection with the Addis Ababa Master Plan, which envisaged steady expansion of the metropolis into surrounding areas inhabited mainly by Oromo farmers. (The master plan potentially encompassed an area at least ten times the current size of the capital.) In November, Oromo in and around the villages of Wolenkomi, Yubdo, Chanqa, Finch'a, Ginch'i, and some other places protested publicly against encroaching private investors who said they were acting under the Master Plan. Their slogans were: "Oromiya is not for sale", "Killing is not an answer to our grievances", and "We want genuine self-rule". With all land in Ethiopia being state-owned, the Addis Ababa Masterplan was legal, and failed only in its authoritarian implementation and by not providing compensation for farmers losing their land. Students at Addis Ababa, Haromaya and other universities staged protests in solidarity.

In the ensuing clashes, around *400 people were killed by the security forces*, including children and pregnant women, and in some confrontations several policemen also died. About 3,500 people were arrested. Journalists covering the protests, including Feqadu Mirkana of state-run Oromia Radio-TV, were also arrested. Among the foreign-owned farms that were attacked and burnt down was Solagrow, a Dutch farm that had fenced off 100 ha of communal grazing land from local people. The owner, operating under a government lease, lost a $ 300,000 investment. There was criticism within the EPRDF of its Oromo branch, the Oromo Peoples' Democratic Organisation, and some of its 'corrupt members', who were said to be responsible for the problems. The prime minister said on 20 December that the "recent question raised by the people of Oromia was a legitimate one", and that the Master Plan should have been drawn up "in consultation with the people of Oromia". But he added that "merciless legitimate action against any force bent on destabilizing the area" would be used. The Master Plan was suspended, but of consultations nothing was heard. The prime minister's statement that "the ruling party has never imposed a single developmental plan on the public without its will" was incorrect and accepted by few.

Press and media freedoms continued to suffer, with no real independent opinions allowed to flourish. Internet, telephone and e-mail traffic was seriously monitored with the help of sophisticated surveillance technology (e.g., with Chinese expertise and Germany's Trovicor data interception software) and a repressive police apparatus, leading to the arrest of more independent journalists and bloggers as well as periodic closures of social media sites. The state-run Ethio-Telecom Corporation was the only Internet provider that was allowed to operate. A widespread network of paid informants and an extensive phone tapping system restricted free speech, even in the private sphere and security forces generally acted with impunity.

Ethiopia was 4th on the global list of *'most censored' countries* drawn up by the Committee to Protect Journalists, with 17 journalists in jail, others forced into exile, and court cases ongoing against several bloggers. A prominent jailed journalist, Temesgen Dessalegn, was denied medical treatment. Five of the 17 in prison were released before a visit by US President Barack Obama in July. Evidence of reporters' wrongdoing was very slim if not non-existent, and their convictions reflected government/party intolerance of any criticism.

Political freedoms further declined on all indexes, with the Freedom House Index again rating Ethiopia 'not free', with civil liberties and political rights a low 6 on a scale of 7.

In July, the *Federal High Court sentenced 18 Muslim activists* connected to the wave of Muslim public protests against "government interference in their internal affairs" in 2012–14. While these protests had been largely peaceful, the government saw elements of radicalisation and threats to public order and the delicate balance between faith communities. It had condemned the ideological and financial links of Muslim institutions such as the Awoliya Muslim College and some Muslim NGOs with foreign powers such as Saudi Arabia and Qatar. While the evidence against the Muslim leaders, detained since late 2012, was slight and circumstantial, they received jail sentences of five to 22 years for "terrorism and conspiracy to create an Islamic state".

In the domain of higher education, *academic freedom was restricted*, and university teachers and students walked a tightrope. The government continued to put party members in charge of university presidencies and suppressed critical public discourse, regularly accusing the university community of being 'pro-opposition'. Several academics critical of the government were denied tenure or contract renewal after retirement age. In March, philosophy professor Dagnachew Assefa was fired, apparently for criticism of the government. There was also strong pressure on students to join the EPRDF, with the prospect of securing a job. Curricula and research were increasingly monitored by the Ministry of Education, and freedom of assembly of staff and students was restricted.

The political situation in the rest of the country was marked by armed peace but also by several *low-key armed insurgencies*, with the *Ogaden problem* in the Somali Regional State continuing. While a part of the Ogaden National Liberation Front (ONLF) submitted and sought a compromise with the government after negotiations, another part continued its rebellion, but much weakened. The government played on clan-group differences in the Somali population (about 45% of the Somali Region's population belong to the Ogaden clan-family). On 26–29 May, armed clashes led to dozens of people being killed, with accusations of mass repression and rape of civilians, including, for example, in Shilaabo district, where government special forces, the 'Liyyu Police', were said to be involved. Its former commander Abdi Mohamed Omar (of the Reer Abdullah–Ogaden clan) continued as Somali Region president. The federal government was bent on keeping this region under complete control because of its proven large natural gas deposits and expected oil finds.

In the restive *Gambella region* in the West, insurgency by disgruntled and marginalised Anywa people (who had lost much of their land to government-supported investors and were threatened by the ongoing influx of Nuer people into their area) continued. Tensions between Nuer and Anywa remained at dangerous levels. The Majangir minority in Gambela also continued to suffer from government repression and land dispossession. In South Omo, a violent clash in May led to the security forces killing about 50 local people.

As well as the ONLF, there were smaller movements such as the Benishangul People's Liberation Movement, the Gambella People's Liberation Movement, the Oromo Liberation Front and the Sidama National Liberation Front. In October they concluded an alliance, the People's Alliance for Freedom and Democracy. In the north there was a movement allied to the Ginbot-7 party, with a base in Asmara (Eritrea). But none of these insurgency movements were regime-threatening.

Ethnic clashes occurred here and there in the country, revealing the unresolved problem of ethnic conflict management in the political system. On 12 December, a major confrontation between Oromo and Amhara in Ameya *woreda* (district) of Oromiya State erupted, with at least five people killed, ten houses burnt down, and many families dispossessed and fleeing. It was allegedly instigated by local (Oromo) government officials. Ongoing clashes also occurred between some ethnic groups in the south-west.

On 21 April, *public protests* erupted in Addis Ababa, following the circulation of a disturbing video recording of ISIS ('Islamic State') adherents decapitating what were probably Ethiopian Christian migrants in Libya. Demonstrators took to the streets and scuffles with the police followed, ending in a repression of the protest, with 48 people injured and hundreds arrested.

Overall, *religious relations* were accommodative, but tensions between Orthodox Christians, Pentecostal-Evangelical Christians and Muslims of various denominations remained present; strong rivalry continued under the surface and openly on Internet sites, with harsh polemical attacks. Several groups of ISIS sympathisers emerged and a number of them were arrested. On 11 December, a grenade exploded in the compound of the Anwar (Grand) Mosque in Addis Ababa, injuring 24 people. The attack was probably related to intra-Muslim rivalries.

Foreign Affairs

Ethiopia maintained good bilateral relations with Somaliland, the Somali Transitional Federal Government (TGF), which it supported militarily, Kenya, Djibouti and Sudan. It opened new talks with *Somaliland* on the future use of Berbera port. With *Kenya* there were some tensions over policy in southern Somalia.

Relations with *Eritrea* remained at a low ebb – in fact were absent – because of the continued stalemate on the border demarcation issue, now entering its 13th year. There were no new initiatives or pressure to resolve the matter, except that the Ethiopian prime minister said he would be prepared to meet and talk with the Eritrean president. The latter refused. The stream of Eritrean migrants/refugees into northern Ethiopia continued (although the majority exited via Sudan). Refugee camps were maintained in the Tigray region to accommodate them. In September, a remarkable episode unfolded when the core of the Tigray Peoples Democratic Movement (TPDM), a formerly anti-Ethiopian government group located in Eritrea under the protection of the Eritrean regime, defected to Ethiopia. Under its leader Captain Molla Asghedom, the force of about 700 men battled Eritrean border forces near Umm-Hajer and Seq al-Ketir, and entered Ethiopia via Sudan. The background to this event seems to have been the refusal of the TPDM to ally with the anti-EPRDF Ginbot-7 movement led by Berhanu Nega, which operated from Asmara, and wanted to unite all factions.

There were government negotiations with *Sudan* on finalising border corrections on the 725 km border between the two countries, including in the Al-Fashaga agricultural area east of Gedaref. Informal reports of Ethiopia giving land to Sudan led to these negotiations being contested.

Ethiopia remained the *key player in* IGAD. Ethiopia's representative Seyoum Mesfin (ambassador to China) was involved in IGAD-sponsored mediation talks between the combatants in South Sudan (SPLM and SPLM-In-Opposition) to reach a compromise, but these talks ended in failure early in the year.

The *Nile issue* stayed high on the agenda, with Ethiopia making conciliatory noises to Egypt but not changing its policy of unilateral hydro-thermal energy structure expansion via the Grand Renaissance Dam, about 45 km from the Sudanese border. The work on this project progressed, but slowly because of insecure funding (mainly domestic, as international partners had withdrawn). Egypt's concerns about the water level of the Nile were not alleviated, despite a rhetoric of cooperation and 'win-win'. On 23 March, the leaders of *Egypt, Ethiopia and Sudan signed a Declaration of Principles* in Khartoum (Sudan) on the regulation of Nile water use. It was a political deal, sidestepping the controversies ahead. Under the declaration, a technical committee was appointed by the three countries to oversee the dam's construction, but it would "... not be allowed to visit the dam or to witness the work on the site", thus precluding an evidence-based assessment of the dam's environmental impact.

With Addis Ababa as the *headquarters of the* AU, Ethiopia played a prominent role in Africa, but one growing problem, also voiced by some African diplomats, was the restrictive security regime around the AU, with the Ethiopians monitoring and screening visitors, suppressing free reporting and constraining media. This had a negative effect on the AU itself.

China, the EU and India remained major economic and trade partners of Ethiopia, providing most of the FDI, although the Chinese involvement was slowing down.

Ethiopia was visited by a number of *foreign dignitaries and delegations*. In January, Egypt's President Abdel-Fatah al-Sisi was in Addis Ababa to attend the AU summit opening session and consult with Ethiopian leaders (his visit being cut short by terrorist attacks in the Sinai by ISIS-affiliated groups). In the same month, Turkish leader Recep Tayyip Erdoğan paid an official visit, accompanied by ministers, bureaucrats and businesspeople. On 13–17 February, Seán Sherlock, the Irish minister of state for development, trade promotion and north-south co-operation, visited Ethiopia for talks on trade and investment opportunities, and Irina Bokova, head of UNESCO, visited on 23 March. She participated in the Women in Parliaments Global Forum Summit at the AU headquarters, and also met with Ethiopian Prime Minister Hailemariam and President Mulatu Demeqe. Also in March, Gil Haskel, head of Israel's Agency of International Cooperation MASHAV, came for a tour of agricultural projects, on which he was accompanied by Israel's ambassador in Ethiopia, Belaynesh Zevadia, and met with Ethiopia's Foreign Minister Tedros Adhanom.

On 16–17 April, Rwandan President Paul Kagame made a state visit, to discuss regional cooperation, trade and investment and "learning from both nations' experiences in peace and security", in which these two authoritarian governments did indeed have much in common. July saw a visit by two ministers of state from India.

A Japanese Development Ministry team including the permanent secretary of the Ministry of Industry and Trade (MIT) and the deputy permanent secretary of the Ministry of Finance visited Ethiopia from 28 September to 1 October to promote the *Kaizen* management system among government and companies. (The Kaizen system was included in the GTP II Plan.)

On 20–21 October, EU foreign affairs representative Federica Mogherini visited Addis Ababa for meetings with the AU (on the African Peace Facility, AMISOM and other security issues) and the Ethiopian government to discuss "economic growth, investments, climate change and migration issues". On 23 October, a Swiss delegation led by President Simonetta Sommaruga arrived to discuss the intensification of Swiss-Ethiopian bilateral relations. In December, French Minister of State for Foreign Trade Matthias Fekl visited the country for similar purposes, accompanied by a delegation representing some 40 French businesses.

October also saw a visit by fashion and entertainment world icon Victoria Beckham, active in philanthropic work, who visited youth groups and met with the Ethiopian minister of health. Another humanitarian visit was by Belgium's Queen Mathilde, honorary chair of UNICEF-Belgium, who was in Ethiopia on 9–12 November, visiting projects regarding the survival and wellbeing of children.

From the north-east African region, Addis Ababa was visited by politicians from *Somalia*, including on 9 March the new Somali TFG prime minister, Omar Abidrashid Ali Sharmarke, to discuss regional security and defence issues, and later in the year Abdikarim Guled, head of the Galmudug Interim Administration, and Puntland leader Abdiweli Mohamed Ali.

Prime Minister Hailemariam made a number of foreign visits. On 7 February, he was in Djibouti for talks with President Ismail Omar Guelleh, concluding cooperation agreements on economic integration, transport (new railroad links), power and energy, and foreign

relations. On 8 June, he was present for the second day of the summit of G7 nations in Germany, and he visited Rwanda in August, following up on Kagame's visit to Addis Ababa in April. He went to
China in September, for talks on economic cooperation and to attend the 70th anniversary of the end of WWII in Asia, and was in
India on 26–29 October for the India-Africa Forum Summit. Finally,
in December, Hailemariam attended the UN COP-21 Paris climate
change summit.

A foreign policy highlight of the year was the visit on 27–28 July
to Addis Ababa by US President Barack Obama, as part of a brief
African tour. His planned visit was contested by a large part of the
Ethiopian-American community, which in general remained very
critical of the Addis Ababa regime. Obama was the first US president
to visit the country. He met with Hailemariam and addressed the AU
meeting at AU headquarters on 28 July on the subjects of economic
opportunities in and for Africa and the need for the continent to
have a democratic political future. In what was widely seen by opposition groups and analysts as a propaganda coup for the Ethiopian
government, Obama gave a speech on Ethiopia in which he spoke of
the "legitimately elected government" and referred in only subdued
terms to the problematic human rights situation and political and
media repression. He lauded the country's major role in battling *al-
Shabaab* terror in the region.

Socioeconomic Developments

A *major drought* severely impacted food production and threw millions of people into dangerous, food-insecure conditions. According
to UNICEF, toward the end of the year the total number of people
affected was 10.2 m (of whom 5.7 m were children). Food, clean
water, medical treatment, etc. had to be provided in aid. Cognisant
of Ethiopia's problematic image as the perennial hunger country of
Africa, the government was reluctant to publicise the situation, but

again asked international donors for massive *food and humanitarian aid*, requesting $ 596 m in October. It said it had itself allocated $ 192 m to combat the crisis. In December, the government revised the amount needed to $ 1.4 bn, with a request that donors please pay.

The 'El Niño-effect' was blamed for the drought, but the crisis showed again that *agricultural production* and distribution were still not effective. The systemic lack of land property rights and the restriction of the small-holder sector did not stimulate local agrarian entrepreneurship and disadvantaged small farmers, and agro-pastoral production systems were similarly undermined. In addition, uncontrolled population growth played its part.

The various large-scale *land investment schemes* by both foreigners and local investors were not universally successful, and many collapsed for lack of preparation and failure to realise investment plans. Domestic agrarian investors tended to be urbanites who acquired land lease concessions for investment through agencies in the capital and engaged local former farmers and labourers for low wages, which only partly compensated them for the attendant loss of their land. The government became more cautious regarding allocation of land for investment and formulated somewhat stricter conditions for those leasing it.

An important development was the promulgation in September of the second phase of the *Growth and Transformation Plan* (GTP II). In this new five-year plan (2015–20), further GDP growth was foreseen, with expansion and commercialisation of agriculture, and infrastructural and hydro-energy construction, despite the criticism of social and ecological impacts by experts over recent years. More emphasis was also placed on industrial development and the interest of foreign parties in industrial investment steadily grew over the year. The GTP II also hinted at a renewed emphasis on manufacturing, with top party people and policy advisors aiming at a ten-year trajectory to make Ethiopia a major manufacturing hub with the sector as the main absorber of the approximately 2 m people entering the labour market every year. Major attractions for global investors were the very low wage costs and the availability of subsidised facilities in the first few years. Hindrances were the difficult and unpredictable regulatory environment and the government obsession with control. Industrial development was manifested in the planned construction of several new industrial parks in the cities of Hawassa (built by the Chinese and to be inaugurated in 2016), Dire Dawa, Kombolcha and Meqelle (in the north) and Adama (or Nazret). They would offer land at $ 1 per square metre a month to factories investing.

On 21 September, the Chinese–built Addis Ababa Light-Rail was opened in the capital, a two-line 34 km urban transport system, and one of the first in Africa, built with a Chinese loan of $ 475 m. Tickets were affordable at ETB (birr) 6 ($ 0.3) and state-subsidised.

The 1,870-MW *hydropower dam Gibe-III* reached completion and started producing electricity in October. Fears were expressed by various experts that it might suffer from silting up, as had happened with the Gilgel-Gibe I dam, and be vulnerable to periodic droughts. The reduction in the downstream flow of the Omo River had already affected various local peoples: the pastures and food retreat cultivation systems of the Bodi, Mursi, Kara, Nyangatom and Kwegu were impacted, with food insecurity and hunger as a result. The previously announced 'controlled flood release' did not occur, further undermining agriculture. Plans for building the *Gibe-IV* and *Gibe* V dams on the Omo, south of Gibe-III, were reconfirmed, again with a non-transparent bidding process and informal consent given by the government to the Italian construction company Salini to build the Gibe IV as well. Nothing was heard of environmental and social impact studies. Not all water management experts understood the logic of this dam, and local people were again shocked at these non-negotiated plans and the possibly devastating impact on their lands and livelihoods.

On 28–29 October, an 'Ethiopia Summit' was held at the Sheraton Hotel, Addis Ababa, organised by the UK's *Economist Intelligence Unit* and attended by government officials, global business executives and leading journalists, on the country's prospects for 'market potential', the telecoms sector, energy policy and manufacturing.

In March, Hailemariam announced *gas production and exports* from the Kalub and Hilala fields in the Ogaden Basin (estimated reserve: 4.7 trn cubic ft), scheduled to begin in 2017. The Chinese company GCL-Poly Petroleum Investments was the partner, and a $ 4 bn pipeline would be built to export the gas via to Djibouti.

In the south, relentless but risky *restructuring of the countryside* continued, including relocation and resettlement of local peoples, massive land clearance and the expansion of sugar plantations along the Omo River, run by MeTEC, the military-industrial complex of the EPRDF party, and the state-owned Ethiopian Sugar Corporation. It was a conflict-ridden process, strongly opposed by native populations in the area, who stood to lose everything in return for only marginal jobs for some of them – as guards, for example. Reports of abuse of local populations' rights in the Omo Valley induced the global retail company Hennes & Mauritz to state in January that it would stop using any cotton from this area, following a similar statement by the German company Tchibo a week earlier, and Turkish Ayka Investment was contemplating doing likewise.

Ethiopia's *economic growth*, as measured in GDP increment, continued; the IMF figure (not corrected for 2.7% population growth) was 8.7%, and GDP reached about $ 61.5 bn. The GDP per capita (current prices) was reported to be $ 597. Annual inflation was still high, at 10.4% (IMF figure). The World Bank (again) noted that the Ethiopian birr was overvalued.

Estimates of development were again variable and primarily measured quantitatively, based mostly on local data provided by the Central Statistical Authority and the IMF and World Bank figures. These showed that poverty, defined as $ 1.25 a day purchasing power, fell during the year by 2%–3%, and applied to 29.5% of the total population. Good qualitative measurements of poverty and well-being were, however, lacking or not considered, and some groups (the urban poor, pastoralists, some farming and occupational groups, and the unemployed) experienced a decline in food security, income and level of well-being.

External debt grew to about 23.4% of GDP, while the budget deficit (budget year ending 30 June) was limited to 2.8%, due to significant capital inflows (mostly donor money to the tune of $ 3.8 bn, of which about 10% was 'humanitarian aid') and an alleged 50% increase in FDI, which reached about $ 2.2 bn. Ethiopia retained one of the highest aid-per-capita ratios at $ 40.5. This was explained by its being seen as the most prominent country in Eastern Africa due to its relative stability and the size of its population, economy and army, and its role in African peacekeeping missions (including AMISOM, and in Darfur-Sudan). The government again effectively harvested the donor money, but this meant in effect that the country was as dependent as ever on external support, while at the same time its totalitarian state-developmental regime was further entrenched.

Remittances from Ethiopians overseas via the Commercial Bank of Ethiopia, the country's largest bank, reached a record estimated $ 3.7 bn, some 40% from the USA. This far surpassed export revenues, and was thus was the country's largest source of income. In addition, substantial unregistered sums also entered the country.

In January, it appeared that the World Bank, a major supporter of Ethiopia's authoritarian development trajectory, had ignored an internal report from its own Inspection Panel on the *abuse of World Bank funds* for Ethiopia's alleged forced relocations/evictions of local people. The report had said there was an 'operational link' between the World Bank-funded programme called 'Protection of Basic Services' and the controversial government 'villagisation' campaign, and noted that "failing to acknowledge this link and take action to protect affected communities constituted a violation of its own policies on project appraisal, risk assessment, financial analysis and protection of indigenous peoples". Similar criticism of the World Bank's involvement in other southern regions, jeopardising the rights of local people, were also heard – and ignored.

In general, the paradox of GDP growth amidst conditions of serious agrarian under-production, food insecurity and outmigration of unemployed and dispossessed people was again stark, showing the serious imbalances and inequalities in the national economy, which benefited some sections of the population and hurt others. Ethiopia ranked 173rd of 197 – countries on the HDI. The GINI-coefficient went from 30.1 to 33.3 (for what the incomplete statistical data are worth), indicating increased income inequality.

Ethiopia's *main exports* were gold (21% of total exports), coffee (19%) followed by flowers, live animals, oilseeds and khat. Export revenues totalled caround $ 2.9 bn.

On the *Index of Economic Freedom* (Heritage Foundation), Ethiopia's position was unchanged: 37th in Africa (and 148th in the world), meaning '*mostly unfree*'. Some progress was achieved in public finance management and trade freedom. On TI's Corruption Perception Index, it was 103rd of 168 countries, statistically a two place improvement, but not matched in the public's perception, especially regarding the elites / ruling party members, who had unfair privileges in access to credit, land lease contracts and jobs. A consistent though subdued stream of complaints about this was registered, and much everyday corruption and nepotism stayed out of the books.

Financial freedom was restricted by government efforts to keep a grip on the national economy. Negotiations on WTO membership were again stalled, with Ethiopia – taking a nationalist economic stance – not prepared to open up its financial and banking sector to international capital.

In September, the IMF concluded its 2015 *Article* IV consultation, which, while praising overall 'macroeconomic performance', resulted in warnings of too high inflation and high borrowing by public enterprises "with attendant risks of external debt distress". They also advised "decisive action to strengthen the business climate" and "enhance external competitiveness, less burdensome regulation, and easier private sector access to credit and foreign exchange". This was directed at the very dominant hold that the party-state retained over the national economy to the detriment of the private sector. Again, in good IMF fashion, nothing was said on the social and environmental aspects of the growth model, or about overall developmental equity or income distribution patterns.

On 13 August Ethiopia announced a climate resilience strategy plan for the agriculture, forestry, water, irrigation and energy sectors at a meeting with a delegation of the Global Green Growth Institute. It was said to be part of the government's vision to build a climate resilient green economy.

Ethiopia's *population* reached an estimated 92.3 m, continuing a major growth rate. Urbanisation accelerated.

Outmigration, aided by human traffickers, continued in the tens of thousands. UNHCR figures revealed that 82,268 Ethiopian migrants made the crossing to Yemen (70,845 of them young men), the highest number on record apart from in 2012. The numbers were surprising in view of the great domestic turmoil and insecurity in Yemen. Motives were repression, exclusion, poverty, lack of jobs and the indebtedness of farmers (who were unable to pay back obligatory loans for fertilizer, for example). Ports of embarkation were Obock and Bosaso. There was also legal out-migration of young Ethiopian females for domestic work in the Gulf States. In the context of migration, human trafficking remained a serious but under-documented problem.

Ethiopia itself also accommodated around 100,000 *new refugee arrivals* from neighbouring countries (mostly South Sudan), bringing the total number to 773, 759 (UNHCR figure), who were cared for with a UNHCR budget of $ 270 m.

Ethiopia in 2016

All the year's events were overshadowed by persistent demonstrations and protests by, mainly rural, people against political repression and perceived inequalities in land allocation and against dispossession. The lives of hundreds of people were lost in violent repression, and there were also tens of thousands of arrests. Bloodshed and anger dominated the country for months, and demonstrations and pockets of armed resistance persisted even after the declaration of a 'state of emergency' in October and the instalment of a new ruling body, the 'Command Post', which took extrajudicial authority to "restore public order" and suppress activism. The overall situation was one of political stalemate, disarray and distrust.

In international affairs, Ethiopia kept its prominent position in the Horn region, via IGAD, in the AU and as a participant in AMISOM in Somalia. It maintained its links with major donor/investor countries and concluded a new 'cooperation deal' with the EU.

Economic growth – GDP and infrastructure investments – continued, although at a slower pace. Industrial projects slowly expanded, accompanied by FDI. Population growth remained high, as did outmigration, running at close to 100,000. Food insecurity due to both natural and political-economic causes remained a serious problem and endangered the lives and livelihoods of an estimated 5–6 m people.

Drought again struck in some areas, necessitating substantial food aid. The militant protests and the damage they caused to domestic- and foreign-owned companies, notably large-scale agrarian businesses, shook investor confidence and led to complaints and criticism, albeit short-lived, from donor countries. Investors' hesitation did not prevent most of them from continuing their economic planning and partnership with government agencies. The political system, however, faced unresolved problems in accommodating people's grievances and addressing issues of lack of accountability and socio-political inequality.

© KONINKLIJKE BRILL NV, LEIDEN, 2017 | DOI 10.1163/9789004346826_015

Domestic Affairs

Ethiopia's political system continued to be marked by autocratic rule, with a one-party government and parliament since the last elections in 2015. The Ethiopian Peoples Revolutionary Democratic Front (EPRDF) also retained in control of all public officers and the army. No opposition representatives led any public body or administration. The political process and national policies remained top-down dirigiste and strongly controlled. Domestic tensions over lack of accountability, few media freedoms, politico-economic inequality, corruption and the absence of political dialogue perpetuated discontent below the surface. In rural areas, tensions were fuelled by large-scale land deals and land alienation, which victimised locals by side-lining small-holders and agro-pastoralists. New enterprises only absorbed a fraction of these people.

The year saw dramatic civil unrest and repression, with at least 800 (and according to some opposition circles, several thousand) public protesters killed, and more injured. Tens of thousands were arrested, often arbitrarily. Such numbers had never been seen before, and the unrest – due to people clamouring for land rights, justice and government accountability – persisted throughout the year, with many attacks on property. Later in the year, some protesters turned to sporadic armed resistance, but had little organisation or opportunity to effect systemic changes. The protests were concentrated in the Oromiya and Amhara regions, but there was also unrest in Benishangul-Gumuz, Afar and the Southern regional state, where 'ethnic clashes' and repression occurred. The Somali Region saw a low-key rebellion continue, but without major armed clashes. Core issues underlying the year-long protests were: lack of political freedoms, loss of (access to) land, poor compensation for land loss, and identity issues, which played out against perceptions of a government seen as arrogant, intimidating and routinely overreaching its powers.

The protests in Oromiya, the largest region, were a continuation of the 2015 rebellion against the (now suspended) Addis

Ababa Masterplan, which had aimed to expand the metropolis into Oromiya farmlands. During the year, protests spread to other towns, including Woliso, Chiti, Wonch'i, Ambo, Ajo, Hagere Mariam and Shashemene. Government vehicles were stoned and destroyed on the roads and government offices and enterprises were looted or torched.

A major drama occurred on 2 October in the town of Bishoftu (Debre Zeit) in Oromiya on *Irreecha* day, an annual Oromo cultural festive to mark spring, instituted in the 1990s. An estimated 80–90 people died and hundreds were injured. The proceedings had turned political, and security forces fired teargas and live ammunition into the crowd. Panic followed, and in the stampede many died, being trampled to death or falling into ditches. Messages of condolence were issued by Amhara and other protest leaders, and popular anger, notably in the Oromo areas, rose rapidly. This incident and the shockwaves it sent out were the probable trigger for the government's declaration on 9 October of a *state of emergency* (SoE) across the entire country.

The protests in Amhara Region and elsewhere were caused by feelings of political marginalisation, economic inequality and, more particularly, identity issues, including, for example, the status of the Wolqait region, historically part of Gondar (Amhara). July saw the arrest of Colonel Demeqe Zewdu, a retired military officer and a key member of the Wolqait Identity Committee, which was agitating for the return of this area to the Amhara Region from Tigray (to which it had been annexed in the 1990s). During the arrest, a fight ensued between his armed escort and the police/security forces, and several people were killed. Unrest spread against a background of already long-standing issues of land loss, perceived marginalisation and lack of freedoms. Other Wolqait Identity Committee members and leading young demonstrators, including Ms. Nigist Yirga, were later abducted.

In the weekend of 6–7 August, protests took place in several locations in Amhara, and some 100 demonstrators were shot and killed.

In the same month, protests also flared up in Oromiya and the South (Shashemene town). Dozens of farms and businesses were attacked and damaged, among them the Esmeralda flower farm near Bahir Dar, the FV SeleQt vegetable farm, the Africa Juice company and the Turkish textile firm Saygin Dima. In addition, more than 60 trucks and cars seen as belonging to the government or to certain state-linked companies were torched and destroyed. The protests hit not only foreign farms perceived to have neglected the rights of (displaced) locals, but also state/party enterprises. On 4 October, an animal farm in Wonji owned by the tycoon Mohammed Al-Amoudi, who was close to the regime, was torched and, the next day, a gas depot in Dire Dawa was damaged. In early December, a 60 ha state sugar plantation constructed by TPLF's metals and engineering company MeTEC in Jawi, Gojjam, was partly burned down (for the second time).

Security units used lethal force to subdue the protests. They usually gave protesters one warning to disperse or turn back and opened fire on the crowds if they did not obey, which led to high numbers of deaths. The units (often special federal forces, not the regional police) also avoided communication with protesters.

The SoE affected not only the regions in turmoil but all other areas too, both rural and urban, although some parts, such as the Southern capital of Hawassa, had not seen any protests at all. The new authority structure under the SoE was the *'Command Post'*, a unit consisting of the prime minister, chief-of-staff, minister of defence, a Tigray People's Liberation Front (TPLF) vice prime minister and one senior TPLF Central Committee ('Politbureau') member. This junta-like committee, as some called it, had supreme authority and behaved like a new 'sovereign'. It could act at will to restore order and suppress unwanted protests, some of which had taken on a violent character. Under the Ethiopian Constitution – a product of the ruling party in 1994 – an SoE could be declared under conditions of: external invasion, a natural disaster, an epidemic, or "a breakdown of law and order which endangers the Constitutional order and which cannot be controlled by the regular law enforcement

agencies and personnel" (Art. 93). Observers both within and outside Ethiopia doubted the validity of declaring a (nationwide) SoE,
because the protests, in so far as they damaged property and constituted public protests against failing governance, could also have
been tackled through law enforcement under the Criminal Code.
But the government identified the unrest as a *systemic threat*: people wanted to change the political system. In general, the Ethiopian
people responded with scepticism, defiance and a sense of humour
to the impositions of a regime of exhaustive restrictions, with online
parodies on the SoE proclamation appearing.

The emergency regulations led to an increased military presence,
mass arrests and even house-to-house search campaigns in all areas
of unrest, although protesters developed alternative methods of resistance, such as the 'dead city' campaigns – wholesale strikes that
paralysed public life. Even some religious festivals were boycotted.
This led the security forces again to try and force people to open
their businesses and offices.

Despite the SoE, protests went on in subdued forms in many
areas. Some armed resistance took place in isolated parts and border areas of the north and west. The low-key insurgency of Ogaden
rebels in Somali Region 5 also continued.

Foreign NGOs and aid workers complained of the restricting impact that the SoE had on their work; they felt they could not report
on the real needs of the people (in the face of impending drought)
or had to slow down their activities.

As part of its campaign, the government, using the sole Internet
and telecoms provider Ethio-Telecom, repeatedly *shut down the
Internet and social media* (Facebook, Twitter, WhatsApp, Instagram,
etc.). On 7 June, the government had rushed through Parliament
a 'computer crime law' with very restrictive clauses that provided
for even more government control over the Internet, including
Facebook posts. Internet shut-downs caused significant damage
and delay to the business sector because essential communication
was hampered. This became worse under the SoE.

In general, *media freedoms and civil society organisations suffered.* On 27 May, the journalist Muluken Tesfaw (of the weekly '*Ethio-Mihdar*') was arrested when interviewing people evicted in connection with the Blue Nile dam construction. On 1 October, a critical blogger, Seyoum Teshome, was arrested and other journalists remained in jail. Prime Minister Hailemariam said on 6 December in an interview with the BBC: "We are ready to be criticized by any journalists because we know we are not perfect", but the practice did not match the rhetoric.

At the end of the year, government figures stated that *some 2,400 people were to appear in court, and some 9,800 of those arrested had been released.* The opposition gave much higher numbers of arrests. The prisoners held in camps were subjected to a "re-education, training and disciplining" campaign. They were forced to 'repent' and ask for pardon before being released. Descriptions of life in the camps by former inmates spoke of intimidation, humiliation and abuse. By imposing this form of punishment, the government in effect denied that those arrested had any legitimate grievances and implied that they were just 'criminals'. It was clear that correct mechanisms for accountability and dealing with criticism and grievances were not in place. Opposition parties had no demonstrable connection to the protests. One opposition leader said: "We were unprepared for this and we could not influence events." Most protests were spontaneous and sudden, although they had become contagious, spreading via word of mouth and social media. As they went on, a degree of coordination and local organisation emerged, but trans-regional or 'Oromo-Amhara' alliances did not materialise, due to distance, somewhat different agendas, organisational problems and preventive action by the authorities. In some areas, local authorities and militia joined the protesters and some local self-government units were set up.

Business life suffered many setbacks as a result of the unrest. The situation also led to absurd practices, such as flower producers in the Sebeta, Tulu Bolo and Adama areas transporting their produce in *armed convoys* to the export points. In many areas, agrarian enterprises and state plantations had been provided with armed guards before.

The unrest also caused power vacuums in which *'ethnic' animosities* were whipped up and played out: some minorities were routed, as in Dilla town, for example, where Gurage and northern traders and shopkeepers were attacked by local Gedeo people, and in Gondar, where 'Tigrayan' businesses – or at least TPLF-linked interests – were targeted. In ugly violence on 6–7 October, dozens of people, mostly of Amhara descent, were killed in the town of Arsi Neghele (Oromiya). Superficial Western journalism sometimes appeared to 'ethnicize' the protests, framing them in terms of ethnic oppositions, but this was a misjudgement of the fundamental *social and economic contradictions* of Ethiopia's developmental model, which had led to the marginalisation of people.

On 13 September, more than a dozen people were killed by security forces in Konso, where local people had petitioned and demonstrated for separate district status. Some 4,000 people also fled the area. The Omo Valley saw continued tension due government investment projects such as sugar plantations displacing and cowing local people. There also was continued resistance to (forced) villagisation. In March, shocking photographs of slave-like abuse of local people in the South appeared in social media and on some Ethio-diaspora websites. There were also *clashes between 'rival' ethnic groups*, such as in February in Gambela Region, a very volatile region due to the displacement of many Anywa to make way for commercial, state-supported agricultural enterprises and the influx since 2014 of around 250,000 Nuer refugees fleeing South Sudan's civil war. Anywa and Nuer people clashed, leading to dozens of deaths, even among the regional police force, which split along ethnic lines.

The government's economic policy under the Growth and Transformation Plan II focused on large-scale commercial agricultural development and on 'transforming' the smallholder sector. The land taken from smallholders and agro-pastoralists leased to investors or exploited by state companies reached an estimated surface of more than 2.5 m ha (of the projected 3.5 m). The vast majority of small-holders affected were displaced and poorly compensated, which fed resentment. Only a few found jobs on the new farms, and new farm-land elsewhere was not given to them.

International criticism from foreign donors and institutions of the way the authorities handled the protests fell on deaf ears, and the latter predictably rejected any intervention by international and UN observers to investigate the killings. Criticism soon subsided: donor statements again had no bite due to lack of interest, lack of com-mitment to a rights agenda and an overemphasis by Western and other donors/trading partners on Ethiopia as a "strategic partner and emerging economy". The government saw its harsh repression to stop the protests at all costs as justified and continued to repeat its refrain against 'illegal protests' by 'anti-peace elements'. No ac-countability probes into excessively violent army, federal police or militia practices were carried out. In general, there were no political structures or procedures in place to account for abuse or respond to charges, grievances or even alternative views and policies. In in-terviews with global media (as on 9 March with 'The Guardian'), PM Hailemariam showed nominal awareness of Ethiopia's prob-lems, such as 'lack of a democratic culture', 'bad governance', cor-ruption and youth unemployment, but his government's policies to deal with those problems were falling short. His remark in the interview that Ethiopia was "an island of stability in a troubled re-gion" rang hollow at the end of a year that was marked by domestic repression and the curtailing of civic freedoms.

On 12 November *Merera Gudina, leader of the legal opposition party, the Oromo Federalist Congress, was arrested,* a politician not known for any violent or insurrectionist agenda. He was detained at Bole Airport on his return from a meeting at the European Parliament, where he had been invited to testify on the unrest in Ethiopia. The government claimed that he had met and 'conspired' with two declared government opponents, Berhanu Nega (of the Ginbot-7 movement) and the 2016 Olympic 10-km silver medallist Feyissa Lilesa, who had made the crossed-arm protest gesture after his race. Merera's arrest and other measures against opposition voices seemed to reveal the government's insecurity and fear of any dissenting opinions. The SoE was thus used to interpret the clauses of the already extremely strict anti-terrorism law of 2009 very stringently and to declare critical voices as criminal, if need be. It appeared to many observers that the government was again revealing that it was aware of its unpopularity but incapable of cultivating dialogue or negotiation.

After the wave of open protests had subsided toward the end of the year, Hailemariam announced a "new approach" and promised to weed out government officials who "had abused the public's trust" by their corrupt and illegal practices. He also said talks would be held with excluded groups that had grievances. On 1 November, the government announced a reshuffle of cabinet ministers: 21 new appointments were made, bringing the total, including both new posts and replacements, to 30. In a televised presentation of the new ministers, the prime minister explicitly mentioned their 'ethnicity', presumably to show that the government was responsive to ethnic inequalities, but this was felt by many to be embarrassing and irrelevant.

Under the SoE, those arrested had limited recourse to the usual rights, such as *habeas corpus* and appeal. While many thousands were detained, put in prison camps and subjected to forced 'rehabilitation', none of the people's concrete grievances were addressed, except rhetorically. The prime minister and government spokespersons repeatedly muttered about "the need to be more attentive to the people", and "to address the problems that were overlooked", but no comprehensive solutions or new policies were forthcoming by the end of the year; it was all about restoring order and the *status quo.*

Internal relations between the four constituent parts of the ruling EPRDF were sometimes tense, and rivalries as well as disagreements on how to handle the protests and address the apparent popular grievances were evident. Some leading members of the Oromo People's Democratic Organisation (OPDO) and the Amhara National Democratic Movement (ANDM) were accused by the leadership of sympathising with the protesters. At the same time, the leadership, notably of the ANDM and the OPDO constituent parts, tried to operate more independently from the EPRDF overall structure.

Although the overall system of governance itself was not reformed, selected (former) high-level party members were charged with crimes and sentenced, including the former head of domestic intelligence (Ethiopian National Intelligence and Security Service or NISS), Woldeselassie Woldemichael, who was convicted on charges of corruption and sentenced to ten years in prison.

After the death of numerous protesters in Oromiya and Amhara in early August, even *the UN High Commissioner for Human Rights called for a probe by international observers*, decrying the impunity, but to no avail. Ethiopia lived up to its reputation as a 'hard-line autocracy', as it was classified by the German think-tank BTI. The US State Department's annual report on human rights also confirmed a string of abuses, bad prison conditions, torture, disappearances and impunity of the security forces.

Inter-religious relations between Christians, Muslims and traditional religionists, despite a general accommodative attitude, were often marked by underlying tensions and rivalry, but no large-scale violent clashes occurred. In the countryside, however, Protestant Evangelicals (many of whom were recent converts) and followers of traditional religions were engaged in frequent conflicts.

Foreign Affairs

Foreign policy was made by the ruling EPRDF without interference from other groups, either domestic or foreign. Ethiopia's regional role in Eastern Africa was recognised and it remained a partner in global efforts to stem Islamist terrorism. At the same time, it was strongly dependent on humanitarian aid and development funds from donor countries and institutions. The government manoeuvred between new donors and partners such as China, India and Turkey and the traditional Western and other donor countries. In March, Ethiopia began its campaign for a non-permanent seat at the UNSC for 2017–18.

On 21 September, the EU, mindful of the growing migration threat and the unrest fuelled by the 'youth bulge', concluded a $ 500 m job-creation scheme deal with the government to be implemented in the coming years.

Ethiopia retained its prominent position in the IGAD, the AU and the AMISOM force in Somalia and maintained its contingents (around 8,100 personnel) to various UN missions (including in Sudan's Darfur and Abyei regions).

Relations with Kenya, Somaliland, Sudan and especially Djibouti were peaceful and fairly close, with mutual agreements, cooperation and high-level visits. South Sudan was problematic because of that country's internal disarray. Ethiopia favoured Salva Kiir to continue as leader and on 28 November refused entry into Ethiopia for rebel leader Riek Machar.

There was no improvement in relations with *Eritrea*. On 12 June, armed clashes, resulting in a "significant number" of casualties, were reported between Eritrean and Ethiopian forces near the border town of Tsorona, with each side predictably blaming the other for starting the incident. Eritrea claimed to have killed over 200 Ethiopian troops. In February, Ethiopia had accused Eritrea of fuelling anti-government protests in Ethiopia. It later also accused Egypt of supporting the protesters – without any evidence.

Prime Minister Hailemariam made various foreign trips. On 7–9 April, he visited Ghana to strengthen bilateral relations. On 14 June, he was in Brussels and signed a joint declaration with the EU, 'Towards an EU-Ethiopia Strategic Engagement', on security matters, migration and economic cooperation. He went to Kenya on

22–24 June for talks on security issues, border management, economic relations (with a business forum) and the on-going Lamu Port-South Sudan-Ethiopia-Transport (LAPSSET) Corridor project. On 28 October, he went to Juba (South Sudan) to press for calm in the border area, for a peace deal, and for improved economic relations. On 20 November, he visited Saudi Arabia, meeting with King Salman and business people.

Ethiopia received visits by a significant number of *foreign dignitaries. Brazil's Minister of Foreign Affairs Mauro Vieira* visited Ethiopia on 8 March and met with the prime minister and with AU leaders, and an Ethio-Brazilian business seminar was held. On 7 July, the *Israeli Prime Minister Benjamin Netanyahu* visited with a delegation and discussions were held during an Ethio-Israel business summit on more future cooperation in agriculture, water management, technology and tourism development. Several agreements were signed. *German Chancellor Angela Merkel* came on 11 October for a visit to the AU headquarters in Adis Ababa and for talks with the government. Merkel declined to give a speech to the one-party dominated Parliament and in a conversation with Hailemariam advised him to open up political dialogue and reduce the costly repression in the country. On 11 November, *Canada's Foreign Minister Stéphane Dion* visited during an African tour, appealing for proper handling of the political unrest and for opening a dialogue process. A Saudi business delegation headed by the chairman of the Saudi Development Fund paid a visit on 14–16 December for a meeting with the Ethiopian prime minister that focused on 'investment opportunities'.

The Nile question remained a bone of contention. Although in March the 'Declaration of Principles', a tripartite agreement on the Nile waters, was concluded between Sudan, Egypt and Ethiopia, misgivings were not resolved, especially between the latter two countries. Egypt continued to be fearful of expected negative effects of the huge Renaissance Dam on levels and quantity of water reaching the country downstream. Sudan tended to favour Ethiopia, as it would have future benefits from the use of the accumulated water and the electricity generated by the Ethiopian dam. Egypt hinted that if there were no guarantees regarding its share of the Nile waters – its essential lifeline – it would keep all options open. In the wake of this Declaration of Principles, it was agreed that there would be a comprehensive scientific investigation of the dam project and its likely effects on the Nile water flow, but this had not started by the end of the year.

On 21 July, Ethiopia, Djibouti and China announced the launch of a *$ 4 bn natural gas project*, based on future exploitation of the large Ogaden gas reserves.

An unexpected armed incident occurred on 15 April, when a well-organised party of *Murle raiders* from the Pibor area in South Sudan crossed the border into western Ethiopia (Gambela). They raided 20 villages, took hundreds of cattle, kidnapped 108 children and killed 208 local people (from the Nuer). Before the Ethiopian army could retaliate, they withdrew to South Sudan, which was in turmoil because of the civil war. In the subsequent weeks, the Ethiopian army unilaterally crossed the border and retrieved some children and cattle. In the south-west (Bench-Maji Zone), there were repeated violent incursions and cattle raids by South Sudanese Toposa into Ethiopian territory – a long-standing problem.

Socioeconomic Developments

The country's population, economic output and GDP all increased, although investments, exports and imports slowed down, partly due to world market developments, climatic problems and the social unrest, which also hit tourism revenues. However, figures cited on the country's economy were often approximations, and different sources showed remarkable divergences.

The country saw continued drought and related climatic challenges, leading the government, as in previous years, to appeal for aid for around 9 m *people in need of food* at the beginning of the year. Later, this figure fell to 5.6 m. The areas most affected were Somali Region, Afar and Central-East Oromiya (including Arsi). Tens of thousands of livestock were reported to have died and crop production was affected. The government spent some $ 380 m on the problems itself but, despite increased agrarian production, 'productive safety net' programmes and an improved early warning and logistics system, no durable solution to the recurring El Niño-driven challenges was in place. High population growth contributed to the problem. The food relief industry, led by WPF, USAID and the EU, again came to the rescue.

GDP at year's end was around $ 62.5 bn, having shown a real-terms growth rate of about 6.5%, significantly down from previous years. Apart from world market developments, this was partly due to the unrest and mass protests, which led to damage and shook investor confidence. A stiff state-led economic policy restricting the role of the private sector did the rest. Various state ventures did not produce expected profits, either. For example, the huge sugar plantations in the South did not come out of the red, due to massive costs, the declining world sugar price and looming global over-production. Per capita GDP was said to be $ 719.

Agriculture's share in GDP was 36% (still employing about 80% of the population), services represented about 47%, and manufacturing 17%. Industrial production grew at an estimated 9%, so above the GDP growth rate. Agricultural growth was down to 2.9%.

The *state budget* (the Ethiopian budget year runs from July to July) reached $ 10 bn, while expenditure amounted to $ 11.8 bn. The *current account deficit* was stood at 10.2%–10.5% of GDP. Taxes and other revenues generated some 14.6% of GDP.

The annual *IMF Article IV consultation* was concluded in October, and the IMF warned that debt increase was a risk, exports had underperformed and the current account deficit remained high. It blamed the region's drought for "... supply shock, necessitating scaled-up food imports". Again, nothing was said on the state-dirigiste economic policies and the lack of political and economic freedoms, despite that fact that they impinged on the performance of the national economy.

On 17 December, the 1,870 MW *Gibe III hydro-electric dam* was officially opened, although it had gone on the grid earlier. In December, it was reported that water levels in the Omo River and of Lake Turkana (in the Ethiopia-Kenya border area) had already dropped by 1.7 m., affecting downstream fisheries, river-bank cultivation sites and other sources of livelihood for local people. Kenya's government, having little interest in the arid northern frontier areas and its populations near Lake Turkana, did not respond.

Work on the huge $ 4.8 bn, 6,000 MW Renaissance Dam on the Blue Nile progressed slowly, but was said to be 70% complete at year's end.

Another infrastructure project, the Chinese-financed 700 km, $ 4 bn *Addis Ababa-Djibouti rail link*, was completed and formally inaugurated on 5 October in Addis Ababa by Prime Minister Hailemariam and President Guelleh of Djibouti. Additional railway lines were planned.

The new $ 300 m Hawassa Industrial Park was officially opened on 13 July.

According to Prime Minister Hailemariam's six-months' report to Parliament on 10 March, *export revenues* had reached $ 5.3 bn, but the IMF and other sources referred to a sum of around $ 3 bn, with coffee still as the top crop (27% of exports), followed by oilseeds (17%), vegetables, including *khat* (17%), gold (13%), and flowers, live animals, raw leather products and meat products (about 20%). This represented a decline in exports of around 7% compared with the same period in the previous year.

Low export revenue-generating capacity remained the economy's Achilles heel and had not shown a structural breakthrough in recent years. Export was again dwarfed by *imports* to the tune of $ 14.5 bn, although this was $ 1 bn down from the previous year. The large trade deficit thus continued, compensated for by foreign aid flows and remittances from the Ethiopian diaspora. The country struggled with foreign currency scarcity.

Inflation went ahead at an estimated 9% per year, with the birr (ETB) reaching 22 to the dollar. Experts estimated the currency to still be *overvalued* by around 20%-40%. Real estate prices and house rents in Addis Ababa rose very rapidly.

The *public debt* at year's end stood at slightly over $ 36.9 bn, or 54.2% of GDP (up from about 49.6% the previous year, a 12.8% rise). The amount of *external* debt reached $ 23 bn. China was the largest creditor, with about $ 17 bn in outstanding loans, followed by India, Turkey and the World Bank. The rapidly mounting debt (from $ 14 bn in 2011) caused several Ethiopian and international economic experts to express concern about the sustainability of Ethiopia's financing model, all the more since the profitability of various new major projects and enterprises left much to be desired. The IMF, however, stated that, despite increased vulnerability, Ethiopia's "risk of external debt distress remains moderate" (in part because 70% of the debt was owed to 'official creditors', not trade and commercial-based ones). The previous budget (of July 2016) reserved a substantial chunk of around $ 633 m (or ETB 13.9 bn) for debt repayments.

There were estimates of *illegal money transfers* – capital flight – out of the country of some $ 2–$ 2.5 bn – representing a higher share of GDP than in any other SSA country. The organisation Global Financial Integrity suspected that, as in other countries, import-export businesses and some government officials were involved – both regularly conniving with the banks. As the government (ruling party) controlled close to half of the Ethiopian economy, their involvement was more than likely. Export or import trade misinvoicing and 'leakages' in the balance of payments were the predominant tricks.

Remittances by overseas Ethiopians – both declared and undeclared – amounted to $ 3.4 bn, much more than annual export revenues, and again showing the developed world's extra impetus to the country's economy. On 8 June, it was announced by the

US Securities and Exchange Commission that Ethiopia's electric utility ETTC had agreed to pay them nearly $ 6.5 m to settle charges that it had violated US securities laws due to failure to *register* bonds sold to US residents of Ethiopian descent.

In the Heritage Foundation's annual *Index of Economic Freedom*, Ethiopia again came out as 'mostly unfree' – a qualification highly familiar to private-sector business people, small entrepreneurs and traders. The ruling party and its large business conglomerates were still seen as dominating the economy, using insider knowledge, patronage and often unfair business practices. The country continued to suffer from *corruption*, buttressed by the stories of ordinary people, office workers and business people. On TI's Corruption Perception Index, Ethiopia was 106th of 176 countries, a slight drop, but still comparatively modest for Africa.

Social and income inequality increased somewhat, with the GINI coefficient reaching 33.6, slightly higher than in 2015, but the data on which this was based were shaky. A small party-linked and business elite continued to increase its wealth rapidly. On Oxfam's Multidimensional Poverty Index (MPI), Ethiopia had an 87.3% 'MPI poor' population, higher than East Africa's average (70%).

Most economic figures confirmed the picture of a skewed, externally dependent economy that lacked sufficient export revenue-generating capacity and was propped up by remittances from the Ethiopian diaspora, donor aid money, and loans, particularly from China. The long-term vulnerability of the economy remained.

Population growth remained at a high 2.7%, and the total population, according to the UN Population Division, reaching 101 m, though other sources put it some 5–6 m lower. The increase for the year was more than 2.2 m people – reflecting a basically unsustainable pace in view of the limited resources and economic prospects. The birth rate in urban areas fell slightly, but the urban population increased by about 4%, mostly due to rural-urban migration.

Population growth went along with a rapidly *dwindling agrarian/ natural resource base*: in many parts, land scarcity became more acute, leading to group conflict, attempted cultivation of marginal areas, loss of vegetation, drying out of the land (due also to excessive planting of eucalyptus), and water scarcity. Efforts to reclaim eroded land were successfully undertaken in some parts of the northern highlands, but in other regions erosion continued unabated.

The number of *refugees* in Ethiopia reached about 783,000, 45% of whom were from South Sudan. UNHCR again bore the major responsibility for assisting them, with a budget of $ 280 m (but with a funding gap by October of 62%). An estimated 38,000 Eritrean refugees/migrants crossed the border into Ethiopia (paying an average of $ 2,500 each to smugglers), bringing the total to some 163,000. Most of them stayed in camps, while others moved on to Sudan and the Mediterranean coast, heading for Europe. About 94,000 Ethiopians migrated (fled) to Yemen, remarkable in view of that country's heavy suffering from armed conflict and severe economic decline. The migrants hoped to move on to Saudi Arabia or the Gulf States. The risks were high, but the reason most given was to "… seek the opportunity to have a better life", at whatever cost. In a reverse movement, some 3,400 Yemenis fled to Ethiopia.

Contraband and illegal economic practices were on the increase, among them human trafficking, and smuggling or illegal sales of wildlife products. The latter sector increased significantly, amidst slackening prevention policies. At a meeting of the Horn of Africa Wildlife Enforcement Network on 7–8 December, it was said that cheetahs and animal products such as ivory, rhino horn and antelope skins were most traded, notably to countries in the Arabian Peninsula and Far East. This was a further sign of the precarious state of Ethiopia's ecology and environmental situation.

Further Reading

This list[1] contains suggestions of important background literature, roughly since 2000, on Ethiopian society, politics and socio-economic affairs, as well as on the changing role of Ethiopia in international relations. Journal articles and book chapters treating detailed aspects of Ethiopian society and history were omitted.[2]

Abbink, J. and T. Hagmann, eds, *Reconfiguring Ethiopia: The Politics of Authoritarian Reform*. London – New York: Routledge, 2013.

Ambrosetti, David, Jean-Renaud Boisserie, Deresse Ayenachew and Thomas Guindeuil (eds), *Climatic and Environmental Challenges: Learning from the Horn of Africa*. Addis Ababa: Centre Français des Études Éthiopiennes, 2016. (E-book, http://books.openedition.org/cfee/101>. ISBN: 9782821873001.)

Aregawi Berhe, *A Political History of the Tigray People's Liberation Front (1975–1991): Revolt, Ideology and Mobilisation in Ethiopia*. Los Angeles – New York – Pretoria: Tsehai Publishers, 2009.

Bahru Zewde, *The Quest for Socialist Ethiopia. The Ethiopian Student Movement, c. 1960–1974*. Woodbridge, UK: James Currey, 2014.

Campbell, J., *Nationalism, Law and Statelessness: Grand Illusions in the Horn of Africa, 2014*. London: Routledge, 2014.

Desplat, Patrick and Terje Østebø (eds), *Muslim Ethiopia. The Christian Legacy, Identity Politics and Islamic Reformism*. New York: Palgrave-Macmillan, 2013.

---

1 Ethiopian authors are cited on first name.

2 See also: J. Abbink (2016), *Ethiopian-Eritrean Studies: a Bibliography on Society and History, 2010–2015*. E-book (Leiden: African Studies Centre), vii, 283 p. ISBN 978-90-5448-151-5. (download: https://openaccess.leidenuniv.nl/handle/1887/37415).

Dessalegn Rahmato, *The Peasant and the State. Studies in Agrarian Change in Ethiopia 1950s–2000s*. Addis Ababa: Addis Ababa University Press, 2009.

Dessalegn Rahmato, Mehret Ayenew, Asnake Kefale and Birgit Habermann (eds), *Reflections on Development in Ethiopia. New Trends, Sustainability and Challenges*. Addis Ababa: Forum for Social Studies – Friedrich Ebert Stiftung, 2014.

Erlich, Haggai, *Saudi Arabia and Ethiopia. Islam, Christianity and Politics Entwined*. Boulder, Co.: Lynne Rienner, 2007.

Fantahun Ayyele, *The Ethiopian Army: From Victory to Collapse, 1977–1991*. Evanston, Ill.: Northwestern University Press, 2014.

Ficquet, Éloi, Ahmed Hassen Omer and Thomas Osmond (eds), *Movements in Ethiopia – Ethiopia in Movement*. 2 volumes. Los Angeles: African Academic Press – Tsehai Publishers, 2016.

Heinonen, Paola, *Youth Gangs and Street Children: Culture, Nurture and Masculinity in Ethiopia*. Oxford – New York: Berghahn Books, 2011.

Mains, Daniel, *Hope is Cut: Youth, Unemployment, and the Future in Ethiopia*. Philadelphia: Temple University Press, 2012.

Marcus, Harold G., *A History of Ethiopia. Updated edition*. Berkeley – Los Angeles – London: University of California Press, 2002.

Markakis, John, *Ethiopia: the Last Two Frontiers*. Woodbridge, UK: James Currey, 2011.

Mattes, Robert and Mulu Teka, *Ethiopians' views of democratic government: Fear, ignorance, or unique understanding of democracy?* Afrobarometer (www. afrobarometer.org), Working Paper no. 164, 2016.

Milas, Seifulaziz, *Sharing the Nile: Egypt, Ethiopia and the Geo-Politics of Water*. London: Pluto Press, 2013.

Mohammed Hassen, *The Oromo and the Christian Kingdom of Ethiopia: 1300–1700*. Woodbridge, Suffolk: James Currey, 2015.

Munro-Hay, Stuart, *Ethiopia Unveiled: Interaction between Two Worlds*. Hollywood, Ca.: Tsehai Publishers, 2006.

Prunier, Gérard and Éloi Ficquet (eds), *Understanding Contemporary Ethiopia. Monarchy: Revolution and the Legacy of Meles Zenawi*. London: C. Hurst, 2015.

Seidel, Kathrin, *Rechtspluralismus in Äthiopien: Interdependenzen zwischen Islamischem Recht und staatlichem Recht*. Cologne: Koeppe, 2013.

Toggia, Pietro, Melakou Tegegne and Abebe Zegeye, eds, *Ethiopia in Transit: Millennial Quest for Stability and Continuity.* London – New York: Routledge, 2011.

Tronvoll, Kjetill and Tobias Hagmann (eds), *Contested Power in Ethiopia: Traditional Authorities and Multiparty Elections.* Leiden – Boston: Brill, 2011.

Waal, Alex de, *The Real Politics of the Horn of Africa: Money, War and the Business of Power.* Cambridge: Polity Press, 2016.

Woodward, Peter, *Crisis in the Horn of Africa: Politics, Piracy and the Threat of Terror.* London: I.B. Tauris, 2012.

Index

Printed in the United States
By Bookmasters